Laughing Saints and Righteous Heroes

MORALITY AND SOCIETY SERIES
Edited by Alan Wolfe

RECENT TITLES

*Moral Communities in Medical Science: Managing Risk in Early
Human Experiments*
Sydney Halpern

Soft Patriarchs, New Men: How Christianity Shapes Fathers and Husbands
W. Bradford Wilcox

Citizen Speak: The Democratic Imagination in American Life
Andrew J. Perrin

The First Year Out: Understanding American Teens after High School
Tim Clydesdale

*God and Government in the Ghetto: The Politics of Church-State
Collaboration in Black America*
Michael Leo Owens

*The Catholic Social Imagination: Activism and the Just Society in Mexico
and the United States*
Joseph M. Palacios

The Making of Pro-Life Activists: How Social Movement Mobilization Works
Ziad W. Munson

For a complete list of series titles, please see the end of the book.

Laughing Saints and Righteous Heroes

Emotional Rhythms in Social Movement Groups

ERIKA SUMMERS EFFLER

The University of Chicago Press Chicago and London

ERIKA SUMMERS EFFLER is assistant professor of sociology at
the University of Notre Dame.

The University of Chicago Press, Chicago 60637
The University of Chicago Press, Ltd., London
© 2010 by The University of Chicago
All rights reserved. Published 2010
Printed in the United States of America

20 19 18 17 16 15 14 13 12 11 10   1 2 3 4 5
ISBN-13: 978-0-226-18865-2 (cloth)
ISBN-10: 0-226-18865-5 (cloth)
ISBN-13: 978-0-226-18866-9 (paper)
ISBN-10: 0-226-18866-3 (paper)

Library of Congress Cataloging-in-Publication Data

Effler, Erika Summers.
   Laughing saints and righteous heroes: emotional rhythms in social
movement groups / Erika Summers Effler.
       p.   cm. — (Morality and society series)
   Includes bibliographical references and index.
   ISBN-13: 978-0-226-18865-2 (cloth: alk. paper)
   ISBN-10: 0-226-18865-5 (cloth: alk. paper)
   ISBN-13: 978-0-226-18866-9 (pbk.: alk. paper)
   ISBN-10: 0-226-18866-3 (pbk.: alk. paper)   1. Social movements—
Case studies.   2. Social groups.   3. Altruism.   4. Emotions.
I. Title.   II. Series: Morality and society.
HM881.E33   2010
303.48'4—dc22

                                                      2009022450

⊚ The paper used in this publication meets the minimum requirements
of the American National Standard for Information Sciences—
Permanence of Paper for Printed Library Materials, ANSI Z39.48-1992.

For Aaron and Alexander

Contents

Preface

This project began as any other ethnographic project would. I gained access to a Catholic Worker community and to STOP, an anti–death penalty group, and I went about the business of conducting fieldwork to answer the question: How could apparently failing, high-risk, altruistic social movement groups maintain commitment?[1] As my work proceeded, the project started to feel like sand slipping through my fingers. While the project developed, the groups sometimes shrank to one person; at other times they grew to twenty or more people. Some members left when they became annoyed or busy—hardly examples of commitment. I struggled to make sense of what I was seeing. Then I

1. Studying small groups has certain advantages. One of the most significant is the capacity to directly view processes of social organization (Hare, Borgatta, and Bales 1955; Fine and Fields 2008; Fine and Harrington 2004; Stolte, Fine, and Cook 2001). Studies of organizations or neighborhoods, for example, do not lend themselves to the thorough observations of social organization that are possible when one studies a small group. Small social movement groups offer an even richer opportunity for one to observe multiple group dynamics. To work for change means to frequently run up against obstacles that represent serious threats to the survival of these groups. As Fine and Stoecker note (1993, 274), small groups dedicated to working for change are likely to be more intense, concerned, motivated, and active than groups that are not focused on generating external change. Observing intensely motivated and frequently frustrated action provides opportunities for examining the relationships between the internal group dynamics, the external dynamics in which groups are embedded, and the long-term consequence for the ways in which groups negotiated these relationships. The Catholic Worker community and STOP are not only social movement groups; they are altruistic groups—they work toward causes that do not immediately benefit them in an instrumental or rationally calculated way. Because both groups are altruistic, they had a utopian quality to them, although during this study this quality eventually faded at STOP.

gave a talk, and someone asked me the question I had been dreading: "How can you claim these groups are maintaining themselves when they lose members?" It was a fair question—how could I? Certainly Weber was right, organizations remain despite changes in membership.[2] After I was asked this question, I saw clearly that I was interested in *how* they remained.

It took awhile to experience the gestalt shift that allowed me to see that these groups didn't *have* processes; they *were* processes. Once I embraced this perspective, a completely different picture of the social world emerged. The persistence of individual membership became far less important than the persistence of the group as an emergent actor. I realized I had been asking the wrong questions. Rather than asking how groups maintained membership, I should have been asking how they persisted as centers of action despite political changes and fluctuations in member involvement. Over time, I could see that what we generally think of as "groups" are rhythmic patterns of organization. Sometimes these groups were entities within fields of action, other times they were contentious fields where members vied for power, and still other times they were coalitions focused on distant goals.[3]

My two groups *felt* very different from each other, and their emotional tones were central to their different styles of persistence.[4] I not only occupied different roles in these groups; I was literally a different person in these two settings. I thought different thoughts, felt different emotions,

2. Continuity beyond specific individuals' involvement is central to Weber's definition of organization ([1914] 1978: 49).

3. Sociological work on small groups tends to approach the investigation of groups with a set of assumptions: boundaries of groups are generally taken to be self-evident or created through experimental design; small groups are understood to be comprised of individual persons; and the focus of investigation is on dynamics that unfold over minutes or hours. This work takes a different approach to the investigation of both the Catholic Worker community and STOP. The boundaries of both groups are not given. In fact, this work focuses on the internal and external dynamics that contribute to the expansion and contraction of the groups' boundaries. The approach taken here also differs from much other small group research, because it does not assume that either group is comprised of individual actors; rather, the groups are treated as social actors. Just as shifts in boundaries are a focus of investigation, so too are the dynamics that lead to individuals precipitating out of the group. The assumption is that group dynamics drive this precipitation. For more thorough treatments of social scientific approaches that focus on interaction over and above individuals, see Abbott (2001b), Bales (1949), Bourdieu (2000), Collins (2004), Douglas (1966), Durkheim (1997, 1995), Goffman (1974), Lefebvre (2004), Mead (1932). Finally, the perspective taken in this volume is on dynamics that unfold not only over hours, but also over years.

4. During the bulk of the time I spent with these groups, STOP embodied the reformist position that seeks legitimacy according to the prevailing legal and religious systems. The leaders gained facility with the legal system and relevant laws and did not hesitate to turn the system back on itself when possible. The Catholic Workers, on the other hand, worked to live up to the spirit rather than the letter of the law. Their conviction that they could embody their ideals, and in their best moments that they did, drove the community's continued involvement (Riesebrodt 1993, 16–18).

and interacted in different ways. Eventually I understood that the difference in my position in the two groups was data in its own right.

I came closer to full-member status at the Catholic Worker house, while I never moved beyond my position as a helper in STOP. My time at the Catholic Worker house was compelling and overwhelming. While there, I was often moved to tears, both from touching stories and from uncontrollable laughter. The Catholic Worker community attracted people who became deeply attached to the group and who spent large amounts of their time with the group for many years. Participation in STOP, on the other hand, was far less captivating. I rarely saw participants finding emotional satisfaction or relief in the immediate experience of involvement. Participating in STOP riled them up, pricked them, tempted them with promises of fulfillment and rest, but seldom delivered. Those who enjoyed deep fulfillment and passion imported it. Thus, involvement was at the cost of these outside psychic resources. Some members primarily found satisfaction after the fact, when they reflected upon past moments of alignment between their values and action. Compared to the Catholic Worker community, STOP was more of a revolving-door organization.

The difference in my experience leaving these two groups also illustrates my different position in the two groups. When I told the Catholic Workers that it was time for me to go, they openly conveyed their sense of loss at my leaving. They told me repeatedly that I would be missed and that I was welcome back at any point. They made sure I understood that I had been an important part of the community and that I would be remembered long after I was gone. STOP's staff, on the other hand, thanked me for my efforts, wished me well, and saw me to the door.

———

I tried several different styles of writing as I looked for a way to convey the emotional dynamics that enabled the groups to persist as centers of action. I found it nearly impossible to capture the emotional tones of interactions with abstract description. Not only were these descriptions—such as "Then Linda got angry and shamed the group, lowering their enthusiasm for the afternoon"—not very interesting or compelling; they also seemed to ask for too much trust from readers. Why should readers believe me that these were the emotional dynamics shaping that particular afternoon? Even if they did believe me, how could they use my work to investigate emotions and groups for themselves? These inadequacies became all the more apparent when I tried to convey how histories of varying durations influenced unfolding emotional dynamics.

If a reader would hesitate to accept my description of a fairly short scene, why should they believe that a particular moment was linked to a conflict that fractured the group five months before? Even if a reader accepted my conclusions, how could such abstract claims offer insight into how social scientists can think about and examine the processes through which such groups persist?

After trying multiple styles for organizing and communicating the findings from my fieldwork, I found that I could communicate emotional dynamics most directly by writing stories. Although I had not set out to write this book as a memoir or creative nonfiction, through trial and error I found that I only could convey the emotional dynamics of these groups by writing about my own experiences. The stories evoked the feeling of my experience in the field far better than abstract description.[5] By highlighting my range of experiences within and between the two groups, my intention is to convey how the groups' emotional rhythms produced the different tempos and feelings of involvement in these two groups.

Each chapter of this book contains a story from the Catholic Worker house and a story from STOP,[6] followed by a theoretical section based on a comparison of the two. Each set of stories unfolds over longer periods of time, revealing dynamics that emerge at increasingly longer timescales.[7] The comparative theory-building sections lose some of the complexity that the ethnographic stories capture. However, in return, they provide a more abstract account of the processes depicted at the different timescales.[8] My expectation is that in providing both richly de-

5. The stories about the groups were based on my field notes. I did not tape-record while I was in the field, so all quotes have been reconstructed from the dialogue I recorded in field notes. Although I did my best to represent the voices that I came to know so well, my own voice undoubtedly comes through in my re-creation of their verbal exchanges. Thus, the quotes that appear in the stories should *not* be treated as direct representations of what was said, nor should they be used for linguistic purposes.

6. In order to preserve anonymity, in some cases I have changed the gender, ethnicity, race, or age of the people who appear in my stories. All names have been altered, and physical characteristics have been radically altered in some cases, in order to maintain privacy.

7. Ethnography offers a window into a visceral and intuitive understanding of a scene that cannot be achieved with analytic reasoning alone (Wacquant 2004; Eliasoph 2005). At their best, ethnographic accounts tell a story that allows readers to use their own senses to develop a visceral feel for the rhythmic dynamics of a particular situation, scene, group, organization, or neighborhood. As Lefebvre points out, "No camera, no image or series of images can show these rhythms. It requires equally attentive eyes and ears, a head and a memory and a heart" (2004: 36). This work contributes to the emerging multidisciplinary literature on studying and conveying sensory experiences in qualitative work (Stoller 1997; Desjarlais 2003).

8. Ethnographers may point out, and quite rightly, that important information is lost in the further abstractions of the theory sections. Alternately, those who are accustomed to using data that appears more solid and concrete in their theory building may find the analytic leaps in the comparative theory sections a bit slippery. From particular points of observation, both critiques would be accurate. Ultimately every social scientist makes choices about what to foreground; this

tailed stories and abstract theory, the reader can gain a feel for exactly what happens when trading visceral complexity for abstract elegance.[9]

It is important for me to note clearly that the stories in this volume do not reflect the entirety of my experience in the field. On the contrary, the stories were crafted from vast numbers of interactions in order to illustrate the most prominent emotional patterns within these two groups. As this book highlights, not only did each unfolding interaction have multiple meanings; any past interaction also could take on radically different meanings in future interactions. This is to say, every scene depicted in this book did in fact occur, and the scenes did influence the dynamics that follow in the story. However, one should keep in mind that these scenes meant very different things to participants in still later interactions. Indeed, taken as a whole, the stories from each group illustrate how the different meanings for interactions emerge and collapse. Detailing the dynamics that shape changing meanings is, in large part, one of the main theoretical points of the book.

While writing this book, I thought of a collage of pictures that one of my father's friends from graduate school gave him when I was about ten

---

book foregrounds complex nuances in the story sections and abstract patterns in the comparative sections. As Polanyi explains, "Intellectual commitment is a responsible decision, in submission to the compelling claims of what in good conscience I conceive to be true. It is an act of hope, striving to fulfill an obligation within a personal situation for which I am not responsible and which therefore determines my calling. This hope and this obligation are expressed in the universal intent of personal knowledge" ([1958] 1962, 65).

9. Dilthey (1996) argues that we do not understand new information in translated bits and pieces but rather through entire worldviews. In order to take up a new worldview, actors need more than access to relevant content; they need to share position and history to develop a worldview that will enable them to make sense of a scene. Thus, the more effective social scientists are at evoking the feeling of a shared position and the *emotional* and *sensory* information associated with that position, the more effective they will be in conveying worldviews to outsiders. Dilthey and Dewey (1934) wrote extensively about the processes through which intense emotional experiences can be evoked through art. Dewey argued that effective art is not the display of the artist's impressions. Rather, "[art] consists of objective material by means of imaginative vision. The subject matter is charged with meanings that issue from intercourse with a common world" (319). Borrowing a page from Dilthey and Dewey's work on the power of prose and poetry to evoke emotional responses, I suggest that social scientists need to think not only about the content of their findings and arguments, but also about forms that will most effectively enable them to convey this content. I argue that stories are particularly powerful tools for conveying experience to readers. Once one commits to a process-focused evolutionary perspective where the connectedness of events is the focus of analysis and theory-building, storytelling offers a particularly good fit between epistemological assumptions and methods for representing findings and theoretical insights. Stories not only proceed along the same logic that is the foundation for an ethnography focused on the evolution of social processes; when done well, they hold the power to evoke strong emotion in readers, and in doing so, draw readers into sympathy with the dynamics depicted in a way that static representations never can.

years old. It had precut matting for arranging a series of photos in which the friend had placed pictures of parties, most of which occurred at my childhood home. In the middle, the friend placed the title "The Syracuse Scene" and the dates they had been in school together.

Shortly after my father received the gift, another friend stopped by the house. "*That* was the Syracuse scene?! That was *not* the Syracuse scene," he'd scoffed when he saw the collage.

I remembered thinking, "If the Syracuse scene wasn't at my house, where was it? How would I know if I saw it? Who decides where the real Syracuse scene is?"

The stories in this book are like the pictures in that collage; they were taken with one person's camera—mine. My pictures are of the things that interested me the most. I tell sociological stories; the activists would likely tell other stories about themselves. This is not an apology for my lack of objectivity. I am convinced that telling these stories from my own perspective is the most honest and interesting way to depict the emotional dynamics that shaped both groups. My hope is that in being open about the process of interpretation, analysis, and writing, readers can have a more accurate sense of what they are reading, and thus how they might interpret the material in this volume for themselves.

––––––

I did not directly seek out the Catholic Worker community or STOP when I went looking for field sites. I knew that I wanted to study two altruistic social movement groups, one with a loose structure and another with a formal structure.[10] An activist friend suggested a number of groups when

10. I began this project with an interest in the non-rational motivations for high-risk and chronically failing altruistic behavior. My reasoning was Durkheimian—if I could understand how such unlikely social patterns persisted, I would also learn a lot about how less extreme and more typical social patterns persisted. The very existence of the groups I selected belied the notion that rational choice assumptions could explain social behavior, especially behavior organized around social change (McCarthy and Zald 1977). Identity was hardly a better explanation since many people foster identities as sympathizers with these movements without any regular participation. Thus emotion was the likely suspect for explaining this unlikely persistence. Structural theories of emotions (Kemper 1990) suggest that social organization and emotion shape each other in direct ways, so I looked for groups that had drastically different styles of organization. The Catholic Worker community was chaotic and self-consciously attempted to maintain an anarchist spirit where community members stepped right in and took responsibility for the action they felt needed to happen. STOP was a formal nonprofit with a board of directors, a director, and employed and volunteer staff. The drastic differences in structure suggested that both groups would likely go about solving their shared problem of maintaining involvement in a chronically failing altruistic group in very different ways. Such structural variation in emotional dynamics made these two groups particularly informative comparisons for each other. Beyond their important differences in regards to the emotional implications of the organization of the groups, the groups approximated Durkheim's *organic* versus

I told him what I wanted to do. I am forever grateful to him because there is no doubt in my mind that my connection to him helped me gain access to both of the groups that I ultimately ended up studying. Although I had been much more involved in other social movements, I had personal experience with both the Catholic Worker movement and the anti–death penalty movement before I started my fieldwork for this book. The stamp of my history undoubtedly permeates the text.

I grew up in a Catholic family in upstate New York, an area of the country with a long history of radical Catholic activism and rich in Catholic Worker houses. I do not remember when I first learned of the Catholic Worker movement, but I remember very clearly my initial experience at a Catholic Worker house. The sacrament of confirmation in the Catholic Church requires community service. My parish arranged for groups of candidates to help at Unity Kitchen, a Catholic Worker house in Syracuse, New York. Unity Kitchen served dinner nightly to a regular group of homeless men. Our job as candidates was to help the Workers prepare and serve dinner.

As soon as I entered the building, the mystical weight of the Workers' routine activity fascinated me. We were called to prayer during the preparation of the meal. Each table sat six people for dinner, a Worker and five guests. The Workers served, and the guests were exactly that, guests. We learned to set the wooden tables, which looked like they had been scrubbed every day for at least fifty years with tremendous attention to detail. I remember being corrected for my placement of the place mats and told that they should be positioned an inch from the table's edge. When I asked why, I was told that the Workers tried to treat all guests as though they could be the Second Coming of Christ.

After the meal, the candidates sat with the Workers and listened to them discuss their upcoming Stations of the Cross during Holy Week. Their stations wouldn't be held in a church; rather, one station would be at a homeless shelter, another at a prison, still another at the welfare offices, and so on. Just as preparing and serving the meal were both prayer and mundane activity, the Stations of the Cross would be both prayer and public protest.

Some of the other confirmation candidates left talking about the poverty of the people we had served, but I had seen poverty before; the

---

mechanical solidarity (1997), Apter's *telic* versus *paratelic* action (2007), Weber's *bureaucratic* versus *charismatic* organization ([1914] 1978), and Aristotle's *doing good* versus *being good* ([1925] 1990). Thus the comparison of these two groups not only provides an opportunity to gain insight into my original question, but also to gain insight into many of the social dynamics that have been at the heart of sociology since its inception.

xv

Workers were the ones who fascinated me. Who were these people, and how could they be so apparently happy with so little? How did they continue to purposefully live such an austere existence for so many years? I talked about my experience at the Catholic Worker house for a long time afterward. I remember my mother teasing me when she bought a set of stoneware to replace our random mismatched plates: "We've got try to live up to Catholic Worker standards."

As for the death penalty, I do not remember a time when I didn't think it was a grisly business for the state to be involved in killing people, even before I knew about the social context shaping capital punishment in the United States. The formative moment for me, however, was when in 1993 on St. Patrick's Day Sister Helen Prejean came to speak to a class I was taking. I remember the date because I was a student at Notre Dame. The date and location explained why, on a traditionally Irish Catholic campus filled with conscientious students, only four students out of a class of thirty-five had turned out for her talk.

I never had heard of Sr. Helen Prejean before that day. It was the year before her book *Dead Man Walking* (1994) came out and three years before the movie based on her book was released. The few who had come to class sat in a circle around her, and she told us her story of befriending a death row inmate. Her story was long, complicated, and emotionally overwhelming. In graphic detail, she described the brutal rape and murders to which the inmate she had befriended had confessed. She told us about the father of the murdered boy who had told her he had forgiven the perpetrators when he had knelt over his son's dead body and prayed the "Our Father" as he identified his son in the field where he had been murdered. She also told us about the parents of the raped and murdered girl, who had expressed a deep sense of betrayal toward Sr. Helen for her closeness with one of the perpetrators. Sr. Helen concluded her story by describing what it felt like to accompany the man who was both a perpetrator of these horrific crimes and her friend to his death.

Three years after Sr. Helen's talk, I became friends with a man who had worked with Sr. Helen. He had become involved with the anti–death penalty group Murder Victims' Families for Reconciliation following his sister's murder. My friend asked me to accompany him to *Dead Man Walking* (1996) on the day it opened. On a bitterly cold winter day, I took a train to Chicago and sat with him as he endured one of many crucibles in his struggle to forgive the man who had murdered his sister.

A reader should not conclude from this account of my personal history with the anti–death penalty movement that the stories about STOP are tearjerkers. On the contrary, the stories about STOP highlight the difference between the day-to-day emotions of mundane activity and the stirring emotions of intense involvement.

Beyond this personal history, my intellectual history also clearly marks the book. Certain work has influenced me far beyond what I could communicate by merely citing it. Erving Goffman's (1959, 1963, 1967, 1974) and Randall Collins's (1998, 2004, 2008) work on interaction, as well as Durkheim's ([1912] 1995) work on ritual,[11] comprise the most basic lens through which I learned to think about and observe the social world. Their influence, Collins's in particular, permeates the most taken-for-granted assumptions that ground this book. In examining relatively extreme and small cases to develop theory, my methodological approach follows Durkheim's in *The Elementary Forms of Religious Life* ([1912] 1995). Jonathan Turner's *On the Origins of Human Emotions* (2000) and *Human Emotions* (2007) informed my thinking about the dynamics of emotions. Harrison White's *Identity and Control* (1992) was my constant companion as I worked out the theoretical details. Finally, Andrew Abbott's *Time Matters* (2001b) and T. F. H. Allen and Thomas B. Starr's *Hierarchy* (1982) sharpened my analysis of time immensely. Both helped move me from plodding descriptions of the relevance of timing to far sharper theoretical statements about the central role of timing in social organization. As I said, these works so permeate this volume that citations alone cannot account for their influence.

In conclusion, I should say a few words about studying altruistic social movement groups. In revealing the emotional dynamics of these two groups, both positive and negative, there are sections of the text where it may seem that I make people who mean to be helpful look disingenuous or selfish. This is not my intention. Despite the fact that groups similar to the ones described in this volume have improved the quality of life for countless people, this book is not intended to serve as homage or exposé. Instead, my goal is to describe the processes that support collective efforts to work toward visions of the common good. I tell stories about moments of both inspiring strength and all-too-familiar human frailty in order to communicate how it *feels* to do this work over time. By painting a complex picture, I explain how ordinary people can become and remain involved in extraordinary efforts.

11. The work of Mary Douglas ([1966] 2002), Victor Turner (1969), and Anne Rawls (2004) has also greatly influenced my work here.

Acknowledgments

Although one name appears on the cover of this book, countless people have made this book possible. First and foremost, I must thank the activists who let me become a part of their world for almost three years. They invited me into their lives because they wanted people to know about their work and the causes that mean so much to them. I hope I do justice to their effort, their missions, and the generosity that they showed me.

This book benefited tremendously from the guidance of a number of people—Robin Liedner, Diana Crane, Charles Bosk, Silke Roth, David Grazian, and Randall Collins were enormously generous with their time and attention. Randall Collins in particular has guided my academic development with a light touch, lots of emotional energy, and more faith in me than I had in myself. I am endlessly grateful for the opportunity he has given me to learn through vigorous intellectual discussion. Elisabeth Clemens, Andrew Abbott, and Gary Alan Fine were also very generous with their time and advice during different stages of this project.

The University of Notre Dame, with its strengths in the sociology of religion, social movements, and culture, has been the perfect environment for working on this volume. I have benefited from the resources and intellectual vibrancy of both the Center for the Study of Social Movements and Social Change and the Center for the Study of Religion and Society. I was also able to refine my ideas in a year-long faculty seminar on human personhood. Lynette Spillman,

Christian Smith, Janis Hausmann, and Robert Fishman generously took the time to read my manuscript, and they gave me invaluable feedback. I presented part of this work at Princeton's Weekly Seminar on Culture, and participants gave me very useful feedback.

Simone Polillo was the most steadfast of intellectual companions throughout this process. He gave me thoughtful and challenging feedback and, more importantly, moral support every step of the way. My aunts Diane and Lynne read my manuscript in its entirety and gave thoughtful comments and moral support. Two exceedingly talented research assistants, Chris Hausmann and Carl Neblett, helped me during the writing stages of this project. Alan Wolfe saw value in my work in its initial form; I am tremendously grateful for his support for this project. Doug Mitchell and Tim McGovern helped me to clarify my arguments.

I received support for the research I conducted for this book from the Social Science Research Council's Program on Philanthropy and the Non-Profit Sector, the Charlotte W. Newcombe Doctoral Dissertation fellowship, and the University of Pennsylvania's dissertation fellowship and Pollak Fellowship.

Several women in my life, my grandmother, Catharine O'Donnell, my aunt Lynne O'Donnell, my mother, Kathleen Mary O'Donnell Effler, and my good friend Donna Kaplan did me the honor of praying at the shrine for Blessed Marianne Cope, Donna Kaplan's cousin, to ask her to intercede on behalf of my efforts to write this book.

I cannot communicate the depth of my appreciation for the untiring support and care that my friends and family gave my son throughout the researching and writing of this book. My son is a well-loved child, and for that I am eternally grateful.

Finally, without the love of my parents, Kathleen and Steve, my brothers, Damian and Adam, and, most especially, my husband, Aaron, and my son, Alexander, this book would never have been written. One cannot deserve such love, support, and sacrifice; one can only appreciate it.

ONE

Introduction: How Do Chronically Failing Altruistic Social Movement Groups Persist?

This book is an investigation of altruistic social movement groups. I studied the day-to-day interactions in two altruistic social movement organizations in order to understand how such groups maintain intensity of involvement. My focus was on the process of maintaining the energy required to do the work, a sense of responsibility for others, commitment to the work, cooperation among group members, and the ability to deal with failure. The purpose of this study is to understand the emotional dynamics of such groups, and how group dynamics either motivate the production of collective goods or drain participants of their feelings of efficacy and enthusiasm.

I conducted ethnographies within a Catholic Worker house and an anti–death penalty group. In this volume I compare findings from these ethnographic studies to develop theory about the role of face-to-face interaction in building group culture and generating group emotion.[1] This

1. In this volume I take an ecological approach much like the one Robert E. Park proposed early on in the development of Chicago school sociology (1936a; 1936b). In particular, my focus on the evolution of action in groups follows the emphasis on succession that Park lays out in "Succession, an Ecological Concept." In this article Park states the practical and intellectual goals of studying succession from an ecological approach. "Studies of succession . . . seek less to predict

1

research has significance for understanding the sources of emotional exhaustion or burnout associated with helping work, as well as the emotional dynamics and organizational patterns that support the continued efforts of charities, social movements, and other nonprofits dedicated to helping others. The findings from this research are also relevant to the recent and increasing focus on the role of emotions in social life within the field of sociology.[2]

This book is based on three years of ethnographic research of two groups that were intensely involved in altruistic causes despite minimal success: a Catholic Worker community and STOP.[3] The Catholic Workers sought to bring about a radical transformation of society by living in voluntary poverty and serving their neighbors. STOP, the anti–death penalty group, worked to change capital punishment laws and achieve a moratorium on the death penalty.

This book illustrates how these groups survived unfavorable political conditions, internal conflict, and fluctuations in their resources, through

---

the course of change than to make change intelligible, so that it can eventually be controlled by technical divides or political measures. For these reasons studies of succession are concerned not only with the form which change takes but even more with the circumstances and events which precede, accompany, and follow change—in short, with its natural history. The study of succession involves, it seems, not merely the life-cycle of individual types of institution and society, but eventually a study of processes by which new types of society are incubated and eventually, by which a new social order emerges from the lap of the old" (1936a, 178). George Herbert Mead's definition of knowledge fits well with the expectations for what counts as knowledge in Park's ecological approach. Mead defines knowledge as "a process in conduct that so organizes the field of action that delayed and inhibited responses may take place. The test of the success of the process of knowledge, that is, the test of truth, is found in the discovery of construction of such objects as will mediate our conflicting and checked activities and allow conduct to proceed" (1932, 68). Like Park, Mead does not hold up the capacity to predict change as the standard for useful knowledge. Rather, both suggest that knowledge should add a level of reflexivity about a particular phenomenon, and that this reflexivity should enable us to control how a succession of events unfolds by either inhibiting certain types of responses or reconciling conflicting responses that can stall responses. As Park and Mead put forward, the goal of this volume is to deepen the reader's understanding of the process of group evolution. Success will result in a greater depth of knowledge—knowledge that should enable those concerned with the dynamics of altruistic groups or groups working for change to gain insight that will enable them to anticipate, and thereby potentially avoid, dynamics that could lead to the collapse of such groups.

2. Clemens illustrates how a group's relationships to other groups and their shared expectations for what they should look like and how they should run influence the type of group structure that will emerge (1997). The work in this volume builds on Clemens's argument by suggesting that the microtemporal organization of a group is also a key factor in the form that a group will take. As Nina Eliasoph points out, "What is funny at one moment and in one place is rude in another; timing and placing are all, even for normal interaction" (2005, 161).

3. Despite the fact that this study is an ethnography, it differs from many ethnographies in three primary ways: one, the field sites are smaller and there are fewer people involved in the interactions I depict; two, each chapter tells two separate stories from the two sites; three, I compare the stories from these sites in much the same way that historical sociologists use cases to build more abstract theory.

a combination of adjusting to their local environment and working on their local environment so that it adjusted to them.

As I indicated in the preface, my attempts to understand how these two groups persisted led me to a surprising conclusion: I could not find persistence when I looked closely. Indeed, I saw mostly change. Still, if someone asked me, "Did the Catholic Worker community and STOP persist?" I would answer easily and honestly, "Yes." Ultimately I concluded that the notion of "persistence" only made sense if I understood the groups not as solid "things" but rather as flows of activity—like rivers.[4]

Like a river, the groups were ever-changing and unpredictable. Even the most veteran members of the groups could not predict what would happen during any particular interaction. However, there were some aspects of the groups, like the physical limits of the spaces the groups moved within or their most basic ideological commitments, which changed more slowly than other aspects. These slower-changing patterns constrained the flow of day-to-day activity within the groups like riverbanks constrain the flow of a river. However, the relationship between face-to-face interactions and other slower-moving aspects of social organization—like physical space, ideological commitments, or local expectations—did not look like simple reproduction. Rather, it looked like the flow of a highly viscous fluid.

By resisting the flow of activity, physical, interactional, and emotional limits created a sense that events unfolded according to logic. As is the case with a highly viscous fluid, pressures against current physical, interactional, and emotional limits built up and then released as new limits were established. This cycle of constraining limits, building pressure, release, and formation of new limits created a punctuated feel to the flow of activity.

To return to the river analogy, the answer to the question "Is the riverbank or the water more powerful in determining where and how the river flows?" depends on the period of time with which we are concerned.

---

4. Both Mead (1932, 147) and Weber ([1951] 1978, 26–27) define the "social" as the readjustment to the present and anticipation of future interaction with others based in an understanding of the past. For both, the "social" is fundamentally historical. Building on the insight that social organization is fundamentally dynamic and historical, I seek to capture the evolution of social organization over time. Conceptually, my goals here are similar to Mische (2009), Moody (2002), and Moody, McFarland, and Bender-deMoll (2005), who all attempt to examine patterns of social relations over time. However, my work differs from theirs in some significant ways. I do not develop innovative ways of conceptualizing networks, nor do I put existing network approaches in motion by taking measurements at particular intervals of time. Instead, I use my comparison of the evolution of social dynamics in these two relatively small and contained sites to examine the process through which meaningful "events" are created. This approach enables me to investigate what the relevant units of time are, and the experiences through which they arise, stabilize, and transform.

If we want to know if a canoe trip will take us past a particular point, the answer is "the riverbank." If we want to know where the river will be located in 10,000 years, the answer is "the water." Similarly, the answer to the question "Are day-to-day activities or longer-term ideological commitments and political and material constraints more powerful in determining the flow of social movement group activity?" depends on the period of time with which we are concerned.[5] Rather than assuming the importance of one timescale over others, the book will illustrate and explain the relationship between different timescales of social organization within the Catholic Worker community and STOP.[6] In doing so, it will suggest a more general picture of the relationship between different timescales of social organization within social movement groups and groups more generally.[7]

In response to their highly unstable conditions, the Catholic Workers counted on little, had modest goals, and kept their attention physically close to the group. In other words, the Workers became adaptable so that they shifted to accommodate environmental fluctuations. This resulted in rapid shifts in the meanings and an inability to maintain a consistent sense of time, both of which made it difficult for newcomers to become involved in the Catholic Worker community.

STOP, on the other hand, responded to a history of intense internal conflict and increasing access to steady resources and political opportunities by attempting to grow both their numbers and their political power. As STOP trained its attention farther from the group and further into the future, it became larger and more hierarchical. In other words, STOP developed a rigid form to resist environmental fluctuations. STOP's distant focus created more durable meanings, an emphasis on the historical development of the group, and a sense of time that coincided with standard

5. Just as the aggregate force of water molecules can erode a riverbank, the flow of group activity held the potential to shape the very constraints that channeled it. Joas quotes Simmel as making much the same point: "That life is a continuous flowing and at the same time something contained in its carriers and contents, something formed around centers, individuated, and for this reason, as seen from the opposite point of view, a forming that is always limited yet which continually surpasses its limitedness—that is what constitutes its essence" (2000, 77).

6. Whereas network theory has treated social relations as static (see Moody 2002 and Moody, McFarland, and Bender-deMoll 2005 for exceptions), this work here focuses explicitly on change over time. In doing so, it provides a picture of social organization where speed and rhythm are as important as the ties themselves in determining the influence between social actors. See Park for early examples (1936a, 1936b) and McFarland (2004) for a more recent example of an ecological approach that accounts for succession and change over time.

7. In the social world, small groups are connected with many other small groups, and these connections shape processes within groups (Fine and Kleinman 1979; Fine 1987). Thus, as Fine and Harrington (2004) point out, a full understanding of the role of groups in political life requires researchers to account for how groups are a cause, context, and consequence of civic engagement.

clock and calendar time. Compared to the Catholic Worker community, it was easy for newcomers to move in and out of STOP's lower ranks, but difficult for lower-level office workers to break into the leaders' ranks.

The following chapters illustrate how involvement within these two groups unfolded in cycles of routine structured times and intense unpredictable times.[8] Progressing through these cycles established a speed and rhythm of involvement in the groups. When the groups pulled their attention closer to their physical boundaries, their involvement sped up and became more chaotic. When the groups pushed their attention farther from their physical boundaries, involvement slowed down and became more predictable. The groups shifted their attention toward or away from their own boundaries in response to changes in their environment. For example, successful conclusions to concerted efforts, new political opportunities, or windfalls in resources allowed the groups to imagine more extensive influence and longer-term more ambitious projects. Alternately, disappointments, unfavorable political conditions, or a sudden loss of resources led to shorter-term and more modest expectations and projects.

Neither of the groups was particularly aware of the ways in which their shifts in attention influenced the speed and rhythm of involvement in their groups. Despite the groups' lack of awareness, both the speed and rhythm of involvement were critical for the groups' capacities to synchronize activity both within the groups as well as between the groups and other actors in their environment.[9] This capacity for synchronization in turn affected the groups' capacities to take advantage of access to resources and political openings.[10] Thus the groups' day-to-day and

8. See Durkheim ([1912] 1995) and Turner (1969).

9. The capacity for synchronization worked much like the traffic laws that Goffman uses as an analogy for the tacit responsibilities that actors have for the flow of events that occur during interactions (1967, 12, 9). Like merging onto an expressway, social actors must accurately identify an opening in the flow of interaction and get up to the appropriate speed. While the appropriate speed does not guarantee coordination, enduring successful coordination is impossible without sustaining the appropriate speed. Not all social action requires joining in an already established flow; sometimes new action takes off. In this case, dancing would be a better analogy for coordination. To the extent that successful dance emerges as a single activity, actors must be able to adjust their timing mutually so as to create coordinated action where there is usually separate action.

10. This volume contributes to the long-standing interest in the ways in which the timing between movements and political conditions influence political opportunities (McAdam 1988) and cycles of protest (Tarrow 1994). This volume explains how the timing of *interaction* also is central to understanding the dynamics of social movement groups. It is central as well to other processes that social movement scholars have identified as crucial for mobilization and success, such as framing, grievances, ideological commitments, emotions, networks, and the capacity to effectively maintain and gain access to material resources and political opportunities (see Goodwin and Jasper 2006).

moment-to-moment activity within these groups was influenced far more by the speed and rhythm of involvement than the groups' ideological commitments. Indeed, despite both groups' ideological commitments to gender and racial *equality*, the temporal and rhythmic constraints on interaction contributed to the unintentional reproduction of gender and racial *inequality*. More specifically, the closer focus and faster speed of the Catholic Worker community obscured the importance of race in interaction. Alternately, the more distant focus of STOP's leadership and the slower speed of involvement for STOP office staff reproduced gender inequality within the group.

A Glimpse of the Catholic Worker House

Three months after I started spending time at the Catholic Worker house, I took my habitual driving route to the neighborhood. A mile past the center of the city, the height of the buildings dropped off precipitously as high-rises became endless blocks of tiny row houses. The farther I drove, the more boarded-up houses and burnt-out cars I saw. Farther yet, increasing numbers of weedy lots where homes had been demolished made the city blocks look like smiles with missing teeth. I crossed a wide and busy street where most of the businesses had hung Puerto Rican flags over their storefronts. I drove under a banner in Spanish announcing the dates of a Puerto Rican festival and entered the fuzzy boundary between an African American and a Puerto Rican neighborhood. A few blocks up, I turned the corner at a neighborhood bar where a rotating group of racially diverse men usually could be found drinking, talking, and drumming outside.

The narrow street I turned on housed the Catholic Worker community that I had studied for three years. Amateur murals promoting cultural diversity and peace decorated the sagging four-story row house that served as the group's primary residence. To the side was a lot that looked like a tiny urban jungle. It brimmed with hearty-looking weeds that grew in defiance of the hard-packed earth that was littered with broken glass and trash. On the other side of the lot stood a converted garage that housed the Workers' after-school program for neighborhood children.

I knocked to announce my arrival and let myself in. Joan, a White community member in her early fifties, waved me in while she continued to talk on the phone. I threaded my way through the piles of recent donations and pulled out a chair to sit across from her at the dining-room table.

Before I could sit, she hung up and looked at me, saying, "That was someone named Gordy. He's offering us couches if we can get them this afternoon. You're the only one here who can drive. If you want to get them, you need to leave right away."

I had grown accustomed to the flash of irritation and disorientation that I felt in response to the chaotic demands of participating in community life. I knew I would somehow get the couches—I could not very well deny the neighbors the windfall just because coordinating the donation felt like too much of a hassle. I called Gordy and found out that he was a superintendent for a high-rise furnished apartment building. He needed to get rid of about thirty couches by the end of that day. He would rent us a U-Haul that we could reimburse him for later, but I needed to be at his building on the other side of the city in half an hour.

"You here for the couches?" asked a short White guy in his early twenties jangling his keys impatiently.

I told him I was, and he turned and gestured for me to follow. He led me to a basement room filled from top to bottom with small, worn, industrial-looking couches. "I need them out of here today," he said.

"Did you get the U-Haul?"

"Yeah, well, that didn't work out."

I forced a smile and called Joan to work out a new strategy.

"Let's see," Joan hesitated. "We'd have to be able to fill in for Linda during after-school . . ." Joan muffled the phone for a few seconds, then said, "Linda will be there with a truck in an hour."

I went outside to wait on the steps for Linda, a White woman in her early twenties who, like Joan, was a member of the Catholic Worker community.

As the end of the hour drew near, Gordy came out to the front of the building where I was waiting on the steps. "Are you sure you're going to be able to get these out of here today?"

Before I could reply, Linda pulled up on the narrow two-way street in front of the building so that she was effectively blocking traffic. I ran up to the U-Haul truck and found her laughing as usual.

"Want a ride?" she said with a grin.

I climbed in the truck, and Gordy indicated that we should drive around the back.

"This certainly is an adventure! Did I tell you it took me three times to pass my driving test?" Linda asked, cracking herself up.

"They're in there," Gordy called out, and gestured to the back door, letting us know that he would not be helping us to load the truck.

We started carrying the first one to the truck and passed a man who appeared to be on Gordy's crew. He made a sound of disgust, shook his head, and walked away.

"Friendly place, no?" Linda laughed as we hoisted the couch into the truck.

When we returned to get another, we found the grumpy crew member plus four others standing around the couches. Linda and I slid past them to grab a couch, and one of the guys turned and told us brusquely, "It will go faster if you just let us do it."

I was not surprised by how put out the crew members were by helping us, despite the fact that we were not the recipients of the couches and their sacrifice was, by any standard, fairly inconsequential compared to Linda's years of living in voluntary poverty. I saw Linda watching the activity serenely and noted that I had never seen this common incongruity bother her.

Gordy was nowhere to be seen when his crew finished loading the truck. Even though they were still grumbling and doing their best to avoid us, I felt we owed Gordy's crew our thanks, so I shook their hands and I thanked them. The first few seemed startled, but they all softened in response.

Linda grinned and waved at them as she climbed into the truck and said, "Thanks so much! We couldn't have done it without you!" Four out of the five men waved back. Turning to me, she added, "We'd better watch out, or they might actually start liking us!"

Linda had trouble putting the truck in gear, and the momentary goodwill of the crew evaporated as they pantomimed disbelief at our unending incompetence.

"Do you want me to drive?" I asked.

"Absolutely not! How else am I going to get practice?" She wiggled her eyebrows and gave me an impish grin. "I told you about all of my failed drivers' tests, right?"

When we arrived back at the Catholic Worker house, we found many of the neighbors anxiously waiting for us. A married couple—Lucy, a Latino woman in her early forties, and her husband, Owen, an African American man also in his forties—climbed into the back of the truck and started handing down couches. Spirits were high, and no one seemed to pay attention to Jenna, a young Latino who was a mother of one but became a guardian to six after her brother went to jail and her sister-in-law abandoned her children. She kept repeating, "I need a navy blue one. We're doing our living room in navy blue, so I need a navy blue one."

Ten or so children burst through the door of the after-school building. "What's going on?" one boy asked.

"Where'd you get the couches?" asked a girl.

"Can I get one?" asked another.

The scene became loud and chaotic until the college-aged volunteers shepherded the children back into the building.

Blueberry—a forty-year-old intermittently homeless White woman from the neighborhood—showed up just as the last couch was handed off the truck. She grabbed Linda in a bear hug when she saw her, leaving Linda stumbling, breathless, and laughing. Then Blueberry turned to me and took my hands. "I remember you! Ooo! Girl, you need to get yourself some good gloves. Your hands are freezing!"

Blueberry was still smiling at me and holding my hands when Lucy came up behind her and hit her on the head with one of the cushions from a couch. Blueberry ran for cover behind Linda. "Please don't beat me. I've never done you any harm. Now everyone knows what a mean woman Lucy is. Isn't that right?"

"Great, now I'm going to be hit," complained Linda with an exaggerated sigh.

"You people are crazy. You're just crazy," said Jenna, who was now openly impatient to get her new navy blue couch home.

The group reloaded the couches the neighbors had chosen. Linda asked me to stay behind and watch the remaining couches while they delivered the others. I watched the truck pull away, shivered, and contemplated the irony of guarding free unspoken-for couches that were supposed to be going to needy people. But guarding any property was a habit in this neighborhood. Even the Workers' trash cans were frequently stolen.

About twenty minutes into my wait, Paul, a twelve-year-old Latino boy, and his cousin Devon, a thirteen-year-old African American boy, spilled out of the after-school building muttering accusations and threats and throwing punches at each other. I had become increasingly fond of these kids as I got to know them. I had the distinct sense that the violence was a show for my benefit. I recognized their game of luring me into attempting to control their behavior when I was outside and I was outnumbered, so I attempted to ignore them. Moments later the volunteers ejected two of Paul's sisters, ten-year-old Maria and eight-year-old Lydia.

The two girls also came out swinging at each other while casting surreptitious looks in my direction. Devon went after his cousin Maria, and Lydia called to me, "Hey, are you going to let Devon get away with hitting a girl?"

Maria looked like she could hold her own, so I just raised an eyebrow.

Lydia complained to the others, "This is boring. Let's get out of here." She started walking away from the after-school building, stopping first to make sure I was watching her as she spit on one of the couches. Paul, Devon, and Mary followed Lydia's example.

Paul was the first to give up on waiting for my response. He hit Lydia on the head and took off running. Maria caught him most of the way down the next block, put him in a headlock, and gave him a punch to the head.

As I was watching the excitement, an African American woman who looked like she was in her mid-thirties pulled up in an ancient station wagon.

"Are you giving those couches out?"

I considered waiting for Linda's approval but decided I didn't need to. Besides, I wanted to get rid of them so I could go inside and warm up, so I answered, "Yup. Would you like one?"

"Let's look at them." She climbed out and inspected the remaining three. "Well, this one's the nicest, but it has a rip over here . . . I can sew that up, though." She turned to the teenage boy who was sitting in the front seat with his head turned in the opposite direction. His body language suggested he might die of humiliation, but when she asked, he climbed out to help without complaint.

We hoisted the couch on top of her car with the help of her son, and she began to climb back into her car. Concerned, I asked, "Do you think it's safe to drive without strapping the couch to the car? Let me see if I can find some rope."

"I'll drive slowly, and Derek will hang on to it," she responded with confidence.

She drove down the street at a speed that couldn't have been more than ten miles per hour. I watched, waiting for the couch to either slide off the car or Derek to dislocate his shoulder, until she rounded the corner and drove out of sight.

The sky grew darker and the temperature dropped. People began lining up outside of the Catholic Worker house for dinner sandwiches. Looking at my watch, I noted an hour had passed and wondered how much longer the delivery group would take. I decided to give up and headed into the house. When I walked through the door, I found Joan, Blueberry, Lucy, and Ms. Beth laughing and teasing each other as they made sandwiches. An older African American woman from the neighborhood who spent most of her days helping at the Catholic Worker house, Ms. Beth was the self-appointed sage of the neighborhood, the judge of character and realist who told the rest of the community when they were being taken for fools.

"I couldn't see protecting the free couches any longer. Would you like help with the sandwiches?" I asked.

"Of course!" Joan beamed at me. "Wasn't today great? What a great day. We helped so many people. *So* many people. This is the way the Catholic Worker is meant to be, chaotic and busy and helpful. Truly a blessed day."

Lucy added, "It was really great. Very nice. Very nice. So nice to see so many people working together."

A Glimpse of STOP

I walked to the Afghani restaurant below STOP's offices. I still didn't have a key, so I rang the bell next to the entrance.

I watched for the flash of Todd's bright white cross-trainer sneakers, usually the first thing I saw when Todd, the current director of STOP, bounded down the stairs to let me in. He might have identified with the neighborhood anarchists' politics and lifestyle, but he wore his hair cut short in a standard barber style and wore loose jeans and a T-shirt that looked almost stiff in their newness. Todd tended to look more like a middle-class professional in weekend wear than the other local activists I had met.

He gave me a brief distracted glance and said, "Come on in," as he gestured for me to go ahead of him up the steep stairs covered in industrial gray carpet, piles of advertising flyers and phone books, and so much debris that it looked like they'd never been swept.

When we arrived at STOP's office space three floors up, Todd gestured to a stack of water-wrinkled paper with smeared signatures and addresses next to one of the computers. He asked if I would mind entering contact information into STOP's database. Todd was the only other person in STOP's office for most of the morning. He attended to various activities and stopped to talk to me every so often as I typed in addresses.

"I'm going to [local state senator's] fund-raiser this week. He's going to be running for lieutenant governor. This guy is really cool. He's definitely the most liberal Democrat in the state senate. The tickets are $250 a piece, but he knows who his base is, so activist leaders get tickets for $50 apiece. Sometimes I stop and go, 'Wow, I just got involved with this group looking to do a little civil disobedience, now I'm getting phone calls from politicians to help get them elected.' If you want an activist ticket, I might be able to get you one."

I made some noncommittal murmur as he walked toward the front of the office without waiting for my response.

Later in the morning the office quickly went from quiet to chaotic as the other staff members started to arrive. There was a lot going on that day: a staff meeting, the group's monthly vigil in front of city hall, and Lucas, a White high school student who was in charge of student organizing for STOP, was going to receive an award that evening for his work with STOP.

When it was time for the staff meeting, I looked up from my data entry to see if they were going to let me go with them this time. Todd looked like he was trying to avoid my gaze. When I caught his eye, he asked me if I would be willing to stay and finish the work I had begun. "We really need that as soon as possible because we have a mailing going out soon," he explained.

The office was quiet again for the hour they were gone, and then the activity returned in a flurry. All the staff members apparently had tasks that had to be done before the vigil, and everyone seemed to be in everyone else's way.

Todd had been looking for information about another group's protest schedule on a radical political website when he called out, "Hey, look, they have some video of our last protest on the independent media website." He turned up the audio so that the sounds of protest filled the room. "Five, six, seven, eight, stop the killing by the state. One, two, three, four, it's racist, cruel, and anti-poor."

We could hear Todd's voice saying, "Are we going to stand for state murder?" and the crowd responding, "No!"

Lucas was the first to come to sit by Todd at the computer. "Listen to that crowd!" he said.

Marge, an African American woman in her early fifties who was in charge of organizing friends and family of people on death row, moved to stand behind them and looked over their shoulders. I waited to see if Doreen, the White woman in her early twenties who served as STOP's live-in intern office manager, would also join the group around the computer, but she continued to slouch in her seat in front of another computer.

"This isn't the sort of speaking that you would do for a class or a lecture about the death penalty; it's for whipping up a crowd. People should take a lesson from pro wrestling," Todd explained. He imitated a segment where a pro wrestling referee talks about the upcoming match between the Avenger and the Claw, and the Avenger breaks in, grabs the mike, and says, "Hear *this* Claw, your days are numbered! The Avenger is coming, and the Claw won't be able to crawl when I'm done with him!" Todd said, using the voice, passion, and anger associated with pro wrestlers.

Marge pointed out a section of the audio when the lead death penalty prosecutor walked out of the building, and the crowd started booing on its own. "Lock him up! Lock him up!" the crowd yelled.

Todd smiled and said, "God, you got to love these moments!"

The doorbell rang, and Lucas ran back down the stairs and came up with a young Asian man who looked to be about Lucas's age. Lucas called out, "I've got the signs," and turned around to leave.

Marge muttered, "We shouldn't be having staff meetings on vigil days. That's for sure."

"It snuck up on me," Todd explained defensively.

Everyone filed out of the office except Doreen. I was not sure if I was supposed to go with the group. Doreen looked over her shoulder and seemed surprised to see me standing there. "Oh, I'm not going today. You'd better hurry—they'll leave without you."

I jogged down the stairs to the sidewalk and caught the group as they were getting into their cars.

Marge called out that she had to stop somewhere afterward as she slid into her car, so I followed Todd, Lucas, and Lucas's friend to Todd's car.

I was reaching to open the door for the back passenger-side seat when Lucas interrupted what he had been saying to Todd, gestured toward his friend and me, and said, "You guys get in back; I have some stuff I need to talk about with Todd."

I swallowed feelings of annoyance and humiliation and a desire to point out that I had been opening the door to the backseat already. I climbed into the car and I looked over at Lucas's friend. He seemed unfazed as he silently looked out the window.

"Tonight, when I accept the award, I'm going to make sure that I mention how we've been making connections with the African American community." Lucas was referring to the acceptance speech he was planning for that evening's ceremony when he would receive an award for his work with STOP from the regional service organization associated with his church.

"There are going to be a lot of important people there. A lot," Todd said as he drove wildly, nearly hitting a couple of cars as he adjusted his seat while negotiating dense urban traffic.

"Like I said, I'll make sure to mention how we've been making connections with the African American community in my acceptance speech."

Lucas's assumptions about my value to the conversation proved correct; I didn't recognize enough of the names to follow their conversation. Judging from Lucas's friend's continued silent stare out the window, he didn't either.

When we were almost to our destination, Lucas turned in his seat and said, "We got a lot of signatures at the Indigo Girls concert, didn't we? You tabled for that, right?" I must have looked as confused as I felt because he started to ask me again.

Todd interrupted him. "No, you *remember*, it was the woman *who used to be an assistant district attorney*."

Lucas gave Todd a look that indicated that Lucas clearly knew this, and that Lucas was basically asking if I was that woman.

Todd gave Lucas a meaningful look, silently pleading with him to be quiet, likely to prevent Lucas from further revealing that he could not keep track of who I was, even though he had known me for months.

Todd talked quickly. "Yeah, she was really great—very aggressive. She talked to everyone. She didn't wait for people to come to her. She went right up to them. She didn't wait to see if they were against the death penalty or not—just went right up to them. No waiting for them to come to her."

Todd stopped for a moment as he pulled up next to a parking spot on the street that had a "reserved parking" sign on it. "Should we take his spot today?" he asked with a sardonic laugh as he peeled out and drove away.

Until Lucas said, "Excellent idea! God knows how many people we could keep alive by making him take an extra ten minutes on his way to work," I didn't know Todd was referring to the local district attorney.

Todd found a free spot a couple of blocks from city hall. We climbed out of the car and went to grab the signs for the vigil out of the trunk. Todd took out his phone and made a call while Lucas handed stacks of signs to his friend and me. Once his friend and I had all of the signs, Lucas announced, "I'll meet you guys at the vigil. I have to go and talk to someone about tonight," and walked off in the opposite direction. Todd turned and continued his phone conversation as he walked toward city hall.

Lucas's friend and I followed silently behind.

Organization of the Book

This book is organized to address the question "How do such chronically failing, high-risk, altruistic social movement groups persist?" This larger question is broken into three interrelated subquestions: (1) How do such groups attract involvement into risky action? (2) How do groups recover when risky action ends badly? (3) How do such groups' histories shape the groups' styles of persistence? Answering these questions requires detailing group dynamics over successively longer periods of time, thus the book also proceeds according to a temporal logic.[11]

Chapters 2 and 3 address the first two subquestions with stories from each group followed by more general exploration of the dynamics illustrated in the two stories. The stories provide detailed pictures of processes of persistence and transformation in the Catholic Worker community and STOP. Each story illustrates the fine-tuning of an emotional dynamic *within* one of the two groups.

Chapter 4 builds on the previous two chapters to answer the third question: How do such groups' histories shape their styles of persistence? This chapter compares stories about the evolution of emotional dynamics in the two groups over my three years of observation. It offers a general explanation for how these groups persist through either speeding up or slowing down their internal emotional dynamics.

Chapter 5, the conclusion, explores the implications of the theory developed across the earlier chapters to suggest a general theory of social organization. The "Methods Appendix" discusses methodological considerations for investigating the evolution of emotional dynamics.

The stories in this book are written to evoke the groups' emotional experiences in the reader and to highlight the relevant patterns of action.[12] These sections resemble creative nonfiction or memoir, meaning

---

11. I think about the approach that I take as "modest realism." By this I mean that I work under the assumption that there is a relational and contextualized but also very *real* reality out there to be known. Mead puts forth a similar qualified realist empiricist position. He states, "It may be thinkable that viewed from some vast distance the order of some of what we call the same events might differ in different perspectives . . ." (1932, 13). Yet such limits do not mean that the social scientist need to give up the assertion that there is something real to be studied and that scientific investigation contributes to this knowledge. "[The scientist] recognized far more adequately than the layman the insurmountable obstacles that defend the cognizable world from any complete comprehension by . . . science; but he has never relegated the object of his knowledge to the creations of his own perceptions and thought" (1932, 95). Every position offers only a limited view of this reality, so every attempt to represent this reality is necessarily incomplete—not completely subjective, but influenced by the positions of the observer (myself) and the observed (the Catholic Worker community and STOP) and incomplete (Lefebvre 2004, 25; Mead 1932, 13, 95).

12. Stories' potential for systematic exploration and representation of experience is particularly relevant for the sociology of religion. James's *Varieties of Religious Experience* marked a burgeoning social scientific exploration of religion. Although religious experience was the focus of James's work, ironically *experience* became off-limits for social scientific inquiry (McGuire 2000, 204; Yamane 2000). An exception is Dawn Moon's work (2004). By revealing how her personal identity influenced her experience in the field, she makes claims about experience that resonate beyond the specific setting. Recently there has been a push to understand and convey the mechanisms of religious experience (McGuire 2007; Bender 2007; McRoberts 2004; Smith 2008). In the methods appendix, I explore how Lefebvre's *Rhythmanalysis* ([1992] 2004) offers useful methods for exploring

that although they depict social processes, they are uninterrupted by sociological commentary and are relatively long compared to traditional ethnographic accounts.[13] This literary style is well suited for depicting interconnected sensory experiences and emotional processes. Read as a whole, these stories illustrate the dynamics driving the evolution of such groups' emotional logics. Although the stories highlight the fluidity of social organization, they also reveal patterns in the chaos. They should be read with the goal of discerning these patterns.

However, unlike a novel where each chapter contributes to the overarching story that unfolds over the course of the whole book, the goal of each chapter is to convey social dynamics at a particular timescale, *not* to convey a section of a larger story. In a novel, events generally unfold sequentially, but the stories here are like nested Russian dolls—the first stories unfold over a couple of months, the second ones over about six to eight months, and the last stories over about a year. Because the chapters are crafted to communicate dynamics at different timescales, they do not have the same temporal connections between chapters that you would find in a novel. For example, some of the events depicted in chapter 4 actually occurred before events depicted in chapter 3. In order to avoid confusion over the temporal order of events, it is best to read each chapter as a stand-alone story told from a different temporal perspective.

The theory sections that follow the stories use the logic of comparison as scaffolding to move from the local and visceral to the general and abstract.[14] By comparing the modification of emotional processes *across* the two groups to provide a general view of the groups' *emotional techniques*, *expectations*, and *adjustments of speed* over time, these comparative sections highlight the role of *history*, *timing*, and *distance* in negotiating moral action.[15] Although the dynamics explained in these sections are

---

religious experience, as well as how social scientists can draw on literary tools to convey findings about many types of experience to readers in meaningful ways.

13. This book is a product of ethnographic investigations of emotional dynamics as they unfold over time, and this process has resulted in a text that is, in large part, literary in form. In order to highlight the role of *time*, I had to link scenes *across time* without interrupting them with sociological narrative. The end result is a book with sections that read like chapters from a novel. Textual analysis and postmodern ethnography *begin* with literary techniques. Although this text shares a general literary quality with both of these other traditions, especially in comparison with approaches that generate sociology that looks similar to natural science, this text arrives at a literary-looking product from a different path. In particular, the assumptions that led to the literary format of this book are rooted in different theoretical traditions, specifically pragmatist and Durkheimian approaches to investigating the social world.

14. The approach to studying groups in this volume responds to Harrington and Fine's call for work that accounts for both the broad conceptual regularities and complexity of interaction processes in small groups (2000, 313).

15. Glaeser, taking up a similarly modest empiricist position, suggests the limits of representa-

clearly central to high-risk altruistic social movement groups, they are also relevant to involvement in religious and other voluntary associations and with work associated with emotional high burnout, such as teaching, social work, and nursing.[16]

My claims in these comparative theory sections must be provisional. As is generally true of theories developed inductively, all of the available data went into generating my theory.[17] Testing and further specification will have to wait for future studies.

Overview of the Chapters

Chapter 2 identifies the emotional techniques the groups used to attract member involvement in high-risk actions and to manage these members' subsequent positive and negative emotional reactions. Both groups attracted involvement by creating opportunities for high-risk action. The

---

tion require us to carefully choose the stories we tell with our data. He suggests three types that ethnographers can tell: "(1) there is first its concrete embodiment in particular people, their actions in concrete time-space in all its singular curiosity. (2) The second is the social formation as the effect of process, its becoming, maintenance, or disintegration understood as a case standing for a class of phenomena. (3) Finally, interest can attach itself to the patterns, principles, or regularities underlying the very dynamics of process" (2005, 32; numbers inserted). This volume develops all three of the types that Glaeser lays out. The stories about each group in chapters 2, 3, and 4 provide particular detail while communicating how the particulars are the product of the social process depicted in the story. The abstract theoretical sections that follow in each chapter, and comprise the entirety of chapter 5, attend to the regularities underlying the dynamics of process. In telling the first two types of stories, this book examines the factors that influence how, where, and when chronically thwarted altruistic social movement groups focus their attention, and the consequences of the habits of attention they develop. In telling the last type of story, this book examines the evolution of social organization. In telling all three types of stories, this book builds on Mead's insights on the role of history in social organization and Victor Turner's and Van Gennep's challenges to describe the overarching patterns that organize the relationships between rites (Turner 1969, 42; Van Gennep 1960, 10–11).

16. I can only claim validity for the two cases I observed directly: the Catholic Worker Community and STOP. Catholic Worker communities in particular are known for being idiosyncratic. Similarly, based on my limited exposure to other anti–death penalty groups, national anti–death penalty groups and explicitly religious anti–death penalty groups operate according to significantly different dynamics than STOP's. I focus less on the symbolic discourse the groups draw on as they negotiate their day-to-day interactions, which is another reason why the analysis here may or may not be directly relevant to other Catholic Worker communities or anti–death penalty groups. These limitations on my capacity to make general claims about Catholic Worker communities and anti–death penalty groups are not of serious concern because my primary goal is not to add to the body of empirical work on either group. Rather than furthering understanding of these two specific movements, I focus on the relationship between interactional and emotional dynamics and the evolution of social organization. My goal is to provide a new vantage point on these social processes (cf. Riesebrodt 1993). As a result, readers may recognize dynamics relevant to groups they know intimately, which are on the surface very different from the ones I studied.

17. See Lewontin (2000, 95) and Spillman (2004, 219).

story about the Catholic Workers illustrates how they continually exposed themselves to the contingencies of poverty when they placed themselves "in God's hands." Sometimes they were able to feed a hungry neighbor, but just as often they did not have the resources to grant such requests. Other times they engaged in potentially dangerous interactions in under-policed areas. The Catholic Workers' uncertain circumstances created intense interactions, exhilarating emotion, a sense of purpose, and, in the most powerful cases, mystical experiences.

The story about STOP in chapter 2 shows how each participant encountered the threat of face-to-face conflict with passersby during the group's sparsely attended public actions. Although these small public actions carried social and even physical risks, face-to-face conflict created opportunities for feelings of moral authority, righteous anger, inevitable victory, and mythic importance.

A comparison of dynamics that attract involvement in these groups suggests how risk followed by success generates feelings of thrilling expansion. Yet risks can end badly. Thus groups' persistence required emotion work beyond the excitement of risky involvement.

Chapter 3 depicts the groups failing and recovering. When these groups failed, they experienced the opposite of the emotional dynamics associated with success: contraction and low levels of enthusiasm. In response to failure, the groups developed emotional techniques for recovering and avoiding future draining interactions.

The story about the Catholic Worker community in chapter 3 illustrates how after each struggle that ended in failure, the Workers redefined what it meant to live up to the Catholic Worker ideal of taking personal responsibility for the poorest of the poor. Despite their continually changing expectations, the community survived as a center of action with a coherent history by courting grief as an indirect route to laughter and mystical awe. Both laughter and mystical awe provided release from routine conflict and frustration over their sense of inefficacy.[18]

The story about STOP in chapter 3 describes how internal conflict followed closely on the heels of STOP's early popularity, eventually contributing to the breakdown of the group. STOP's director renewed in-

18. Although the Catholic Workers often reveled in chaos, at times they became overwhelmed and drained by their inability to control even aspects of their most personal contexts. During these times, they used laughter, storytelling, and religious ritual to reframe their experiences in terms of timeless universals and in doing so create a sense of transcendent timelessness. Hervieu-Léger describes how reframing situations in terms of timeless religious conditions can create this affect: "By placing the origin of the world outside time and by attributing the order of the world to a necessity beyond society, it erases the chaos represented by reality, at the same time removing the reality from the transforming effect of human control" (2000, 84).

volvement by attracting new participants and shifting the group's focus to expanding its networks and influencing electoral politics.

The theoretical section following the stories explains how both groups survived collapse by reestablishing involvement or attracting new involvement. Their negative experiences served as emotional warning signals, so evolving strategies became ancestors of earlier struggles and failures. Thus their strategies lagged behind their unfolding contexts. The comparison of the two groups suggests how such groups can harness the intensity of threatening emotions, like grief and horror, to stabilize themselves.[19] However, the number of anticipated threats increases over a group's history, which leaves fewer paths to action. Despite continually adjusting to shifting demands of changing conditions, such groups inevitably contribute to the conditions that generate their own exhaustion, disappointment, frustration, and loss. By detailing the evolution of emotional processes over time, this book bridges divisions between cultural and structural approaches to the study of emotions (Stets and Turner 2006), a division that has been carried into the recently growing body of work on the role of emotions in social movements (Jasper 1997; Goodwin, Jasper, and Polletta 2001; Flam and King 2005).

Chapter 4 describes how both STOP and the Workers attempted to avoid threats so that they could create stability out of uncertain conditions. Although both groups narrowed their focus and emotional expectations to protect against the drain of future failure, their techniques changed at a slower rate than their contexts, and as a result drawing on these strategies eventually undermined the groups' future stability.

The story about the Catholic Workers in chapter 4 illustrates how they developed aversions to planning and righteous anger in response to numerous failed projects. The Workers' commitment to their internal focus competed with their needs to bring external resources, such as people and money, into the group. For example, the Workers yearned to grow their community, but their emotional strategies often confused and even offended newcomers.

The story about STOP in chapter 4 describes how the group's leaders rejected efforts to establish an internal focus in response to their history of internal conflicts. They maintained their enthusiasm with horror stories about injustices and political corruption, which engendered feelings of righteous anger. The leaders' emotional techniques failed to draw in the

---

19. Douglas describes the power inherent in destructive forces if used successfully: "The danger which is risked by boundary transgression is power. Those vulnerable margins and those attacking forces which threaten to destroy good order represent the power inhering in the cosmos. Ritual which can harness these for good is harnessing power indeed" (1966, 199).

lower-level members who were responsible for managing STOP's mundane internal tasks. As a result, lower-level group members frequently left the group after comparatively short periods of involvement.

The stories in chapter 4 illustrate how the groups' evolving patterns of action generated rhythmic cycles of negative and positive emotions over time. As circumstances changed, strategies and emotional techniques previously developed to protect stability began to weaken the groups. The groups persisted not only by recovering from collapse but also by developing a capacity to minimize these periods of vulnerability. The unfolding cycles of involvement generated emotional rhythms over time. The story about the Catholic Workers in chapter 4 illustrates how they reduced their vulnerability to ultimate collapse by focusing on recovery from frequent smaller collapses. Because of their rapid fluctuation between emergence and collapse, involvement in the Catholic Worker community felt timeless. Their speed of involvement generated quick shifts in expectations that often surprised outsiders or newcomers. By hastening collapse and recovery, the Catholic Workers increased their internal flexibility and decreased the influence of their surrounding environment.

The story about STOP in chapter 4 describes how the leaders forestalled collapse by extending the distance between their mundane internal responsibilities and their external focus of attention. This slowed their cycle of involvement. STOP's increasingly external focus enabled the group to extend their influence in the local political world, but it also undermined the intensity of the members' involvement, putting them at a greater risk of being pulled away from the group into other centers of involvement.

A comparison of emotion management in these two groups in the theory section of chapter 4 reveals how such groups have to contend with their own strategies, which offer protection against past drains but undermine the potential for action that is crucial to the future stability of the group.[20] The long-term evolution of emotional dynamics in these groups illustrates how the histories of such groups influence their focus, emotional expectations, and speed, which in turn influence future conditions on the groups. Persistence requires either developing tools

20. Past work has examined how individual commitment (Kanter 1972), larger cultural discourses (Lichterman 1996), and historical trends (Polletta 2002) have influenced social movement groups. Alternatively, this chapter shifts the focus toward the internal dynamics that shape social movement groups. It does this by examining how processes *within* groups evolve over time. For example, the Catholic Worker community housed guests who stole from them until frustrations about missing items led to infighting that threatened to devastate the community. STOP worked to build consensus on all of their decisions until their inability to achieve consensus led to a lack of organization that threatened to unravel the group.

to recover repeatedly from collapse or forestalling this collapse. The first accelerates the life cycle of a stable pattern to create a stable meta-pattern out of routine collapse. The second slows down the life cycle of a stable pattern.

Because such groups cycle through negative and positive emotions, events affect them in different ways at different times. Changes—such as political shifts, internal conflicts, or fluctuations in material resources—influence groups differently depending on *when* they occur in the groups' emotional histories. Conversely, groups speed up or slow down the rate at which they modify their emotional processes in order to avert conditions they sense are dangerous. In other words, they alter the influence of perceived threats by changing the tempo of their emotional cycles.[21]

Chapter 5 suggests how the theoretical approach developed across the previous chapters might be used to think about social organization more generally, and thus it contributes to general theoretical discussions about implicit processes that influence social action (Durkheim [1912] 1995; Schutz 1967; Bateson 1972; Bourdieu 1977).[22] This chapter describes how stable social patterns can be seen as evolving cycles of emergence, stability, collapse, and reemergence that move at varying speeds and rhythms. I argue that such patterns emerge when anticipation shunts action into increasingly well-worn paths, and that these patterns collapse when increasingly rigid organization limits access to necessary resources.

From a distance, these groups seem solid and stable; up close, they seem fluid and disordered. This book assumes a mid-range position,

21. By depicting the patterned but highly contingent quality of social movement group processes, chapter 4 contributes to the growing interest in complexity in the study of social movements (McAdam, Tarrow, and Tilly 2001) and small groups (Arrow, McGrath, and Berdahl 2000; Farrell 2001). However, unlike many of the previous forays into these territories, the picture I present does not amalgamate multiple perspectives. Rather, it provides an integrative picture of the evolution of complex processes. This evolution is in response to a particular pattern's history of external constraints and internal constraints. Kanter (1972), Jasper (1997), and McAdam, Tarrow, and Tilly (2001) have presented complex pictures of social movement dynamics, but at the cost of a proliferation of processes (emotional, cognitive, structural, cultural, biographical, organizational, group, political, etc.). Although they focus on small groups, Arrow, McGrath, and Berdahl (2000) have similarly taken an additive approach to understanding small groups as complex systems.

22. I did not choose to study these groups because they are representative of small groups or collective action. On the contrary, they are the exception to the apparent rule of rational self-interested action. Investigating such unlikely behavior holds the potential not only for understanding how groups are able to maintain involvement despite few opportunities for success, but also for understanding many everyday aspects of group involvement more generally; by looking at the extraordinary, we gain insight into the most mundane and ordinary aspects of social life. These groups' very existence offers a sort of natural laboratory for investigating the same fundamental social factors that influence us all. As Stolte, Fine, and Cook (2001) argue, because it permits recognition of the dense texture of everyday life, microsociology can be used to gain insight into broader social issues. However, this theoretical potential is all icing on the cake of the intrinsic value of the stories of what it feels like to live everyday life within these groups.

which smoothes processes but does not solidify them into static or discrete entities. The "Methods Appendix" discusses how social scientists can gain analytic leverage by repeatedly shifting focus. It explains how this book illustrates this process by moving closer to convey gritty physical emotional dynamics in a literary style and by moving farther out to develop smooth abstract theory with the comparative method.

TWO

Thrilling Risk Attracts Involvement

In the stories that follow, the Catholic Worker community's and STOP's members' ultimate goals for social change remained relatively constant. Both stories illustrate how the groups felt that their day-to-day challenges followed directly from their ultimate goals, despite the fact that their everyday activities more directly reflected their immediate environments than their long-term political goals. The section that follows the two stories draws comparisons between the two groups to present a more general theory of the relationship between social movement groups' ultimate goals and their day-to-day challenges.

The story about the Catholic Worker community depicts how their lack of stable resources shaped their day-to-day activities. The community relied on small donations. Occasionally they received unexpected windfalls, such as a hundred blankets or cases of string beans. Other times they were unable to fulfill their neighbors' most basic requests for shelter or food. Although their inconsistent access to resources created moments of tremendous stress and strain, the stress of financial uncertainty—and the fear of failure, suffering, and pain that accompanied this uncertainty—left the Workers open to moments of joyous serendipity. An unexpected check from an unknown parish felt like a miracle when the group was down to its last dollar.

The Workers' sense of vulnerability also created opportunities for intensely intimate and surprisingly satisfying interactions between the Workers and their neighbors.[1] In such peak moments, the Catholic Workers did not feel like they were accomplishing things "out there": they saw themselves as expanding "in here." Members lost their sense of themselves as individuals and became part of a burgeoning sense of "we." Feelings of expansion might include a particular person, the neighborhood, the Catholic Worker movement, or even God.

In the story that follows, I describe my initial reaction to the chaos and uncertainty in the Catholic Workers' community. I then detail how living with chaos and uncertainty could create space for potentially thrilling experiences.

————

The story about STOP depicts how the group's changing funding, political attention, and activist attention shaped their day-to-day activities. When initially begun, STOP had no direct connections to electoral politics. In these early days, STOP measured success in terms of protest turnout, number of arrests, and media coverage, and they enjoyed huge success. Eventually, however, STOP lost political and activist attention. Despite these losses, the group continued to grow in membership, access to resources, and political connections.

Eventually, directorship of STOP changed. The new director played up STOP's history of success and its large membership to gain leverage within the field of traditional politics. He worked to transform STOP from an activist-run and focused group, to a professional organization committed to gaining political leverage in order to achieve legal reform. As the group's resources and tactics changed, the organization became increasingly hierarchical. Emotional tone varied by organizational position, so those at the top had significantly different emotional experiences from those at the bottom.

In the story that follows, I describe the intense face-to-face conflict with passersby that group members experienced during their monthly vigils in front of the district attorney's office. I then detail how these high-conflict situations provided different types of thrilling and satisfying experiences for the various types of group members who participated.

1. By living in the same neighborhood and in similar conditions, the Catholic Workers create routine face-to-face encounters and the potential to politicize the everyday experiences they share with their neighbors (Taylor and Rupp 2002, 141).

Draining Helplessness and Chaos at the Catholic Worker House

I answered the knock at the door to find a large, middle-aged, African American man swaying on the stoop. "May I help you?" I asked. Rather than answering me, he tried to shoulder his way through the door. Afraid to let him in, but also afraid my middle-class sensibilities would offend the Workers, I moved in front of him. "Please wait outside while I make you your sandwich," I instructed, but my voice lacked conviction.

"Shut the door! Shut the door!" Linda yelled to me as she ran to the door while wiping her hands on a towel. I slammed the door in the man's face and jumped back, unsure how I had screwed up, but fairly certain I had.

Linda wedged herself in front of me and opened the door a crack. "Hello, John, what do you need?" Linda asked.

John mumbled, "I need deodorant. Deodorant. Can I have some deodorant?"

"I can give you Slim Jims," Linda said decisively as she shut the door on John again.

I stifled a nervous laugh at the incongruity of John's request and Linda's response. Linda seemed unfazed as she put beef jerky and other snacks in a plastic grocery bag for John.

"John used to be a forklift operator with a good job, but now he huffs and he's psychotic most of the time," Joan explained in a tranquil tone. "He's nice, but he's out of it and huge. It's hard to get him out once he's in. On occasion"—she gave Linda a mischievous look—"he's been relentless about trying to kiss Linda."

Linda snorted. "He's not mean-spirited, but he's aggravating nonetheless. We used to give him a food box, but he was selling it before he even got down the street. So now we just give him enough for himself when he comes to the door."

"Sometimes he shows up with a can he wants us to open and warm up for him. Of course, that's fine," said Joan, already turning back to the open newspaper on the table in front of her. "I'm not convinced he has a permanent home."

It was time for me to go, so I left the Catholic Worker house just behind John. I saw Mr. Diaz, a man who had come to the house for a sandwich earlier, and a friend of his laughing and yelling to each other as they pushed shopping carts unsteadily down the middle of the street.

When he saw me leave the house, Mr. Diaz headed toward me. He said something to me in a lowered voice, but I couldn't make it out. I knew he wanted me to move closer, but I was wary of moving much closer to an inebriated man I didn't know. He moved closer and looked at me pleadingly. I hesitated then moved toward him, deciding he was too slight and drunk to represent much of a threat. He repeated himself.

"I'm sorry, I can't hear you," I told him.

He looked embarrassed as he glanced at his friend over his shoulder and turned back toward me with a pleading look again. I moved closer still.

"Underwear?" I heard him ask.

Enormously relieved that I finally understood him and that his request wasn't threatening, I exclaimed, "Ah, underwear! Let me go see!" louder than I meant to.

Mr. Diaz's gaze darted about, as he apparently tried to assess whether anyone had heard my proclamation.

As I turned back to the house, I saw Blueberry, a semipermanent guest at the Worker house, leaning dangerously far out of a third-story window.

Years before St. Francis's Catholic Worker opened their doors, Blueberry made her home in this neighborhood. Blueberry had run away from home when she was thirteen and joined a group of migrant farmworkers who moved up and down the East Coast according to the picking season. This is where she acquired the only name I had ever heard her called, Blueberry. She came to know the Catholic Worker house through the sandwiches offered at lunch and dinner, and the holiday dinners organized for the neighborhood.

Blueberry's face, swollen with alcoholism and damaged from sun and multiple beatings, told the story of a hard life. Sometimes she slept in the park; other times she lived with different men. She usually dressed in multiple layers of dirty clothes regardless of fluctuations in temperature, and she smelled of alcohol, cigarettes, and deep-fried food. Although she was often bleary-eyed, unsteady, and wet-lipped, her keen intelligence, quick wit, and irrepressible laughter made her popular with the older hard-drinking guys who hung around in front of the neighborhood liquor store.

"Get out! Get lost!" she bellowed. "There's no underwear for you here. No underwear for you! You hear me! No fucking underwear!"

"I wasn't talking to you!" Mr. Diaz yelled back, masking his embarrassment with anger.

"No fucking underwear for you!" I heard Blueberry yell as I closed the door behind me.

I must have looked as dazed as I felt because Joan laughed in sympathy. "I know, it's often crazy around here," she said, clearly enjoying my bewilderment.

I went to the kitchen to ask Ramona, a White Protestant extended community member in her early fifties who'd been involved with the Catholic Worker movement for almost twenty years, if there was any underwear around.

"Well, I don't know about that . . . I'll go check in the clothing room. You finish making the veggie meatballs." A few minutes later she returned. "Just as I thought—no underwear. Ridiculous high heels, glittery dresses we have, but no underwear."

I headed back out to tell Mr. Diaz the bad news and found the drunken exchange of insults had continued in my absence. He stopped mid-insult and looked at me hopefully.

"I'm sorry, Mr. Diaz. We don't have any underwear."

"That's OK. Thank you anyway," he said graciously.

I climbed in my car and drove away pondering my futility as I thought, "Even if I could give him underwear, he'd still be moving his belongings around in a shopping cart."[2]

Catholic Worker History

In the early 1930s, Peter Maurin came to Dorothy Day because she was a journalist, political radical, and recent convert to Catholicism. Maurin—a mystic, anarchist philosopher, and revolutionary—had a lot to say about the world, and he was in search of people who would listen. Dorothy listened and wrote as well, and together they launched the *Catholic Worker*, a newspaper they sold for a penny a copy in New York City's Union Square. By living out the beatitudes and organizing their lives around performing the Corporal Works of Mercy (feeding the hungry, giving drink to the thirsty, welcoming the stranger, clothing the naked, visiting the sick, visiting the prisoner, and burying the dead), the founders of the Catholic Worker movement believed they could fundamentally transform society (Day 1939).

The paper advocated Maurin's radical politics, which he based on Catholic theology and personalist philosophy. The Catholic Workers stressed the importance of personal responsibility for the poor, arguing that people should live in community in poor neighborhoods, give hospitality to the otherwise homeless in their community house, share all

2. As Allahyari points out, most of the day-to-day work of feeding the urban poor takes place in small groups where participants develop personal connections to the people they serve (2000, 1). Understanding the emotion work that enables people to manage feelings of being overwhelmed in the face of pervasive poverty is crucial to discussions about those who work to serve those in poverty.

that they have, and protest any institution that negatively affects the poor. Maurin believed that the transformation of society would involve a general move toward community-based sustenance farming. The end point of the Catholic Worker moral vision was a utopian return to the earth.

Soon Dorothy Day was living what she wrote, inviting otherwise homeless people to stay with her in her modest apartment on the Lower East Side of Manhattan. Persuaded by Maurin and Day's vision, others came to live and work with them. In accordance with their personalist philosophy, neither "guests," people who would otherwise be homeless who lived in the Catholic Worker house, nor workers gave formal commitments. People came and went as their conscience and sense of personal responsibility dictated. This continuously evolving group ran up against the limits of Day's apartment, found a larger space, and eventually housed many guests and fed hundreds a day. The paper grew, Day's reputation grew, and others opened Catholic Worker houses across the country and eventually in other parts of the world.

Although the Catholic Worker movement may look like a charity or a lay religious order within the Catholic Church, a commitment to social change and revolution is central to its vision. A priest speaking at the opening of a Catholic Worker house captured the Workers' understanding of their movement succinctly when he said, "The Catholic Worker is not about charity, it's about justice."[3] A dedication to social change is evident in their commitment to protest, but also in the finer points of the movement's philosophy. Activities that many would usually associate with activism, like picketing or acts of civil disobedience, are understood to be a small part of a broader effort to create justice in day-to-day life. Catholic Workers believe serving the poor is both protest and positive action toward change. To them, feeding someone at the door is a revolutionary activity.

It was in this tradition that a peace group affiliated with St. Francis, a parish in a poor urban neighborhood, bought a house, handed the deed to a holding company that holds the deeds to many Catholic Worker houses across the country, and invited a large Catholic Worker community in another city to send Workers to staff this house. St. Francis's house was in a neighborhood with low rates of employment and high rates of drug dealing, drug use, and prostitution. The neighborhood was known for particularly pure and cheap heroin. Although I did indeed

---

3. See Allahyari (2000, 33).

hear neighbors and guests talk about heroin infrequently, as one of the community's guests once told me, "Everyone around here either is or was a crackhead."

Only the buildings remained constant in the ebb and flow of St. Francis's house. Even the buildings, which had long outlasted their inhabitants, changed as members made modifications to suit their current projects and repaired what they could whenever resources permitted. St Francis's community members came and went in revolving-door fashion. Some would arrive explaining they intended to stay for a few months and ended up staying for years. Other times people came with an intention to stay for years and would leave after a week or two. The neighborhood changed quickly as well. Neighbors would come by daily for years and then suddenly disappear. Sometimes they would resurface a few months later, but they often did not. A sense of the community's history tied current members to earlier members they'd never met; but the meaning of this history changed continually as old members left, new members joined, and current members filtered this oral history through their personal experiences. The house was new enough that members had the sense that they knew the entire history of the community, but it seemed to me that this couldn't last much longer.

Joan and Linda led the house during my time with the community, but other extended members—people who involved themselves in much of the house's activities but stayed at the house only occasionally or not at all—were deeply involved. Joan had been living in the house for seven years and Linda had been living there for eight.

Joan, a White woman in her early fifties, was the charismatic leader of the house. Deeply influenced by politics of the Catholic left in the late 1960s, especially the writings of Thomas Merton and Dorothy Day, she converted to Catholicism while in college. But after a period of intense involvement, she drifted away from the Church.

She explained to me, "I'd spent most of my adult life away from the Church, but one day I saw a flyer in that co-op bookstore near the university. It announced a Mass in honor of Thomas Merton at St. Francis," the same church that initiated the Catholic Worker house she would ultimately help to lead. "I was curious. I'd thought the Catholic left just shriveled up and died after the sixties. I hadn't been in a Catholic church for over *fifteen* years, but as soon as I walked through the door and smelled that incense"—she paused—"it brought back religious feelings I hadn't felt in many, many years. In a way, it was like I was coming home to the home I didn't know I'd been missing." Father O'Leary talked about the local Catholic Worker house in his homily that day. "I made the decision right there to become involved. If this movement could survive, I knew right then I had to be a part of it."

Joan began by coming to the community's weekly Mass and potluck dinner and doing maintenance around the house. Like most of the leaders who had come before her, she thought she would serve as a support person, doing work around the house so that others would be freed up to work with the children. But community members left, she moved in, and she soon found herself making most of the decisions. "You know, sometimes I think about what would have happened if I hadn't seen that flyer, but I really don't think that was a possibility. I'm convinced it was part of a plan that's far bigger than me," she said, laughing at herself.

Joan often became grumpy or lost her temper, but she also supplied most of the enthusiasm that ran through the house. She told the stories that inspired laughter, tears, and mystical moments where community members felt that they had found God through serving hungry addicts and neighborhood children. Although she strove to "take things as they come" and "do what we can with what we've got," she had lofty spiritual and service goals for herself and for the house. Unavoidable disappointment provoked her darker moods.

She also suffered from frustration over her increasing dependence on other members of the community. She had significant vision problems when she joined the community, and over the next few years her vision deteriorated to the point where she had become legally blind. For the most part, she was independent, but she had come to rely on community members to help her accomplish an increasing number of the day-to-day tasks of living. As in any group of people who continually interact with one another, her impairment mostly dropped into the background, but occasionally Joan's vision and her resulting dependence sparked frustration and tension in the house.

Like Joan, Linda's role in the house changed considerably over the course of her involvement. Only eighteen years old when she arrived, she had planned to stay for a year. Not Catholic or even religious, and rather politically conservative at the time, Linda came to the house as a chance to do and see something different. She was looking for adventure, to be a visitor in a strange place away from her family before she started college. Many of the original members left during her first year. With each departure, Linda took up more and more responsibility. One year stretched into two, then Joan arrived and Linda began to play a significant role in assisting Joan because of her vision problems.

When I asked her to tell me how she got involved, she answered laughing, "Yes, that's a funny story. I came for only a year. That plan went well, huh? I think I must've scared everyone away! You see the house was full, and then I showed up and away they went." Eight years later she had finished college while continuing to live and work in the house.

In many ways, Joan's and Linda's personalities couldn't have differed more. Linda was much quieter and more cautious than Joan. Where Joan's moods were mercurial, Linda was unflappable. People would go in and out of Joan's good graces, but Linda remained a constant friend—after one passed her long probationary period. She could be distrustful of the well-intentioned middle-class people who tried to help the house in peripheral ways. She sensed that these people didn't "get it," meaning they had little personal experience with poverty and failed to see the radical purpose at the heart of the Workers' activities.[4]

Most of her friends were people from the neighborhood and the Catholic Worker community, even when she was spending much of her time as a student on a college campus. "Oh, they're silly, they really are. Concerned about this and that little thing without having any idea what's really going on." She laughed condescendingly. "What can you do about people who know so little and have seen so little? They think everyone who doesn't live in a nice house, drive a nice car, and have a nice job doesn't work hard or doesn't want these things. They're full of the American dream. Please!" Rather than arguing with or trying to educate those who "don't get it," Linda preferred to shake her head over their ignorance with other members of the Catholic Worker community.

A Theology of Vulnerability

A month after the day of the argument between Mr. Diaz and Blueberry, I spent the afternoon using the last of the food in the Workers' kitchen to make sandwiches for people who came to the door. Two hours passed quickly, and when I went to answer the next knock on the door, I was surprised to hear Joan say, "This will be the last one until we start all over at dinnertime."

A small but massively built Latino man who looked to be in his late twenties stood at the door. "I'm sorry to bother you," he said, looking embarrassed.

---

4. William James describes how such moral efforts can lead to withdrawal: "When the craving for moral consistency and purity is developed to this degree, the subject may well find the outer world too full of shocks to dwell in, and can unify his life and keep his soul unspotted only by withdrawing from it" (James [1902] 2007, 265).

"Oh, it's no bother," I said. "Hold on just a sec. I'll get you a sandwich and a few other things."

I went to close the door, and he quickly moved his head toward the narrowing opening and said, "Oh, no, I don't need food. I was hoping to get a candle."

Surprised, I hesitated for a moment. "OK. I'll check and be right back."

I told Joan what he had said.

"Dammit! He's sleeping in an abandoned house," she said, pressing her lips into a straight line and shaking her head briefly. "He wants the candle because he's cold, even though it won't give off any real warmth. They're going to burn these houses down; it's not safe. Ask him in so I can talk to him."

I invited him in, and he apologized as he entered, saying he wasn't going to be a regular.

"Do you need the candle for warmth?" Joan asked.

He looked uncomfortable but admitted that he did. "The place I stay at has no electricity. I just got out of prison. I earned almost three hundred dollars while I was in, but I've got to make it last until next month. I got a spot in a treatment program with a job placement program. I'm not an addict," he added quickly, "but I need a job. I only have to make it a month."

Joan told me to give him one of the candles sitting on the shelf. He tried to give Joan money for the candle, but she refused. He thanked us for the candle and left.

"They all leave prison like that, with no money and a criminal record that will make landing a job almost impossible."

"Why didn't you want me to give him food? If he has no money, he doesn't have food, right?"

"He said he didn't want it," she said, and shrugged.

"But why give him a candle when you said it wouldn't help and was dangerous?"

"What else could I do for him? Sometimes there's just not much you can do," she said, surprising me with her serenity.

There was another knock on the door an hour later. "Go ahead; they're only a few minutes late." I opened the door to an African American woman who looked like she was in her early twenties. She asked if she could be put on the list for the weekly boxes of food so quietly that I had to ask her to repeat herself.

Joan yelled to me to invite the woman in. The woman thanked me and followed me into the dining room with deference that pricked my conscience.

"How can we help you?" Joan asked.

The woman started to speak, telling Joan about her three children. She had lived in the neighborhood and had gotten food before, but she had only just moved back to the neighborhood.

I went back to the kitchen to make sandwiches for her. It seemed so inadequate, but it got me out of the room, and I didn't want to watch her ask for food.

"Yes, I remember you. I'll put you on the list," Joan said.

"When is the next food day?" the woman asked.

Without skipping a beat, Joan calmly asked, "Are you in trouble right now?" I didn't hear a response, but Joan called out to me, "Erika, put a food bag together for Gloria and her family. Give her whatever you can find."

Although Linda was supposed to return from the food bank with another load at any minute, for the moment the kitchen was almost bare. It had been a week since the last trip to the food bank. After a trip to the food bank, the kitchen and dining room were stacked with food. Huge boxes of Slim Jims and other snacks filled the dining room, and potatoes, onions, and boxes of vegetables sat in piles on the far side of the kitchen floor. Frozen food filled the freezer so full that food would fall out whenever I opened the door.

"Just throw whatever you can find in a bag, don't worry about making it nice and neat," Joan called to hurry me along. I opened the cupboards and eyed the cans of miniature corn, olives, water chestnuts, and sprouts.

As I handed the young woman the food, I apologized that it wasn't all that much and said she should come back the next day when the boxes would be available. Without looking in the bag, she thanked me profusely, attempting to hide relief that could only have followed desperation.

She left and Joan looked at me. "We can never do as much as we'd like to," she said as if she had read my mind.

Only minutes after the woman left, Linda arrived from her trip to the food bank. I went out to unload the car. When I opened the door to the backseat, I saw at least thirty cartons of Ben & Jerry's ice cream and burst out laughing.

Linda laughed as well. "I know it isn't good to be selfish, but in certain cases it just can't be helped!"

"I don't think you even have enough freezer space!"

"Then we'll just have to have an ice-cream party, won't we?"

Ms. Beth arrived as we were finishing unloading. On our next-to-last trip carrying the food into the house, Linda announced to Joan and Ms. Beth, "We will be having a surprise shortly!"

"You know I don't like surprises—tell me what it is!" demanded Joan in staged bad temper.

"You'll just have to be patient."

When we carried in armfuls of Ben & Jerry's, Joan clapped her hands and Ms. Beth chuckled and shook her head.

"Now, what are we supposed to do with all that ice cream?" Ms. Beth mumbled under her breath with a smile.

We managed to find space in the freezer for all but six cartons.

"Well, I'm afraid we have no other alternative," Linda said with a smile. "Spoons are our only recourse."

We passed around the cartons and spoons. Joan read the appeal letter she had just finished for the newsletter as we sat and ate ice cream.

Then Joan announced that a woman with four children was coming to talk to the Workers about staying at the house that afternoon. While Joan was explaining this, I saw a well-dressed, painfully thin, African American woman out the window. She looked at the house and wandered away only to come back again. After another pass, she came back and knocked at the door. Linda opened the door, and the woman introduced herself as Tina. Joan told her to sit with us.

We were still eating ice cream, so I offered some to Tina. She looked thrown and politely declined.

Joan asked Tina to explain what was going on.

Tina sat straight and looked at the table as she talked, occasionally raising her gaze to make sudden and guarded eye contact with the rest of us. "I've been kicked out of my apartment by my landlord. I refused to pay rent because we didn't have any running water. My mom's been helping me out, but she's always yelling at me in front of my kids about trying to steal her husband." She started crying. "My stepfather used to touch me, you know sexually, and when I told my mother about it, she yelled at me and my stepfather. He ended up leaving, and she always said I tried to steal him. Still does twenty years later. I'm not the kind of person who would do that. I promise you I was not trying to steal my mother's husband," she pleaded.

"Of course you weren't," murmured Joan.

Tina went on to say she had money to get an apartment, but she couldn't find one that was appropriate for her four kids. She apologized for crying. Joan gave her a sympathetic look and passed her tissues.

I tried to fight the urge to leave for the kitchen.

"I don't have anywhere to go, and if I go to a hotel, I'll use up all the money I've been saving. I have a fourteen-year-old boy, so he'd go to the men's shelter. People get stabbed and killed in there. There's no way I'm taking my boy to that shelter." She said she wanted to buy a house, that she thought that she might have enough money. "I don't think that I'd need to stay longer than a month—it can't take that long to find an apartment, right?"

The phone rang. "Ah, Ramona! Good timing," said Joan. "I was just going to call you. I wanted to know if it would be all right to use the room you just fixed up as a staff room if there was a pressing need for hospitality?" It was clear Ramona hesitated, but Joan laid on the guilt about the children along with many assurances that the room would be left as it was found. Finally, Ramona agreed.

Joan grinned at Tina, and it was clear the woman would be allowed to stay. Tina looked as though a tremendous burden had been lifted from her shoulders, and she started crying harder. Joan hung up the phone, and the group discussed the logistics of Tina moving in. Ten minutes later Joan said, "We'll see you later tonight. We're happy to have you," with a big smile.

Shortly after Tina left, neighborhood kids started arriving for the after-school program.

"How about ice cream for a snack today!?" Linda asked the kids. They responded with a cacophony of enthusiastic responses. "OK, OK, calm down. Everyone will get some. Today will be an ice-cream party day!"

———————

Over dinner a few hours later, Joan told the group how she had recently heard from a friend of hers who had gone to Rome for the canonization of a saint. "When [the saint] first started serving the poor, she thought that she was going to serve the pagans. But after she had been there long enough, after she had really spent time with the people, she started to see they were all in it together. She saw she *was* them. This is the goal for doing this work—to understand that we're all in this together, working together, helping each other." Linda and Ms. Beth, swept up in Joan's speech, nodded their heads in agreement as she spoke. "That's when you're really able to start doing the work, when you realize that you're not better than the people you help. In many ways, we need them more than they need us. This isn't charity."

Joan was invoking Catholic Worker theology as well as Catholic social teachings on the preferential option for the poor, which argue that God calls followers to advocate for the voiceless and powerless. Christian action demands efforts to restore justice and right relations in this life; consequently, the poor and vulnerable have a privileged moral claim on the community of Christian believers. This reasoning took the form of liberation theology in Central and South America, where the focus was on the poor mobilizing on their own behalf.[5] In the Catholic Workers' personalist theology, the focus is on the poor as other, not self. This theology inverts charity models of helping. The poor not only have a privileged moral claim on the Church; they also have a greater moral independence than those who are not poor. The poor need to advocate for themselves, but those who are not poor *need* the poor in order to live out their religious beliefs.

After dinner I headed home. While I was starting my car, two girls from the after-school program knocked on my car window. I was opening the door to see what they needed when they both dove into the car, grabbing me hard and saying, "Don't go!" Don't go!"

The girls weren't much smaller than me. I was so surprised by their friendly assault that I had to fight my knee-jerk reaction to push them off. I swallowed what I knew was irrational anger and explained that I had to go home, but I would be back.

One said, "Can I just have a hug?" even though she was already hugging me, so I relaxed and hugged them for a moment. I drove off a few moments later flustered. I couldn't tell if the girls were genuine or working me over; regardless, their emotional neediness left me with a sense that even if the Catholic Workers were resource rich, they would not be able to meet some of the most pressing needs of neighborhoods and guests. I thought of how little the Workers could do for the recently released prisoner and the mother who came before Linda returned from the food bank.

But then I thought of how the Workers also offered hospitality to a mother and her children and gave the neighborhood children an ice-cream party.

Still the frustration overwhelmed me. I thought of Joan talking about the recently canonized saint and wondered why such deep identification with suffering people didn't make the work more painful.

5. See Smith (1991).

Moments of Agape

A few weeks later, I heard a knock while I was working in the kitchen. Joan called to me in an aggravated tone, "Erika, can you help Jasmine out?"

I had heard people mention Jasmine. I knew that Jasmine was a prostitute and had been in and out of jail and that Joan found her provoking, but I had not met her.

Not sure whether Joan was irritated with Jasmine or me, I called out, "Sure," and hastily wiped my hands as I left the kitchen. Joan looked seriously inconvenienced as she waved me toward an African American woman who was extremely thin, a look I would later come to recognize as the most evident sign of crack addiction. She wore an obvious wig, a loose dirty T-shirt, and athletic shorts. I could not see her face because she was looking at the floor.

With Joan's request, I felt the full weight of the Workers' lack of bureaucracy. I had never been asked to help one of the guests on my own before, and there was no protocol I could rely on for guidance. I tried to sound less frazzled than I felt as I asked, "What would you like?" I winced, thinking I sounded as if I was taking her order at a fast-food restaurant.

She continued to look at the floor and spoke so quietly I could barely hear her. "I was hoping I might be able to use your shower."

"I can do that!" I said, overly enthusiastic in my relief at finding out I could handle the task. She looked up and smiled, and I could see she was probably twice as old as I thought she was. "Follow me."

"OK, Erika." She tried to flatten herself to the wall as I passed her to head up the stairs.

The linen closet was less than two feet from the second-floor landing. Jasmine stopped abruptly to keep herself from crashing into me and said, "Oh, I'm sorry, Erika," looking at her feet.

I found her repeated use of my name disconcerting and started to sympathize with Joan's irritation. "Don't worry." I rummaged through the closet. Fearing anyone who had come to shower probably would not smell that great, I kept my distance as I handed her a little soap and shampoo from a hotel chain and a threadbare towel with a floral design that suggested it might have been plush in the early sixties. I stopped at the clothing room on the way to the shower. "Would you like some clothes?" I asked her.

"Yes, please, thank you so much, Erika," she responded, this time looking me in the eye.

I unlocked the door to the clothing room and gestured for her to go first. As she passed, I found my earlier assumption was wrong; she smelled clean except for the lingering scent of cigarettes.

She wore a shy smile while I looked for clothes that might fit her frail frame.

I started to understand why Joan found her provoking. Her open vulnerability felt like a bottomless pit of need I could drown in. I wanted her to have more pride.

"How about this?" I held up a gray T-shirt.

"I like bright things," she responded, looking around. Although she called me by name repeatedly and thanked me every few seconds, she was quiet but firm about her taste.

"You're welcome to look," I told her over my shoulder. "The room is organized by clothing type, not size, so we might have to search for a bit."

We both started to loosen up as we dug through the clothes together. Soon it was as if we were shopping. She held up a bright blue shirt. "What do you think?" she asked, this time smiling as she again looked me in the eye.

"Oh, that's cute!" I responded.

"How about this? It's sort of nice."

"Hmm." I wasn't a fan of the color, and this evidently showed on my face.

"You're right. Hey, look at this." She giggled when she found a disco-era dress.

"Absolutely. No doubt, that's the look for you!" I said, and we both laughed.

It began to dawn on me that I'd been metaphorically holding my hands over my ears and squeezing my eyes shut in fear of what I would see, not in response to what I had actually seen. When I really looked, I could see Jasmine only wanted a little kindness and affection, nothing beyond what I was capable of giving her or even capable of enjoying myself. She wasn't uncomfortable with my power and privilege; I was.

As I stopped bracing myself against the discomfort I anticipated I'd feel in response to the distance between our positions, I was actually quite humbled by how small the distance seemed.

We decided on a skirt and T-shirt. "Well, I'm going to go shower, Erika."

As I watched her leave, I was startled by the consuming awareness that if circumstances in our lives had been slightly different, I could have been her and she could have been me. Shaken, I continued to organize the piles of clothes in the clothing room until she returned to show off her new outfit.

"How do I look?" she asked as she preened and turned in a circle. She was looking me in the eye, and her voice held more confidence now.

"Really wonderful." I smiled at her. There was a brief moment of hesitation as I realized she wanted to hug me. I was a bit uncomfortable with the idea of hugging someone I had only known for minutes but reached out and hugged her anyway. She was so vulnerable, thankful, easily made happy, and she felt like a reed when I hugged her.[6] The experience overwhelmed me with a strange combination of joy, pride, relief, humility, and power. I realized that I had been fighting against the exact experience that offered the emotional satisfaction that can be found in such a tragic environment.

As we broke from the hug, I told her, "You look so great, you have to go downstairs and show your new look off!"

"OK, Erika," she said, smiling.

Joan and Ms. Beth sat at the table, absorbed in their reading. I said, "Hey! Doesn't Jasmine look great?"

Neither looked up. Ms. Beth wore a bland look and nodded; Joan gave a distracted " uh-hmm," and added, "It was nice seeing you, Jasmine. I'm afraid we have to get ready for dinner and liturgy now." Their lack of enthusiasm disappointed me. Jasmine, however, appeared unfazed. She thanked everyone again and left with a smile on her face.

As I closed the door behind her, I realized that I had just sent her away clean, proud, and in a new outfit to return to smoking crack and prostitution; her immediate future hit me like a ton of bricks. Sure, she would do many other things besides smoking crack and prostituting herself, but I knew those two activities were inevitable. I felt dazed, humbled in the face of how little I had actually helped her, yet energized and proud of the connection we had forged. I had been afraid that sorrow would overwhelm me if I got too close, but that didn't seem to happen. The emotional connection did make my futility painful, but it also rendered the interaction intensely compelling.

That evening the community read the liturgical readings of the day and discussed them over dinner. "We're here because we truly believe we are more likely to encounter God here."

"I somehow doubt Jesus will head straight for the suburbs when he returns," Linda said wryly.

---

6. Clark describes such moments of physical empathy: "[It] is like a sound striking a 'sympathetic chord' and setting a piano string vibrating" (1997, 37).

"Mother Teresa said, 'The lepers of Calcutta are Christ in his most challenging form.' She wasn't giving charity to lepers; she was serving her beloved." Joan's eyes shone with tears as she spoke. Ms. Beth nodded with her eyes closed.

"This doesn't always happen. God knows it doesn't always happen." Everyone laughed heartily despite misty eyes. "Sometimes you're not serving anyone other than an ornery drunk guy who doesn't want the sandwich you've just made," and everyone laughed again. "But when it does . . ." She paused, closed her eyes, and said quietly, "It is phenomenal."

Little Miracles

More than a year later, Lucy knocked on the door as she let her son and herself in. She had been a regular ever since her family's six-week stay at the house almost a year before. "Do you mind if we look in the clothing room to see if we can find any coats?" she called out.

"I'll check and leave the room open for you if I see some," I said, leaving her to chat with Joan while Linda talked with her son. When I returned and told Lucy there were lots of coats, she left her son to look at some recently donated books while she browsed. Only minutes later she came back, her arms full of coats.

"I hope you grabbed one for yourself," Joan said.

"Oh, you know I'm just focused on getting the kids what they need. They grow so fast! Unfortunately I stay the same every year." Lucy laughed and patted her middle. "Oh, I almost forgot. I know you guys are cut off from the food bank,[7] and I just got a whole bunch of lunch meat, way more than we can use. I figured I'd bring it by tomorrow if you guys can use it."

"Can we use it?" Joan practically shrieked. "Yes, we can use it! Anything you want to bring would be a big help. Ms. Beth and I were thinking about making sandwiches to bring to Blueberry when she's standing out in the cold in front of the liquor store, but then we thought, 'Why don't we bring sandwiches for all the guys who hang out there?'"

As they talked, someone knocked on the door. I answered to find Mr. Diaz and his friend; both smelled and moved as if they'd already consumed a fair amount of liquor that morning. "Could we get some coats and blankets?" Mr. Diaz slurred.

---

7. The Catholic Worker community did not have nonprofit status, so they were not supposed to be using the food bank. Eventually they were "caught" and cut off from the food bank.

"There aren't any blankets." Eyeing the steep flight of stairs they would have to climb to pick coats out, I added, "but I'll get you a few coats to try on."

As usual, it seemed as if the clothing room had a huge selection of everything except what I needed. Middle-class people donated middle-sized clothing; most of the people who came to the house needed the smallest or the largest sizes. Both men were small and excruciatingly thin. The women's coats were the only ones remotely close to the right size, so I picked out a few of the most gender-neutral, hoping the men either wouldn't notice or wouldn't care.

Both men seemed overly pleased with the selection. Each put one on and showed it off to the other and to me. "This is stylish, right?" Mr. Diaz declared.

"I don't know. Mine's very nice," slurred his friend with an exaggerated condescension. I laughed, and the friend turned to Mr. Diaz, saying in a stage whisper, "What, hasn't she ever seen such stylish guys before?" They carried on until I had to wipe tears from my eyes because I was laughing so hard.

Joan interrupted the show, calling out that they should check back in a few days for blankets. I passed the message on as I waved them off. The friend turned his wave into a salute and said, "God bless America," in mock seriousness before cracking up.

I went back to the dining room and found Lucy drinking coffee and telling stories with Joan and Ms. Beth.

A half hour later Nick, a White man in his early sixties who'd become involved in the community over the previous few months, showed up with several boxes of school supplies. "I found someone who wanted to give all this stuff away," he told us. "So I told him, 'I know a place where it would be really useful,' so here I am with a carful," he explained with his characteristic gesture of raised shoulders, upturned palms, and big grin.

Linda came home from school as we were unloading and helped us with the last trip. By the time we were done, there were boxes of school supplies everywhere. We had stuffed them under the table and piled them on top of each other against the bookcases, effectively blocking access to the books. The room was utter chaos, but, like everyone else, I was excited by the prospect of the latest windfall.

Linda got herself a cup of coffee as Lucy said good-bye. As she came back to the table, she asked the group, "Do you think Lucy needs a new fridge?" Everyone agreed that she probably did, and then decided they would somehow move the refrigerator that had just been donated to

Lucy's house. "Can you just strap something like that to the roof of a car?" Linda asked, and Ms. Beth pointed out that Lucy had a minivan.

The easy conversation continued on into the evening, until it was time for the weekly Liturgy of the Word. As I rose to move a stack of notebooks out of the way in preparation, I saw Joan smiling to herself. Noticing my attention, she explained, "This is how it's supposed to be here, exactly how it's supposed to be. This was a perfect day."

Her serene joy no longer puzzled me. Despite these routine frustrations and sorrows, I understood that they did not do their work to congratulate themselves on their moral superiority, to appease a God they feared, or to alleviate their guilt. With time, I began to understand that they did the work because they often enjoyed it. Although the uncertainty and randomness could be draining, the barely tamed chaos they lived with could also generate exhilarating feelings, a sense of purpose, and, in the most intense cases, mystical experiences.

Distress at STOP's Monthly Vigil

Seeing only a handful of people as I approached city hall, I felt a wave of apprehension. This was the first time I had agreed to meet STOP's staff for their monthly vigil in front of the district attorney's office. The few people gathered for the vigil stood around a rickety card table laden with pamphlets and flyers. A pile of weathered signs leaned against the table.

Todd, the second director of STOP who took over after Timothy, talked with Timothy and an elderly White woman whom I later learned was Elizabeth. Although I had known Timothy years before, I had not seen him in years, so I wasn't surprised when I didn't see any glimmer of recognition as he noted my approach.

I began to feel like I was eavesdropping because I couldn't seem to catch Todd's eye, so I turned to look through the stack of signs leaning against the table.

I selected a sign and rested it against the building that housed the offices of the district attorney while I put on my mittens.

"You can't lean it against the building," said an older African American man who was picking up a stack of flyers from the table.

I looked at him questioningly, not sure if he was serious or not.

"If we touch the building, we're trespassing. They can arrest us. We shouldn't get arrested without an audience. It's a waste; don't you think?" he explained, and then walked away to hold his sign.

I turned and saw the civil affairs officers, police officers monitoring and protecting the protestors, looking at me anxiously.

Feeling progressively more foolish, I picked up the sign.

I wasn't sure where to go. The body language of the man who'd advised me about signs suggested that he didn't want company. I decided to stay where I was, partway between the man and Todd, Timothy, and Elizabeth, who were still talking.

I wasn't sure where to look. I wanted to avoid eye contact with passersby, but the sidewalks were so busy, I could only do this by looking above everyone's heads or at the ground, and this felt cowardly. I tried to look at the people passing.

Todd, Timothy, and Elizabeth took up signs with an apparent ease that bewildered me.

Most people ignored us. Only their purposefully blank faces and invisible blinders that kept their gaze carefully away from us suggested that they saw us at all.

"Get a life!" said one man.

"Get a job!" said another.

One woman stopped long enough to yell, "You're not good people! You care more about the lives of murderers than the families of police officers who die to keep our cities safe! What's wrong with you people?!" Then she turned on her heel and started to walk away.

My body buzzed as adrenaline coursed through me. I realized that I had been holding my breath. I tried to recall if a complete stranger had ever yelled at me before. I could think of a couple of instances when I had been on the receiving end of road rage, but those interactions seemed far safer and less personal than this experience on the street.

Another person stopped to disagree, and Elizabeth called after him, "Thank you for sharing your feelings. I respect your feelings—don't you want a response?" The man turned for a second and continued to voice his disagreement from a distance of about fifteen feet. Elizabeth walked after the man. This seemed imprudently brave and aggressive to me.

I was becoming more and more tense as the negative reactions seemed to heap one upon another, each one happening before the effects of the previous one had worn off. The few positive responses did little to counter my mounting desire to flee.

My anxiety and frustration compounded as I became conscious of the fact that I had been so wrapped up in my own experience that I had paid very little attention to the STOP members around me. How was I going to be able to write about their experience if I couldn't keep my focus on them? Even as I made a concerted effort, I had difficulty pulling my attention away from my own discomfort. I looked at my watch and found only twenty minutes had passed—a third of the time scheduled for the vigil.

When the hour finally ended, I helped clean up the supplies and unsuccessfully tried to catch Todd's attention again. Emotionally worn out, I walked to the bus stop feeling humiliated and frustrated. Why had Todd so studiously ignored me? Was I really such a liability? I couldn't figure out how the others had managed to seem so relaxed, comfortable, even excited. Although my sense of self-consciousness all but disappeared in the excitement of STOP's first big protest, the conflicts during this, my first vigil, had felt personal.

The History of STOP

I walked into the lobby of the religious organization's building, signed in, and found my way to a small meeting room five minutes after the first STOP meeting was supposed to start. I saw five people sitting around a table and a man I correctly assumed to be the director standing at the end of the table.

He paced as he began to talk. "I felt momentum in the air for ending this thing. You could feel it. *This* is going to *happen*." He sounded like he'd gotten a tip on a horse and was about to bet on a sure thing. "I'm telling you, we are going to stop the death penalty! This is the new anti–death penalty movement. This isn't just a religious issue—it's a *civil rights* issue. We can fight this on the state level *and* on the local level. We'll use direct action, and they won't be able to ignore us. Everywhere *they* go, there *we'll* be, in their faces, accusing them of their blatant racism. We're going to demand justice!"

Although Timothy didn't come across as particularly power hungry, it was plain that this was Timothy's group. He was committed to direct action, which for him meant protesting aggressively without apology.

The small group discussed tactics. Should they demonstrate against the district attorney at his home? Block streets? Get arrested? Do jail time? They only judged a tactic as too extreme if they believed it would alienate potential supporters.

They agreed that they needed to announce a break from the old movement, particularly what they perceived to be the use of religiously influenced tactics. Instead they would draw from the civil rights movement.

Timothy suggested a large initial protest. "We'll blindside them and get more media attention if we seem to come out of nowhere." The group concurred. They would attempt to attract media attention and send a strong signal to the district attorney's office, announcing themselves as a political force that was willing to "play hardball." Their strategy hinged on the group's ability to capture the attention of the local activist community. The small group compiled a list of activist organizations, planned non-violence training sessions for those risking arrest, and sent founding members out to recruit, not just for the cause in general, but for this initial protest.

———————

Their organizing efforts paid off. On the day of the big protest, I descended the stairs to the basement of the building where they held their meetings. Rather than the mere handful of people who attended the first meeting, it looked like hundreds of people were moving about the basement. The room swam with excitement and a sense of occasion. People moved quickly and with a sense of purpose. I saw people of varying ages and races, but most were White and between eighteen and thirty. It seemed as though many people knew one another, which made sense considering STOP's strategy of recruiting groups.

After completing a lap around the basement, I could see that the action centered on those who planned to risk arrest by committing civil disobedience (arrestees). This group included Timothy and the other members as well as some new faces. The arrestees focused on one another and stood in a tightly clumped group as the action buzzed around them. They talked quietly enough that it was difficult to make out what they were saying from outside the group. Many of them fidgeted, wringing their hands, running their fingers through their hair, or shifting their weight. Even though the arrestees seemed to be at the center of the activity, I only saw their support people—the people who would hold their keys during the protest and receive the arrestees' calls from jail—approach them directly. The rest of the people asked questions or passed along information to the supporters.

"We need the people participating in civil disobedience to form a circle and hold hands," yelled a rather conservatively dressed thirty-something White man. Once everyone was holding hands, he began leading the group in what sounded like a secular prayer. Many of the arrestees closed their eyes and had looks of intense concentration. "Let us remember those who suffer from injustice and the great tradition of people who have taken risks and made sacrifices to resist injustice."

A moment later, Timothy moved in front of the crowd with his bull-horn, exuding confidence despite the palpable nervous energy. "We're

45

here today to tell the district attorney's office we're not going to take it anymore!" He started walking backward out of the building, yelling a chant into the bullhorn, and the crowd followed. The crowd's enthusiasm grew as the group rounded the corner to the district attorney's office and saw another seventy-five to a hundred protestors waiting. Many people from both groups exchanged familiar and enthusiastic greetings as the groups merged.

The police had set up yellow tape between the street and the sidewalk on both sides of the street. A line of uniformed officers stood to the side of the building's entrance and served as targets for the protestors' increasingly enthusiastic chants.

"Those participating in civil disobedience will now cross the street," yelled Timothy through the bullhorn. The ten arrestees separated themselves as the rest of the crowd cheered them. They crossed the street and solemnly took up their positions sitting in front of the entrance to the district attorney's office. Timothy and two of the other original members of the group took turns yelling into a portable sound system, accusing the district attorney's office of murder and racism while they paced back and forth in front of the arrestees. The arrestees continued to look somber as they sat rigidly and successfully blocked the office for almost an hour.

Just as the energy of the crowd began to flag, a large police van pulled up. The police line moved toward the arrestees, warning them that they would be arrested if they didn't move. The arrestees refused to meet their eyes and looked into the distance. Two officers took the arms of an arrestee and attempted to pull him up. The arrestee went limp while continuing to keep his expression carefully blank. The crowd yelled and hooted as the other officers moved in, handcuffed him, and carried him to the police van.

I heard people in the crowd encouraging the group to keep the noise level up throughout the long process. One woman said to another beside her, "It's scary to lose your freedom, even if you're prepared. Lots of people panic. We have to yell to help them stay focused." The van started to shake with a loud metallic noise, and we could see the side of the van repeatedly bulging as if someone was kicking the van from the inside. The crowd cheered in response. An apparently higher-ranking police officer yelled to the others, "Let's go! Let's go! We've got to get them out of here!" The police stepped up their efforts to remove the arrestees from the scene.

The van pulled away, and the crowd started to disperse. There was a sense that something important had happened—the arrestees were the captains of the team that had just won the championship game. The supports were still on alert for their phone calls. Many of the others lingered to gather signs and soak up the last bits of excitement, walking with confidence and talking in loud voices.

———

The protest became one of the "remember when" moments that local activists talked about to secure their position within local activist history. A number of prominent activists spent two weeks to a month in jail for blocking the entrance to the district attorney's office. A widely distributed weekly newspaper put the group's claims about the district attorney on their front page. Attendance at the planning meetings tripled. Grants from a national religious charity enabled the group to pay the director a full-time salary. Eventually this chapter of STOP grew to be the largest and most successful in the state, and in time it took over as the state headquarters for the organization.

Timothy found his long-awaited triumph came at a cost. As he assumed professional responsibility for organizing the state, he felt he'd also assumed personal responsibility for abolishing the death penalty. Those closer to him told stories about how he worked twenty-hour days and often commented that he believed his personal efforts could determine whether someone would live or die. After two and a half years under this pressure, he began to suffer not just emotionally but physically. Eventually both Timothy and STOP's board, made up mostly of those who organized the first successful protest, agreed that it was time for him to step down. Timothy took a position on the board, and under his direction the board agreed to hire Todd, a White man in his early thirties who was new to the activist scene, to replace Timothy. This was the first major turnover in STOP's history.

Todd had been a teacher and most recently a minister, but he'd been asked to leave his congregation after becoming increasingly vocal about his left-leaning politics. Following the loss of his position, he decided he would become a full-time activist. Although he had leadership, public speaking, and organizational skills from his experience as a minister and the fervor of recent conversion, he found the activist scene was a hard nut to crack, making few social inroads in spite of his concerted efforts. Most of the people were younger or had been involved in the activist community for many years, and the networks and boundaries were tight. STOP's activist-centered approach and extensive networks attracted Todd. When the board offered him the job of directing STOP, they offered him not only a chance to make a living as an activist, but indirect opportunities to further integrate into the local activist social scene.

———

On a surprisingly cold late spring morning almost two years and many demonstrations after STOP's first big success, I walked to a park a block away from the district attorney's office where participants were to meet for a brief rally before proceeding to the district attorney's office for another STOP-organized demonstration. I looked around for demonstrators, but only saw the City Service volunteers in their matching T-shirts, looking sleepy as they waited for their daily group exercise to begin. I double-checked my calendar to make sure I had the right place and time, waited for a minute or two, then walked a half a block until I could see the district attorney's office to make sure I didn't have the wrong location. But there was no sign of anyone from STOP.

On my return, I saw the City Service volunteers starting to line up and two small clusters of people wearing clothes that suggested they might be activists. They looked about the same age as the City Service volunteers and just as tired. Many were yawning as they talked. I looked for signs but didn't see any.

I approached one of the groups and asked, "Are any of you here for the anti–death penalty demonstration?" They all turned toward me, several of the people gave me vague nods, and then they all turned back toward one another and resumed their conversation.

I waited for a few awkward beats. Deciding that leaving would be less painful, I wandered away.

I noticed a new group made up of much older people. Their circle appeared closed as well. I settled on standing near the groups but by myself.

"Are you here for the death penalty protest?"

I turned to see a White man who looked to be in his early thirties, tall and thin with dark shaggy hair and a child on his back, looking at me expectantly.

"Yes."

Relieved I was no longer standing alone, I searched for a moment for something to say. "How old is your son?"

"Lawrence? He's eighteen months," he said with a big smile and obvious pride.

"I have a son too."

"It's great, isn't it? I'm a grad student in chemistry, but once he was born, I couldn't resist the opportunity to spend as much time with him as possible, so I'm taking some time off."

I nodded.

"Good morning, everyone! Line up, it's time to get moving," a woman yelled over a bullhorn, announcing the beginning of the volunteers' morning exercise regimen.

Lawrence's father raised his voice to be heard over the group counting off jumping jacks in unison behind him. "I'm guessing it's going to take everything I've got as a parent to make sure he doesn't turn out to be as sexist and hateful as the rest of society. I think it's important for him to grow up going to actions. It's crucial for his moral development."

Surprised by the intensity of his comment, I laughed and said, "Sort of like going to an activist church."

He looked thoughtful and responded seriously. "Yeah, but with the purpose of creating a sense of unity among people, not divisions."

I wasn't sure what to say after that, but I was saved by the sound of another amplified voice competing with the workout behind us.

"Good morning! My name is Todd. I'm the director of STOP." Todd had arrived without my noticing. He was dressed in new-looking jeans, bright white sneakers, and an Amnesty International anti–death penalty shirt.

He paused to give the thirty or forty people who'd turned out time to draw closer. I looked at my watch. The protests had seemed to dwindle over time, but I could hardly believe this was the extent of the turnout.

"We have gathered here this morning to let our DA's office know that we will not tolerate state-sanctioned murder!" If Todd was discouraged by the turnout, I couldn't tell. He interjected fervent commentary with call-and-response cheering, attempting to work up the crowd. A few responded immediately, and more responded every time Todd called for a response.

I had been introduced to Todd at a STOP protest a year before, but the difference between the man I had first met and the charismatic man leading this crowd astonished me. In our first meeting, Todd had seemed friendly but quiet. Medium height, medium build, and dressed like a middle-class professional, his look was more mainstream than any of the local activists I had met. He'd looked slightly self-conscious, yet excited, a combination that led me to believe he had not been to many protests.

A year later, Todd's command of the crowd surprised me. He occupied the center of attention; everything about his demeanor demanded this focus. He announced it was time to start marching to the district attorney's office. I felt terribly exposed as we walked, nostalgic for the size and buoyancy of the first STOP protest.

Again the police were prepared for the demonstration, but this time it looked as though they may have outnumbered the activists. No one was planning to get arrested, but Todd and a few others crossed the street to face the crowd. Yelling into a microphone as he paced in front of the building, Todd alternated between ranting and asking the crowd "yes" or "no" questions.

"Are we going to take this injustice any longer?"

"No!" yelled the crowd.

In the times between leading the crowd, Todd introduced other speakers. Most were leaders in other activist groups, and his pride in their endorsement of his demonstration rang in his voice.

The speakers remained enthusiastic, but the energy of the crowd waned after a while. It seemed to thin, even though I didn't see anyone leave. I looked at my watch and wondered how much longer they would go on and how they would end it.

———

A few months later I went to meet Todd for the first time in STOP's new offices. STOP had recently raised enough money to rent office space in an activist neighborhood that sat at the boundary between a predominantly White professional neighborhood and a historically African American working-class neighborhood. Passing people of various ethnicities in business suits, baggy tracksuits, and the worn black clothing and sneakers cut into sandals that were popular among the neighborhood's squatters, I turned into a shallow breezeway under a sign for an Afghani restaurant.

To my right was the door to the restaurant. To my left, a bulletin board filled with layers of flyers advertising an AIDS benefit, a community-organizing group, a meditation group, a couple of concerts in neighborhood bars, a drumming circle, a massage therapist, and a braiding salon. Straight ahead, a door with three doorbells, two built-in and one jury-rigged. Todd had taped his business card above the temporary bell. He'd crossed out the title "Minister" and wrote "defrocked" next to it. He'd written in "activist" below that and added, "Push bell hard and hold for 5 sec" at the very bottom. Other than Todd's business card, there was no sign that STOP occupied one of the floors above.

I followed the directions for ringing the bell, and Todd greeted me at the door wearing a red stop sign shirt saying: "Stop the Death Penalty," shorts, and no shoes. I followed him up steep stairs, and he explained that the apartment we were heading to on the third floor served as both his personal apartment and STOP's headquarters. We paused at the second landing as he told me the apartment on this floor was now for rent. His neighbor had just moved out, and he was hoping that the organization could rent the space so he could have a separate apartment.

The door at the top of the second flight of stairs opened into a hot small room painted an orange so shockingly vibrant it hurt my eyes. This main room was haphazardly furnished with two computers on card tables and four metal-backed kitchen chairs with cracked vinyl seats. Numerous political posters, Che Guevara and Dorothy Day among others, decorated the walls. Quotes from Audre Lorde, Dorothy Day, Malcolm X, and Che Guevara filled in the spaces between the posters. I scanned for a poster or quotation specific to the death penalty, but I didn't see any.

I could see into the kitchen, which was intricately painted with a complex pattern in earth tones. "That's an amazing paint job."

"Yeah, I did it myself," Todd responded.

He gestured to one of the chairs and picked up a glass of soda with ice as he took a seat himself. He started to talk, and then awkwardly interrupted himself. "You want some water?"

"No thanks."

"Right. OK."

Although I had observed the group off and on since its inception and had met Todd before, he started our discussion by telling me the history of the group, starting with Timothy and the first meeting. He emphasized the continued commitment to direct action. I realized that now even in face-to-face interaction, he buzzed with an angry energy. He held his eyes wide open when he talked, a look that might have made him look surprised if not for the ranting that accompanied it.

Todd explained that their history of large protests and media attention moved the group from the margins to the political fold, from trying to attract the attention of activists to capitalizing on the media's attention with lobbyists and lawmakers.

"It was like they were storming the castle with a battering ram again and again, and finally someone opened the doors and said, 'Hey! Come on in!' It's a transition that we're still adjusting to. Don't get me wrong— we're still committed to radical tactics, we still come out swinging, but now we're meeting with lawmakers and lobbyists. They come to *us* for support. They ask us for our input, or at least acknowledge that they need to listen to us."

He pulled out a photo album of STOP's protests. "Yeah, this photo album's pretty much a 'who's who' of the activist scene around here. See, there's Sarah; she had just gotten out of jail for civil disobedience the week before. We all got arrested for this one," he told me, pointing to a different picture. He showed me more pictures and said that he'd saved all of the materials from actions where he'd spoken. "This stuff will probably be worth something one day."

I thought he was joking. In one of those awkward moments in the field when I wished I'd kept my mouth shut but I didn't, I commented, "That way your great-grandkids can take it to the *Antiques Roadshow*?"

He gave me a chiding look. "No, maybe a rare bookstore or something like that."

After an uncomfortable pause, I asked him if he ever thought about what he would do if the death penalty were abolished, and he answered, "Every day. I make myself think about it every day. This is a temporary organization. We shouldn't be building up complicated structures. We should be as efficient as possible, and hopefully we'll all be out of a job soon."

The phone rang, and Todd excused himself as he twisted around to take the call where he sat. "Bill lies. You can't give him an inch. He's going to come out swinging, so you have to be ready to do the same. Get him on the ropes right away. Go on the attack about legal lynching, state-sanctioned murder, how it's useless as a deterrent, et cetera. Throw the expense in his face."

He stood up and started to pace as he spoke. "You just have to jump right in. That's what they say on the show, just jump right in. Be ready to interrupt. They never stick to the theme of the show, and the questions are never all that thought-provoking, so just jump right in."

He hung up and told me that the phone call was from a STOP member who was going to appear on a local talk show that evening. Poised on the edge of his seat, he looked ready for a fight. "Man, I wish I was doing it. I love taking them on!"

I didn't know what to say. "Wow. I guess you have to be ready for a fight—don't you?"

He looked exasperated by my comment and responded with sarcasm, "Yeah."

Maintaining Connections at the Vigils

Just as I counted down the minutes during my first vigil, I counted down the days until the next vigil, dreading it. While I could have gotten to the district attorney's office more quickly if I had taken the bus, I wanted to avoid showing up alone again, so I went to STOP's offices first. I ran into

Todd on the sidewalk. He wore a suit, trench coat, and dress shoes rather than his daily uniform of jeans, T-shirt, and sneakers. He exuded aggressive confidence, like a basketball player moving from the locker room to the court before the beginning of a game.

His arms were loaded down with signs to take to his car.

"Want help with those?"

"Yeah. Thanks."

We returned to the offices together, where Martha—an African American woman who'd retired early and had just been hired by Todd to organize friends and family members of death row inmates—was just coming out with another armload of signs.

"That's the last of it! Oh, hello! It is so nice to see you!" she said to me with a smile. I loved the fact that Martha always greeted me as though she had not seen me in a year, even if I'd only been away for a day or two. "This is a *very* nice day for a vigil—let's do this!" She normally wore plain pants and shirts, but today she had on a shirt and skirt in bold prints with a matching head wrap. I had been so consumed with my own discomfort at the first vigil, I had not realized they dressed for the occasion.

"Good morning. Everyone looks so nice," I said.

"I've got my Afrocentric clothing on. Someone will always ask me if I'm Muslim when I'm dressed like this. I tell them, 'No, I'm Christian and Afrocentric!' Other people will ask me if I bought this in Africa." She waved off the question. "There are plenty of stores around here where you can buy Afrocentric clothes."

We climbed into the car, and I found I felt less nervous now that I was with the two of them. I hoped it would last throughout the vigil.

We parked a few blocks away, and each took a stack of signs. As we were walking, a street vendor called to us, "Get a job."

"So much for remaining relaxed," I thought to myself.

A couple of the people from the last vigil were already there with the card table and a box of flyers. I helped set these up, relieved that the task allowed me to put off sign-holding, if only for a few minutes. When I could no longer put off the inevitable, I went to the pile of signs to pick one out. The top one said: "Justice for Jack Forest," which seemed too specific to me, so I grabbed the next one, which listed the number of people on death row by race and said: "Stop the legal lynching."

"That's a good one." I was startled; I didn't realize there was anyone standing so close to me. I turned and saw Timothy smiling at me. "That's a good one," he said again. I smiled back and stood next to him facing the people passing by.

The older African American man who'd previously warned me against propping signs against the building was now on the other side of me. He held a small sign in one hand while he passed out STOP pamphlets with the other. Martha stood well in front of the group, in the middle of the stream of pedestrian traffic, as she handed out pamphlets. Two older White women, one of whom I recognized as Elizabeth from the month before, joined the group, first stopping to talk to the man passing out the pamphlets.

Todd came up on the other side of Timothy and engaged him in conversation. After a few minutes, Timothy tried to bring me into the conversation, but Todd walked away as soon as Timothy engaged me. I turned over the possible reasons for his ignoring me.

"So, how'd you get involved with STOP? Are you with other groups too?"

At first I didn't realize he was talking to me because he kept his attention trained on the passing people. "I'm a friend of Joe's. You contacted me a long time ago for the first meeting."

He turned sharply to look at me, then hit his head, "Of course!" He continued to look at me and spoke more quickly. "So, how are you getting money into your house now these days, if you don't mind me asking?" He smiled to let me know he understood he'd just put the common question in a funny way.

I smiled back. "If you'd asked me what I did, I'd tell you I'm a grad student, but since you framed it in terms of money, I'm at a loss."

"Ah, a dilettante?" Even when said with humor, I had come to recognize the test.

"Exactly." I laughed, and he joined me. "Why ask the question that way?"

"Well," he said, returning his attention to the passing people, "if you ask me what I do for a living, I'll tell you I'm an activist and a father, but the answer is completely different if you ask me what I do for money. I try not to confuse my life with what I do to get the money I need to live it . . . I was just giving you a hard time. Do you teach?"

"Not this semester. I'm studying how people become and remain involved in social movement groups." I proceeded to tell him about my research.

"So you're doing research right now! That's fantastic! This is superimportant. You *must* talk to people with children. Yup, that's the group we always lose," he said, shaking his head in consternation. "People are active, then they have kids and they just slip away. Students and retirees make up the backbones of our movement. Everyone thinks they'll stay just as active when they only have one and they're small enough to put in a backpack, but it's difficult when you have more and they're older. Probably the activist community is part of the problem. Parents are in less of a position to get arrested and that's something of a stigma."

"Some people with children go to prison, don't they?"

"The community is deeply divided about this," he said, suddenly looking grave. "It might not look like it from the outside, but people with children, especially small children, who choose to do time are judged harshly, very harshly, by some."

Elizabeth turned toward our conversation. "I agree. The kid issue's really important."

"We need youth camps like the communists used to have," Timothy added.

Elizabeth nodded in agreement. "It's hard on our kids; they don't want to feel like their family's different."

They were friendly, but I couldn't help noticing their continual references to my outsider status. It was clear that the death penalty was part of the constellation of lefty causes that comprised both their larger activist identity and their personal network. The vigil appeared to be a place to sustain their identities and connections with others in the broader network.

This did not, however, account for the dynamics between the people who purposefully kept to themselves during these vigils. I had never seen Todd engrossed in small talk. It almost seemed as though he wanted to disassociate himself from the vigil. The older African American man kept to himself yet seemed to interact warmly but briefly with the others who knew him. Martha interacted with everyone, but she kept herself at a distance and her attention on the people passing by never wavered. I guessed they didn't share the same overlapping involvement.

"My son was mortified when he saw a picture of me in the paper on my knees, face on the rug, and hands behind my back, being handcuffed," Timothy said, drawing my attention back to the ongoing conversation.

One of the civil affairs officers jokingly called out, "Hey, that wasn't us, was it?"

Timothy laughed. "No, have to say that was the county police."

"Figures," said the officer with mock disgust.

A White middle-aged man appeared to be leaning back as he moved down the block with a loping gait. As he read the signs, he sneered and said, "We should kill more."

"So, did you do time?" I asked Timothy, anxious to keep the conversation going.

Elizabeth and Timothy continued to focus on the people, but I found myself turning toward each of them as they spoke so that I faced away from the passing people. As long as I was engaged, I felt protected. I was surprised how willing they were to talk to me. I imagine my mere presence allowed them to impute certain things about my politics, but there was more of an immediate pull than that. People grouped us together; they made negative comments to us as a group, said encouraging things to us as a group, or ignored us as a group. We were together in a very real way that transcended more lofty ideological affinities.

Suddenly Todd started toward a man in a suit walking into the building. I couldn't hear their exchange, but body language suggested Todd had been verbally aggressive. The man in the suit ignored Todd and looked straight ahead. Todd opened his phone again and came back to stand on the edge of the group.

Todd approached Timothy, who moved to include me in the conversation again. Todd nodded but didn't make eye contact, then turned his body so that he was talking to Timothy alone. I wondered if I represented some sort of contamination threat.

Todd spoke in hushed urgent tones, ended the brief conversation with a nod, and took his cell phone back out of his pocket. He talked loudly, pacing up and down the sidewalk as he gestured broadly. Besides his air of intensity and the fact that he wasn't going anywhere, he looked similar to the people in suits walking in and out of the district attorney's office.

On the way back to the car, Todd talked to Martha. There wasn't room for three across the sidewalk, so I trailed behind. I had hoped Todd would warm up to me after seeing the others' acceptance, but nothing about his demeanor had changed. His behavior remained steady over several months of vigils until I grew accustomed to his avoiding me. Cognitively the puzzle preoccupied me, but emotionally I felt like the friend of a cool kid who ignored me at school.

Comforting a Newcomer

Almost a year later, I arrived at the STOP offices on the day of the monthly vigil. While I didn't hunger for the inevitable conflict, I no longer dreaded the small and highly public protests. Rather than feeling frightened and using conversations as lifelines, I had begun to relax and enjoy conversation with the regulars.

I drove to the vigil with Lucas, a White high school student who'd secured outside funding for his position as youth organizer from his church, and with Lucas's friend Hue, and Todd. When we arrived, Lucas told Todd he had to break off to pick up Christina, a friend from his religious youth group who attended a small college in a town outside the city.

Todd, Hue, and I were the first to arrive. The civil affairs police smiled to us in greeting. Hue took a sign and stood where he could be seen but behind me. He looked blankly up toward the tall buildings in front of him and didn't say anything. Lucas walked up with a woman, then turned toward Todd and began an intense conversation, leaving her standing awkwardly near him. She stood facing the group with her back to the street, smiling nervously and looking around as if to see if there were more people.

Lucas bent down and picked up a large painted sheet. "Why don't you take the other end of this banner," he suggested to Christina, momentarily interrupting his conversation with Todd but not looking at her. He held one end, gave her the other, and resumed his conversation with Todd.

Christina walked away from him to spread out the sheet that said: "STOP executions now!" She turned toward me as she walked and introduced herself. Focused on me, she failed to see that she had not walked far enough to stretch the banner out fully, or that she was holding it bunched in the corner, obscuring some of the writing.

"Go a little farther and hold the edge," Lucas absently directed.

"Oh, sure," said Christina, looking embarrassed.

Shame then irritation chased sympathy as I watched her. I wanted to reassure her, but I hesitated for a moment as I realized this would further diminish the standing I worked so hard to gain with Todd. I knew that talking to a true newcomer—a person who had no other ties to any other activist network—would reaffirm my second-class status in Todd's eyes.

I looked over at Todd and watched him approach Lucas again. I couldn't hear what they were saying, but I could see they wore serious expressions and their exchanges were short, almost abrupt; the interactions holding little of the friendly camaraderie that usually permeated their exchanges in the office. I realized most of their interactions at the vigils had this efficient feel. In fact, most of Todd's interactions during the vigils had an efficient utilitarian quality. I had not seen him engage in any interactions that weren't openly instrumental.

In the few seconds I hesitated, I realized that Todd wasn't avoiding me in particular; I just didn't have any valuable information to offer during the vigils. I would never be useful to him, so he would always ignore me. Reconciled with this knowledge, I turned to Christina and asked her, "Are you a friend of Lucas?" even though I knew who she was.

She looked relieved. "Yeah, we're in the same youth group."

"So where do you go to school?" As she answered, she continued to face me—her gaze and body were perpendicular to the crowd.

"Is this your first protest?"

She looked embarrassed. "Yes, but I really believe in the cause."

Christina talked to me nonstop throughout the entire hour of the vigil. She told me about career plans, recent and impending trips, and even her relationships with family members. When the vigil was over, we continued to talk on the way back to the car.

When Lucas turned to take signs from us, he looked taken aback by the intimacy of our discussion. "Did you guys know each other from before?" he asked with furrowed brows.

"No, we just met today at the vigil," Christina answered.

Lucas looked more closely at me. Christina was friendly with me after an hour, and he could barely remember my name after knowing me for more than a year. If I explained how we had forged a connection because I could easily empathize with her discomfort and apparent confusion over Lucas's lack of attention toward her during the vigil, I would have embarrassed Christina and made little sense to Lucas, so I just smiled at him.

The Thrill of Battle

During the next vigil, I watched Todd as he paced up and down the sidewalk, talking on his cell phone, wearing a suit, sunglasses, and a trench coat. As usual, he paid little attention to the group. He looked like a caged tiger waiting for a chance to attack.

An assistant district attorney left the building. Timothy pointed him out to Todd. Todd went directly after this assistant district attorney, yelling at him and calling him a murderer. "We're here to ask you why you put innocent people on death row! Why you stall to keep them from having their day in court! Why you murder and tell the public lie after lie about how your murdering ways will keep them safe!" The assistant district attorney bent his head and walked away, ignoring Todd as he yelled at him for half a block.

Todd stalked away from the confrontation and back to the group, but I could tell he was looking through us. His trench coat was open and blew out behind him as he went, and although he was quite modest in stature, he seemed much larger. "He's not going to get away with putting innocent people on death row while I'm around," Todd announced to everyone within ten yards.

I thought about how most of his behavior had been geared toward performing this sense of power and independence. Todd forced the opposition to pay attention to him and acknowledge him as the opposition in return.

I had previously focused on how participating in the vigils could generate negative feelings of vulnerability and shame, and the positive feelings of solidarity, but successfully demanding attention generated a sense of power. Intimate confrontation provided the thrill of battle and a chance to be a hero. In order to be a hero, one had to slay the dragon—alone. While some found pleasure in the camaraderie that small demonstrations could offer, I could now see that camaraderie repelled would-be heroes.

Times had changed at STOP. Their larger protests had shrunk considerably after their opening success. They weren't the hot center of the activist scene, just one of many causes that claimed activists' attention. Without exponentially increasing numbers of participants, it was difficult for Todd to be a great leader of people. He could, however, be a personal thorn in the side of the opposition, and vigils gave him just the opportunity to remind the opposition that he wasn't going anywhere and he was always ready for a fight.

Toward a Theory of How Thrilling Risk Attracts Involvement

Dynamics of Emotional Vacuums, Relief, and Expansion

Activists rarely have opportunities to directly bring about the change they work to realize. The Catholic Worker community could not end widespread poverty with their generosity alone. STOP could not effectively declare a statewide moratorium on the death penalty. Instead such groups develop proxy goals that stand in for progress toward their ultimate goals. Once challenges are engaged, the situations become risky—outcomes could be dangerous, and emotional consequences could be unpredictable. One might assume that groups would find many of these day-to-day challenges draining,[8] but the stories above illustrate how the challenge of proxy goals can create opportunities for peak emotional experiences.

---

8. Hochschild's *The Managed Heart* (1983) details the ways in which particular types of work, service work in this case, demand emotional labor and the consequences of performing this labor for workers.

Actors' emotions give them a sense of their position in relation to social events. Thus, a change in emotion indicates a change in position in relation to a social environment.[9] In other words, emotion can be thought of as social proprioception.[10] As participants could not anticipate the exact positions they would occupy in these groups' day-to-day challenges, risky situations were emotionally volatile.

Engaging in their day-to-day challenges created emotional vacuums.[11] A heightened awareness of a lack of particular positive emotions coupled with feelings of the complementary negative emotion created tension.[12] When the groups focused on the absence of particular positive emotions, they were intensely motivated to seek resolutions that released these emotional vacuums with the complementary positive emotion. For example, the Workers' awareness of an inability to alleviate suffering engendered an intense desire to relieve their own grief. Similarly, STOP members' awareness of being put on the defensive or feelings of dismissal engendered an intense desire to relive their feelings of righteous indignation.

Because emotion signals social position, appropriate emotional reactions cannot be taught like symbolic content can be taught.[13] For example, Joan could easily convince me of the symbolic meaning of Nick by pointing to him and informing me that he was a group member. However, a similar exchange would have been far less likely to convince me of the emotional meaning of Nick. If she pointed to Nick and informed me that I should admire or dislike him, I would have to ask numerous questions in order to orient myself emotionally in regard to Nick. Does

9. As the following chapters will illustrate, much of the time the groups filtered their experiences through their cultural assumptions. This perspective shares much with other cognition-based theories of emotion (Turner and Stets 2005). However, occasionally the immediate structural context generated emotions directly. Thus, the neat division between cultural and structural approaches falls apart. Rather than focusing on the role of culture or structure in generating emotions, we are left with the question of *when* either will be particularly powerful in creating the emotional experiences of actors.

10. In other words, emotions act as signal functions (James 1890; Freud [1923] 1960; Scheff 1990) that indicate social conditions. Gibson notes that "the activity of orienting and that of exploring and selecting—the commonsense faculty of attending—is seen to be one that extracts the external information from the stimulus flex while registering the change as subjective feeling" (1966, 320).

11. See Lefebvre (2004, 25) and Schutz (1967).

12. The notion of complementary emotions refers to Plutchik's theory of the emotion wheel, where emotions are arranged on a wheel so that emotions that are opposite one another are complementary: ecstasy/grief, vigilance/amazement, rage/terror, loathing/adoration (1980, 157).

13. Hochschild (1979) describes the embodied nature of the training that flight attendants receive for carrying out the emotional labor demanded by their position. They practice by physically enacting how to hold their bodies, smile with authenticity, and modulate their voices so that they are able to successfully carry off their performance as servants while attending to their responsibilities for passenger safety. Similarly, training for civil rights activists often involved extensive role-playing where those who were preparing to commit civil disobedience were able to practice maintaining their composure in the face of taunting and violence.

Nick know and like people that I know and like? Has Nick helped a person that I have perceived to be in need of help? Has Nick been unaccountably rude to a person I care about?

At any given moment, participants occupied countless social positions in regard to the vast number of social relationships in which they were embedded—for example, their family, the group, the movements in which they participated, their city, and so on. The groups shaped participants' emotional experiences through training participants to direct their attention in particular ways.[14]

Anticipating a shared threat directed and sharpened a group's attention, and thus limited the information available for managing challenging situations. In other words, actors traded depth of perception for breadth of perception when anticipating a threat.[15] The uncertainty of risky situations undermined the actors' habitual responses, and the immediate environment absorbed the actors' attention due to the vigilant attention that participation required. When a threat was shared, this narrowing of focus brought participants' perception into line with one another, heightening the mutual awareness of shared position. Thus shared challenges ripened the potential for solidarity among members.[16]

In combination, these factors created conditions where engaging in their day-to-day challenges tended to create a predictable range of emotions within each group. For example, I was initially overwhelmed by the chaos surrounding the Workers' house and depressed by their obvious lack of long-term efficacy. As I learned to focus on the quality of interactions rather than their long-term efficacy, I began to share in the Workers' emotional high points.[17] Similarly, the anxiety I felt during

14. Experience generates an increased capacity to differentiate sensory input and thus enables actors to make finer-grain distinctions: palates become more delicate, hearing picks up finer and finer nuances of musical complexity, and eyes identify breaks in visual patterns more readily (Gibson 1966). Gibson demonstrates that experience also increases the attention span of sensory awareness, creating a capacity to discern certain sensory experiences that require longer amounts of time to unfold (270).

15. Fear and threat narrow awareness (Dewey 1959; Scheff 1990).

16. Participants in more distant involvements faded to the background, time seemed to slow, and interactions felt not only intense, but fresh and heavy with meaning. As Goffman puts it, risk is where the action is, meaning that risk-taking engages and focuses attention such that participants are fully absorbed in the action unfolding around them rather than some other social scene (1967, 149, 185). "An unfamiliar or previously unengaging activity can become intrinsically motivating if a person happens to find flow in it. . . . The motivation to persist in or return to the new activity is emergent, arising out of the interaction itself" (Nakamura and Csikszentmihalyi [2002] 2006, 93).

17. Apter points out that often behavior is means rather than ends focused. "Not only can the activity serve the goal, but the goal can be used to serve the activity. Sometimes the end is primary and the means are secondary; sometimes the means are primary and the goal is secondary. The conventional psychological view, then, is only half-right. It overlooks all those occasions when we do things for their own sake or 'for the hell of it'" ([1989] 2007, 37).

STOP's vigils diminished as I learned to focus my attention on the other participants rather than on the far less predictable passersby.[18] However, in spite of such training, the groups could not ultimately dictate members' emotional responses to their day-to-day challenges.[19]

My experience in both groups illustrates how such groups, by providing social support and training for how to focus attention, facilitate opportunities for thrilling, risky activity that can culminate in a rush of positive emotions.[20] Any resolution, regardless of whether it was a success or failure, ended uncertainty and thus released their emotional vacuums.[21] When risks were *successfully* resolved, the release of tension was accompanied by a flood of complementary positive emotions.[22] Victory filled the void created by vigilant fear. Joy filled the void created by vigilant grief.[23] Risks that ended in success not only generated a flood of

18. Although participation offered opportunities for thrilling expansion for members, these routine risks evoked self-centeredness in newcomers, further increasing the potential for miscommunication between regulars and newcomers. Without emotional support and expectations for filtering experience, participation could actually reinforce the bodily self, in which case the experience is overwhelming and anxiety provoking. Not "getting" these risks created steep boundaries around the groups.

19. Gibson argues that sensory information is not passively received by actors; rather, actors actively go into the world to acquire it. In the language of Gibson, sources are objects, and the stimuli are patterns and transformations of energy at the receptors of the perceiver. Stimuli may specify sources, but they are not the same as the sources. Thus perception depends on far more than the presence of the source of stimulation; it depends on the presence of the observers, their sensory capacity, and their active attention toward the environment (1966, 29).

20. Csikszentmihalyi describes such emotional flow: "In vital engagement, the relationship to the world is characterized by completeness of involvement or participation and marked by intensity. There is a strong felt connection between self and object. . . . Likewise, it is valued aspects of the self that are absorbed or invested in the relationship and realized or expressed through it—a poet's gift, a scientist's iconoclasm, a journalist's belief in democracy" (Nakamura and Csikszentmihalyi [2002] 2006, 86–87).

21. The sheer removal of pain is pleasure in itself. The intensity of the release corresponds to the intensity of need. Dewey points out that "the moment of passage from disturbance into harmony is that of intensest life" (1959, 16). That satisfaction offers release, regardless of success, explains how actors could come to choose a negative resolution over continued uncertainty. On the other hand, the intensity of release also explains how an actor could come to pursue risky action in order to experience such intensity. Psychological stress risk-reduction theories cannot account for risk taking that becomes an end to itself (Escot et al. 2001; Heuven et al. 2006; Jawahar, Stone, and Kisamore 2007). But as Dewey writes: "Only when an organism shares in the ordered relations of its environment does it secure the stability essential to living. And when the participation comes after a phase of disruption and conflict, it bears within itself the germs of a consummation akin to the esthetic" (1959, 14).

22. Dewey talks about this sensation as it accompanies the perception of moving art: "A work of art elicits and accentuates this quality of being a whole and of belonging to the larger, all-inclusive, whole which is the universe in which we live. . . . This work is then felt as an expansion of ourselves. . . . Where egotism is not made the measure of reality and value, we are citizens of this vast world beyond ourselves, and any intense realization of its presence with and in us brings a peculiarly satisfying sense of unity in itself and with ourselves" (1934, 202–3).

23. If we look closely at the emotional dynamics of risk taking, we see a succession of complementary emotions as emotional vacuums that are created and released. *However*, from a distance,

positive complementary emotions; they also generated feelings of expansion.[24] These experiences of expansion created sensations of connection, animation, and becoming larger than life.[25] The result, as Durkheim says, is a feeling of confidence, courage to take action, and boldness in taking initiative.[26] This sense of expansion is a morally suffused energy; it makes actors feel not only good, but exalted with the sense of doing what is most important and most valuable.[27] In such moments, expansion,

---

we see a mingling of complementary emotions during intense emotional experiences. Feelings of grief and joy intermingled in the Workers' moments of agape. Similarly, fear and anger merged during STOP's public protests. This paradoxical mingling of complementary emotions can be found in many of our most moving emotional experiences: finding love in the face of evil, patience in intolerance, joy in sorrow, confidence in fear, compassion in coldness. Thus it should not be surprising that grief is often a stopping point on the way to the Workers' experiences of joy, or that fear is a stopping point on the way to STOP members' experiences of power.

24. James describes how the self simultaneously disappears while one's experience of the world expands during such euphoric moments of expansion: "Religious rapture, moral enthusiasm, ontological wonder, cosmic emotion, are all unifying states of mind, in which the sand and grit of the selfhood incline to disappear, and tenderness rule. The best thing is to describe the condition integrally as a characteristic affection to which our nature is liable, a region in which we find ourselves at home, a sea in which we swim; but not to pretend to explain its parts by deriving them too cleverly from one another. Like love or fear, the faith-state is a natural psychic complex, and carries charity with it by organic consequence. Jubilation is an expansive affection, and all expansive affections are self-forgetful and kindly so long as they endure" ([1902] 2007, 251). Haidt details the recent findings in neuroscience about the brain activity that accompanies these experiences of expansion. "The neuroscientist Andrew Newberg has studied the brains of people undergoing mystical experiences, mostly during meditation, and has found where that off-switch might be. In the rear portion of the brain's parietal lobes (under the rear portion of the skill) are two patches of cortex Newberg calls the 'orientation association areas.' The patch in the left hemisphere appears to contribute to the mental sensation of having a limited and physically defined body, and thus keeps track of [our] edges. The corresponding area in the right hemisphere maintains a map of the space around [us]. These two areas receive input from [our] senses to help them maintain an ongoing representation of [our] self and its location in space. At the very moment when people report achieving states of mystical union, these two areas appear to be cut off. Input from other parts of the brain is reduced, and overall activity in these orientation areas is reduced, too. But Newberg believes they are still trying to do their jobs: The area on the left tries to establish the body's boundaries and doesn't find them; the area on the right tries to establish the self's location in space and doesn't find it. The person experiences a loss of self combined with a paradoxical expansion of the self out into space, yet with no fixed location in the normal world of three dimensions. The person feels merged with something vast, something larger than the self" (2006, 236–37).

25. See Collins (2004) and Lefebvre (2004, 60) for descriptions of the role of energy in generating feelings of connection, growth, and expansion.

26. Mead describes this willingness to take initiative as universal neighborliness, kindness, and helpfulness. He also states that the wider the social process in which one is involved, the more exalted one feels (1934, 274).

27. Durkheim describes the process in *The Elementary Forms of Religious Life*: "In the midst of an assembly animated by common passion, we become susceptible to acts and sentiments of which we are incapable when reduced to our own forces; and when the assembly is dissolved and when, finding ourselves alone again, we fall back to our ordinary level, we are then able to measure the height to which we have been raised above ourselves" ([1912] 1995, 241). A number of social theorists have argued that similar emotional drives motivate social interaction. Collins suggests that individuals

intensity, positive specific emotions, and relief combine to create a sense of mythic importance.[28]

The type of expansion associated with a positive resolution was determined by the nature of the risk. When Catholic Workers witnessed little miracles or made intimate connections with neighbors or newcomers, they experienced a sense of expanding horizontally. In these moments, the distinction between the helper and the one being helped dissolved and both appeared to feel a deeply satisfying sense of expansion.[29] The Workers occasionally experienced similarly moving interactions with those who came to join the community, either as a live-in member or an extended community member.[30]

During STOP's monthly vigils, less than ten people usually turned out. With so few participants, everyone came face-to-face with people who vehemently opposed a moratorium on the death penalty, sometimes an

---

act to gain emotional energy, which feels like enthusiasm, personal strength, and/or willingness to initiate interaction. Actors gain emotional energy from either participation in interaction rituals that generate solidarity or by wielding power in a hierarchical interaction. Alternately, if actors are excluded or subordinated in an interaction, they will lose emotional energy (Collins 1988, 1990, 2004). Gamson (1992) argues similarly, stating that collective identity—the enlargement of personal identity to encompass more people—is intrinsically satisfying. Aron and Aron (2000) propose that people expand themselves both through physical and social influence and through social and bodily identity.

28. The activists in the above stories illustrate what Jasper describes as moments when protestors experience a sense of possibilities opening up, and action seems destined or part of a larger plan of world transformation (1997, 22). In the absence of tangible political or social change, this sense of emerging possibilities offers a satisfying sense of momentum toward the larger goal. The ability to act as an entity within a new field of action requires stabilization.

29. The term "agape" captures the deeply satisfying sense of being one with everything that the Catholic Workers sought in such moments. Traditionally the term indicates Christian notions of selfless love for humankind, but it was also used by C. S. Peirce to refer to a non-theological sense of sympathetic intersubjectivity (Staab 1999; Anderson 1995). Agape is "the sympathetic attraction exerted on us by people, things, or ideas . . . an attitude that something is valuable and desirable in its own right and should be kept around, incorporated into our way of life" (Pape 1997, 59–60). Peirce suggested that true agape is "not directed to abstractions but to persons; not to persons we do not know, nor to numbers of people, but to our own dear ones, our family and neighbors" (Anderson 1995, 105). The connection is not achieved through invoking charity and justice alone. It is a value for a certain type of interaction that generates deep identification and results in care; thus agape is simultaneously an emotion and a value. Frankl does not use the term "agape," but his usage of the word "love" is similar: "Love is the only way to grasp another human being in the innermost core of his personality. No one can become fully aware of the very essence of another human being unless he loves him. By his love he is enabled to see the essential traits and features in the beloved person; and even more, he sees that which is potential to him, which is not yet actualized but yet ought to be actualized. Furthermore, by his love, the loving person enables the beloved person to actualize these potentialities. By making him aware of what he can and of what he should become, he makes these potentialities come true" ([1946] 1984, 134). Also see Haidt (2006, 96–97, 130–31) for discussion of gratification and agape; and (196–97) for discussions of the motivation toward moral elevation and its positive association with intense positive emotions.

30. Interactions with newcomers were most likely to be successful when the newcomers saw themselves as taking up a similar relationship to the Catholic Worker community and the neighborhood rather than seeing themselves as helpers.

attorney from the district attorney's office or just a passerby. Although these confrontations subjected participants to social and even physical threats, face-to-face conflict created opportunities for some participants to enjoy intense and emotionally satisfying interactions. Newcomers found the small, highly visible, and confrontational vigils threatening and exhausting. They visibly contracted, taking up less space, as they endured face-to-face confrontations with hecklers. Vigil regulars, on the other hand, tended to get pumped up by the jeers of passersby.[31] Face-to-face conflicts with hecklers enabled regulars to experience intense feelings of conviction and camaraderie.[32]

————

If we understand an actor to be a history of bounded evolving strategies in response to evolving fields of action, we do not need to presume that actors necessarily correspond to biological individuals.[33] By this definition of "actor," actors can expand and contract so that they could grow to encompass a very large group, even a nation, and shrink so that the body itself could be viewed as an outsider.[34] As the stories above illustrate, the Catholic Workers and STOP's leaders illustrate two different experiences of expansion: saintly inclusive horizontal expansion and heroic dominant vertical expansion.

31. In the case of STOP, the group was a field of contestation in itself. There was limited attention space for heroes, so participants were actually engaged in competition not only with the opposition, but with their own team. Thus, those vying for hero status did not offer solidarity to newcomers, or anyone else for that matter. Participants' divergent positions during the vigils meant that in spite of particular members' experiences of expansion, vigils could pull participants out of emotional sync with one another. The vigil regulars tended to be older and have long careers as activists. Unlike many of the younger activists who lived in the activist neighborhoods and activist collectives, the regulars lived all over the metropolitan area and had families. Thus participation in the vigils provided regulars with some of the thrills of vertical expansion that the leaders enjoyed, as well as opportunities for horizontal expansion that refreshed their identities and emotional and social ties all within their lunch hour.

32. Durkheim ([1912] 1995), Simmel (1964), and Collins (2004) all discuss how outside opposition can increase a sense of solidarity within boundaries.

33. Understanding the process of expansion goes beyond theories of altruism that situate motives solely within individual actors, such as nested interest (Frank 1990) or expressions of individualism (Wuthnow 1991). Instead, it situates the goal that motivates action between rather than within individuals. The emotional current that pulls those participating in the interaction toward involvement and expansion, despite risk and hesitation, grows out of the interaction itself. If expansion is not based in an essential self that is tied to the biological body, time and space are central to understanding actors seeking expansion. The following chapters explore the roles of time and space in the creation, persistence, and transformation of social actors. Chapter 4 illustrates how the achieving and maintaining of stability is a process. Thus the capacity to exert force is the product of multiple indirect forces, so the process can only be understood over time.

34. Eating disorders are an example of a self shrunk below the level of the body (Summers-Effler 2006; Bordo 1995; Bartky 1990).

Table 2.1   Relationship between Type of Risk and the Emotional Consequences of Success

Style	Type of Risk	Emotional Vacuum	Emotions of Success	Type of Expansion
"Hero"	Competition	Fear/threat	Righteous anger/victory	Dominance
"Saint"	Incorporation	Grief/helplessness	Joy/serendipity	Transcendence

The two types of expansion work very differently. Saints selflessly endure humbling hardships with joyful equanimity to find joy in apparently thankless tasks without hope of recognition for their efforts. They must regularly challenge their character limitations by dissolving their sense of self-importance. Like depictions of saints such as St. Francis or Mother Teresa,[35] when the Catholic Workers successfully met challenges, they experienced intense feelings of joy and humility and a sense of dissolving as larger forces worked through them.[36]

Heroes, on the other hand, bravely struggle against insurmountable odds on behalf of the common people. In order to maintain their status as heroes, they must regularly exert their influence across enduring boundaries by taking risks in the face of external threats. They must emerge victorious and earn the admiration of others for their successful risk taking.

35. Although Mother Teresa epitomizes popular notions of sainthood, she is not currently a saint. She has, however, been beatified.

36. James describes the saintly character in the following way: "The saintly character is the character for which spiritual emotions are the habitual center of the personal energy, and there is a certain composite photograph of universal saintliness, the same in all religions, of which the features can easily be traced. They are these:—

1. A feeling of being in a wider life than that of this world's selfish little interests; . . .
2. A sense of the friendly continuity of the ideal power with our own life, and a willing self-surrender to its control.
3. An immense elation and freedom, as the outlines of the confining selfhood melt down.
4. A shifting of the emotional centre towards loving and harmonious affections, towards 'yes, yes,' and away from 'no,' where the claims of the non-ego are concerned. These fundamental inner conditions have characteristic practical consequences, as follows:—
   a. Asceticism.—The self-surrender may become so passionate as to turn into immolation. It may then over-rule the ordinary inhibitions of the flesh that the saint finds positive pleasure in sacrifice and asceticism, measuring and expressing as they do the degree of his loyalty to the higher power.
   b. Strength of Soul.—The sense of enlargement of life may be so uplifting that personal motives and inhibitions, commonly omnipotent, become too insignificant for notice, and new reaches of patience and fortitude open out. Fears and anxieties go, and blissful equanimity takes their place. Come heaven, come hell, it makes no difference now! . . .
   c. Purity.—The shifting of the emotional centre brings with it, first, increase of purity. The sensitiveness to spiritual discords is enhanced, and the cleansing of existence from brutal and sensual elements becomes imperative. . . .
   d. Charity.—The shifting of the emotional centre brings, secondly, increase of charity, tenderness for fellow-creatures. The ordinary motives to antipathy, which usually set such close bounds to tenderness among human beings, are inhibited. The saint loves his enemies, and treats loathsome beggars as his brothers." (James [1902] 2007, 244–47)

Thus heroic behavior requires both opponents and less powerful benefi-
ciaries. Much like mythic conquering heroes, STOP's leaders experienced
a sense of dominance over physical and social space and intense feelings
of victory and power when they successfully took on their opposition.

Conclusion

When actors share risks, they share emotional sequences of absorption,
vacuum, release, flooding of emotion, and sense of expansion. Both
groups took risks in order to maintain a sense of momentum and to buoy
themselves emotionally. Such groups' day-to-day challenges set the stage
for emotional intensity, emotional energy, and a sense of expansion by
generating anxiety that focused attention. The Catholic Workers could
not feel agape without risking rejection and being used for the material generosity that they offered; STOP could not feel victorious without
risking defeat. Regardless of success or failure, taking risks to meet their
challenges generated moments of emotional intensity that lent a sense of
weight and meaning to group activity. And when the groups experienced
success, this intensity was followed by intense positive feelings and a
deeply satisfying sense of expansion. Moments of vulnerability represent
opportunities for social failure, but they also offer the potential for expansion. Such interactions are not only positive and exhilarating; they
create a sense that history or God is on the participants' side.

These two groups took on different challenges, engaged in different
risks, and enjoyed different types of success. We can think of Catholic
Workers as expanding horizontally through solidarity with one another
and a deep sense of identification with the people who come to them for
help—a saintly attraction to involvement. STOP's leaders expand horizontally when they build solidarity with one another by focusing on
outside conflict, but primarily they expand vertically through a sense of
power and importance—a heroic pull toward involvement. The Catholic Workers felt like saints when they made themselves vulnerable and
created solidarity across social boundaries that were difficult to traverse.
STOP members felt like heroes when they took on the opposition and
emerged victorious, when they played David to the system's Goliath.

Although these groups' activities may look masochistic from a distance, their risky actions that left them vulnerable to rejection and failure
allowed them to minimize the threat of burnout associated with helping professions. The commonsense question for high-risk altruistic social
movements is this: How and why do actors want to come to and stay

involved with such groups? But, as the stories throughout this volume reveal, the more pressing question is actually: How could anyone ever leave the roller coaster of altruistic social movement involvement for the humdrum of everyday life?

———

If the groups engaged in risky activity long enough, they experienced failure. When these groups failed, they experienced the opposite emotions associated with success: contraction and low levels of enthusiasm. The next chapter is about how the groups built themselves up emotionally, so that they could once again face the challenges that provided the emotional glue that held these groups together.

THREE

Recovering from Failure Carves Paths to Action

Both the Catholic Worker community and STOP took risks that ended in failure, and these failures represent emotional drains from which the group had to recover if they were to sustain their activities. The two groups went about recovering from these failures in very different ways.

The Catholic Workers had a lofty ideological goal of complete selflessness, a goal that they could not reach for without being hurt. Sometimes neighbors and guests took material goods from the Workers' while rejecting their invitation to emotional intimacy. When the Workers continued to invest more time and emotional energy into failing relationships with guests, they contended not only with emotional drain but also a growing sense of shame over their leniency with problem guests. The Catholic Workers recovered emotionally by turning inward and using religious ritual to sanctify their daily struggles. With enough recovery time, the Catholic Workers were able to interpret their draining experiences within their larger ideology, claiming the experiences as lessons in humility rather than failures.

Sometimes STOP's leaders lost when they vied for public attention. STOP's story describes how despite its early popularity, internal conflict and an unfavorable turn in political conditions eventually led to the breakdown of the group. When STOP suddenly lost the hard-won attention of activists, politicians, and the media, feelings of victorious expansion became feelings of humiliating contraction.

Rather than restoring the group, Todd, STOP's second director, revamped its style, strategies, and goals. A new center of action was created at the site of the old center. He renewed involvement by shifting the group's focus from confrontational protests to efforts to expand its networks and influencing electoral politics.

A Catholic Worker Story of Failure and Recovery

Blueberry Surprise

I made my way through the group of children and the regular field-trip volunteers and let myself into the house.

Blueberry—a fortyish, intermittently homeless White woman from the neighborhood—stood gripping a cast-iron skillet as she served bacon and eggs to Linda, Joan, and Ms. Beth. Laughter usually punctuated these women's interactions, but today they did not banter back and forth or even make eye contact.

Linda and Joan mumbled, "Hello," in my direction. Ms. Beth, who generally said very little but spoke volumes with her expressions, nodded her welcome. Then she momentarily raised her eyes to mine, pursed her lips, and shook her head slightly while giving a partial roll of her eyes, indicating she thought there was some sort of nonsense going on.

Blueberry offered me breakfast with downcast eyes. "You want some eggs and bacon?" I turned down her offer but got myself a cup of tea and sat with the others. More volunteers arrived, and the ones who had been waiting outside followed the newcomers into the house, apparently seeking sanctuary from the impatient children.

While others made small talk, Joan gestured me toward her side. "While we're waiting, will you take Blueberry up to the clothing room? She needs a pair of shoes." I told her I would, and she gestured Blueberry over. Blueberry followed me upstairs.

Unless she was caught up in a novel or a newspaper, Blueberry generally showed her affection by taking up the offensive in lightning-fast repartee. But the heavy silence of the dining room followed us up the stairs. As I fumbled with the keys for the padlock on the clothing room door, she said, "I'm sorry to bother you. Any old pair will do. Really, it doesn't matter, just anything."

"It's no bother whatsoever."

Once in, I eyed the shelves across the room piled high with shoes and asked, "What's your size?"

"I'll take any old thing, doesn't matter. Just something to cover my feet."

"Blueberry," I said in mock exasperation, "you can't wear shoes that don't fit. What size are your feet?" My effort failed to lighten the mood. She wouldn't look me in the eye.

"Eight. But really, I'll take anything. Just need something to cover my feet. Anything really."

I pulled out a pair of white canvas sneakers that did not look too worn and was shocked to see they were size eight. "Hey, they're eights! That never happens in this disorganized mess! I should know; I'm the one who's supposed to be organizing it."

"Wow, yeah, that's something. That's great," Blueberry responded with absolutely no enthusiasm.

I left her to put on her new shoes and went back downstairs. The volunteers were going back outside, so I quickly asked Joan, "Why's Blueberry here without any shoes?"

"Oh, she's staying here for now," Joan said vaguely, looking like she hoped this would suffice as explanation. I waited, and she added in a forced offhand tone, "She doesn't have any shoes because they took them from her in jail. We were up all night bailing her out, and we just couldn't wait any longer for the shoes."

"But I thought you couldn't have her here because of her drinking. I know that you've wanted her here . . ." After a few harrowing experiences with some of their past guests, the group had decided that they couldn't allow people who drank or used other drugs to live in the community, and Blueberry was a serious drinker.

Joan sighed, slouched, and closed her eyes for a moment. "It's a long story, but the long and the short of it is that she's our friend and has nowhere to go. Besides, that's why we're here. Who are we to close our doors to anyone?" She sounded like she was trying to convince herself more than me.

Joan explained that Clint, Blueberry's boyfriend, had come by the house the evening before to tell them about Blueberry's arrest and subsequent incarceration. Clint and Blueberry had fought after drinking. Blueberry had started swinging at him with a box-cutter, so he called the police. When the police arrived, Blueberry took a few swipes at them too. She had been arrested for domestic violence, resisting arrest, and threatening police officers with a weapon.

Larry, a recent retiree and member of the extended community whom the Workers called their "go-to-man," was there when Clint told his story. He, Joan, and Linda had immediately left to bail out Blueberry. Six hours after arriving, they finally had Blueberry, but Blueberry did not have her shoes. Worn out and worn down, all agreed to leave the shoes.

Joan said she and Linda had hesitated to invite Blueberry into their home because of their experiences with Jean, Phil, and Kenny, drug-addicted guests who had caused serious problems in the house, but when faced with turning their friend out of the only place she had to sleep, they had made their decision to take a risk on her with their hearts rather than their reluctant heads.

"I told her, 'In return for bailing you out, I want you to go to AA. I'll go with you. This has to stop. None of us would be here right now if you hadn't been drinking.' She said she'd go." Joan looked hopeful but anxious as she stole a glance at Ms. Beth. When I turned, I saw Ms. Beth was rolling her eyes, pursing her lips, and shaking her head.

Struggling with Boundaries

When I first came to the house, the community had been struggling with Jake, a mentally ill man who had been living at the Catholic Worker house since long before Linda and Joan joined the group. Jake suffered from schizophrenia but had been managing well when medicated. Shortly before I had arrived, he had stopped taking his medication and refused to start again.

The group noticed Jake's declining condition when he started coming to them with get-rich-quick schemes. "He told us he knew where to get his hands on some really cheap bead necklaces. He wanted us to sell them on the street and make a ton of money," Linda explained to me, laughing. Jake's behavior changed from amusing to alarming within a couple of weeks. He accused the Workers of poisoning him, robbed the community house, and called the police on the Workers for various imagined offenses. The more the Workers tried to talk to him about his medication, the more he claimed treachery. They began to fear him, and after much soul-searching and many agonizing conversations late into the night, they decided to have him committed.

I had heard countless retelling of their stories of his behavior and their pain over deciding what to do with him. Their struggle with Jake was a sore tooth that they could not stop probing. Joan in particular seemed to need to turn it over again and again, looking for a possible alternative to their course of action or early signs they had missed. But the continual rehashing did not seem to bring much relief. Although the ones who believed they were capable of housing a seriously mentally ill guest said they had forgiven themselves for having him committed, it was clear that they held their past selves accountable. "We didn't have any business having him here. We never had the resources to deal with him," said Joan in a tone that did not quite ring of certainty.

"He's a nice man . . . He needed help, just not the type we could give," said Linda.

"No matter how much we would like to accept people as they come, we are just not equipped to take in people with severe mental problems. We're just not, we're just not," said Joan.

"God knows they always find us anyway." Linda buried her head in her arms and laughed in defeat.

Her laughter was contagious, and soon Joan was shaking with laughter as well. "There's something about Catholic Workers and crazies. The crazies *always* find us. Remember how we always had to have garlic paste for the one guy?" said Joan, laughing so hard she could barely speak.

"It didn't matter what we were having for dinner . . . 'Excuse me, would you pass the garlic paste?'" Linda said, holding her stomach and gasping for air.

I had never met the man, but I could not help laughing either.

After taking a month break from offering any hospitality, Joan and Linda began to open their house to guests again, secure in the knowledge that they had learned from past mistakes and would be able to avoid situations like the one they had with Jake.

Not long after, a social worker called about a woman named Jean. A nearby hospital was looking for a place for her to stay so that they could release her. The Workers had room, and Jean fit their present criteria for guests—she did not have an overt mental illness—so they agreed that Jean could come to stay when the hospital released her the next morning.

The next day, before Jean arrived, the Workers found a man named Kenny asleep in their after-school building. It was below freezing outside, and the thought of him in the unheated building horrified them; they invited him to stay as a guest as well.

Jean arrived a few hours later with her previously unmentioned husband, Phil, in tow. By the end of the day, three guests occupied their upstairs rooms, and everyone seemed excited that they were back in business.

Not long after, the Workers' belongings—radios, coffee makers, and toasters, among other things—turned up missing. All three of their guests disappeared for the few days after the social security checks came in; behavior the Workers were fairly certain indicated serious drug addictions.

Increasingly frustrated and worried, the Workers began to feel unsafe when they found that Phil and Jean were bringing people into the house late at night.

Exhausted and quick to anger, tensions in the community grew. "The situation is out of control. I never liked them," said Linda.

"Where are they going to go? They'll go to the street. They can't take care of themselves. They're too thin, and Jean's still so sick. They'll die if we kick them out! I, for one, can't live with that. How can we kick them out? They're the reason why we're here," Joan responded.

"Those people are using drugs, and they are lying," said Ms. Beth, clearly disgusted, with Phil and Jean for sure, but possibly with the other members of the community as well.

Ramona stopped cooking dinner long enough to poke her head into the dining room. "You need to kick them out. It isn't safe. This is *not* what Dorothy intended. She kicked people out too, you know."

All of them knew that Dorothy Day, one of the founders of the Catholic Worker movement, had kicked people out, but there was little in the philosophy and theology she developed with Peter Maurin that explained the conditions under which they should feel it was acceptable to do so.

———

While Jean and Phil were testing the limits of the Catholic Worker community, the house hosted eight college students for a long weekend over winter break. They had come to the community to help and learn about conditions in the city. On the last night of their visit, the group sat around playing board games and discussing what they had learned during their visit.

I turned when I heard someone running down the stairs and caught Linda's worried expression as she swung into the dining room. "We have a problem," she said distressed. "There's a twenty missing . . ."

Joan's panicked gaze darted around the group of students, effectively cutting Linda off. "Tell me in my ear," Joan told her.

Linda leaned down between us as an upset and confused college student turned the corner behind her. "One of the students is missing a phone. Another's missing cash."

Both Joan and Linda looked devastated, as if they had been punched in the gut.

We all turned as Kenny walked through the door whistling and smiling. His look quickly changed to apprehension when he saw Joan's face.

"Something missing?"

Joan hesitated for a moment. "Yes, but you didn't do it, right?" she asked, beseeching him with her eyes.

"No I didn't. I didn't take anything," Kenny replied with grave and persuasive earnestness.

"I didn't think you'd do it because you'd tell me, right? You've told me before about things that were difficult to talk about."

"I didn't take anything, Joan."

Joan closed her eyes and nodded her relief. She leaned closer to Linda and me. "I know that Phil and Jean did it. I know they're doing drugs upstairs. Those friends they bring upstairs, they drive a Mercedes," she said, shaking her head in disgust. "Do you have any money?" she asked looking at Linda. "We can't let these kids leave here with this as their last impression." Linda pulled twelve dollars out of her pocket, and I pulled out a ten. Joan collected the money, gave me two back, and turned to hand the twenty dollars to the agitated student. Noting his expensive-looking clothes and watch, I waited for him to refuse, but he pocketed the money.

Joan and Linda let the students continue the game without them and turned back to their conversation about Phil and Jean. I had heard about the loud friends late at night but never the Mercedes. This was the first time that they had admitted out loud that their guests might not be staying with them in good faith. The biggest strike against the couple was that they had never come clean with the Catholic Workers when they had been caught stealing and lying. If the guests could not be model community members, the Workers wanted authenticity at least. The public embarrassment of their theft from the students seemed to be the proverbial straw that broke the camel's back.

Joan hung her head and shook it slowly as she spoke, "This afternoon they said they needed clothes. I should have known. I should have known. I've offered them clothes so many times, but today they needed clothes, and they needed them 'right now.' They took what they could, and they're not coming back."

"They came with nothing but managed to acquire quite a bit of stuff since they've been here. There is no way they have moved out all of their things," replied Linda.

"They certainly left with more than they brought," said Joan in despair.

"I hope they're coming back," said Linda taking a deep breath. "They have a key."

"Well, looks like we'll have to change the locks again."

"You should befriend a locksmith," I commented.

Suddenly, Joan and Linda were laughing hard, doubled over and crying. "God, we just never know what the hell is going on around here! Not a clue," said Joan wiping her eyes.

———

Not long after, Kenny disappeared for a day, and then they got a call saying he had been hospitalized for an infection surrounding his heart—a sure sign he had been using unclean needles. Only a day later, the Workers found out Phil had been pimping for Jean, and Jean had been prostituting herself for drugs out of their room at the Catholic Worker house.

Arguments between community members over what to do increased until it felt as though the community was a hair's breadth from collapse.

Eventually they decided that the guests had to go, but even this did not seem to heal the rifts between them. Ms. Beth stayed away for a few days. Ramona did not come for weekly dinner.

A week later the community was still emotionally raw. Joan told me about how Phil had came back begging to be let in, but the Workers wouldn't open the door.

"He said, 'I just need another chance,' and begged, saying, 'I just need twenty dollars. Just give me twenty.' When we wouldn't let him in, he pounded on the door and kicked it again and again. He yelled at us, 'You can't do this to me! I have rights!' He kept pounding on the door and screaming, 'Who do you think you are? You're not God! You're not God!'"

Then the group was silent. Eventually Joan said to no one in particular, "We're trying to offer a service here. We invite people into our home, and it just feels terribly wrong when someone thinks they've been done wrong by us."

In response to Joan's hand wringing, Linda looked increasingly frustrated until she burst and told Joan bitterly, "You're too idealistic."

Ms. Beth and I were quieter than usual, but Joan and Linda wore particularly guarded expressions and kept their gazes to themselves during the liturgy that followed. Joan continued to grieve openly, not just about the guests, but about innumerable tragedies all over the world.

She talked about suffering, about grandmothers and children being forced to sleep on park benches and in subway stations, and about abandoned children climbing over piles of garbage looking for food in Rio de Janeiro. She grieved for her own inadequacy, telling stories of neighbors who humbled her with their generosity.

Linda slumped lower and lower in her chair as Joan talked; she looked as if each of Joan's stories was a weight, and she was struggling to stay upright under the increasing load. She put her head down and covered her face, as if she were physically trying to avoid what Joan was saying.

Finally, she got up and said to no one in particular, "I have to get some soda for my stomach."

"Where's she going?" Joan asked me, her eyes accusing. I repeated what Linda said, and Ms. Beth turned her head away and sniffed. "Oh, a stomachache," Joan responded, suggesting that Linda often did this to get away from Joan when she did not want to hear what Joan had to say.

Although Joan usually brought the liturgy to a close, the liturgy ended abruptly when Linda returned and suggested we end with a prayer. Joan announced that she would not be holding people's hands during the prayer, saying that she was not physically close enough to hold other people's hands, even though she was an easy reach away from the people on both sides of her. Normally the loudest one praying, this time she did not say the beginning of the prayer at all.

That night the strain continued to build so that it seemed to constrict even movement and air. The group ate in silence until Linda brought coffee out after dinner. Over coffee Joan gave a brief chuckle to herself, and then raised her eyes to the group. She started to tell an old and apparently familiar story, barely suppressing a smile. "One night when I was alone, I heard a knock on the door. It was after the time for sandwiches, but I decided to answer it anyway."

Linda started to smile, clearly recognizing the story. "When I opened the door, a very tiny drunk man fell right though, I mean *right* through the door, and hit his head on those stairs," she said, pointing back toward the stairs. "He just lay there stretched out like that with his head on the stairs for a good long while. I started to worry because I couldn't wake him up. I thought, 'My God, this little drunk man just died hitting his head on our stairs!'

"But after shaking him and yelling at him for a few minutes, he started to move. He groaned and tried to say something. I was pretty annoyed with him at this point, and I told him I couldn't figure out what he was saying and that he was going to have to at least move enough for me to close the door. Then he lifted his head slowly and slurred, 'Cin I geta san'wich?'"

At this point we were all laughing, even Ms. Beth, who always looked like she tried to fight laughter, so that she erupted when she finally gave in. Joan was laughing so hard she could not speak. Linda could barely sit up.

Linda tried to talk a couple of times before she was able to choke out, "One night we came home late, and I realized that the next day was recycling, and I hadn't done it yet."

Joan nodded her head listening to Linda, apparently recognizing her story as well. "And you *know* how Linda is about the recycling," she said with a good-natured eye roll.

"*Anyway*," Linda said, laughing, "I had to get the recycling bins from the shed behind the house. It was dark, and I thought I heard some noises, so I thought I should get a flashlight and check. Joan *begged* me not to go and check."

"I did, but you know how stubborn she is. It's like the horror films—you just shouldn't check the noises!" added Joan.

"But the recycling was the next day, and it had to be done, so I went to get the bins. I heard the noise again and was convinced it was a squirrel or a raccoon or something like this. Anyway, I opened the door slowly, afraid of being attacked by a rabid animal, when out rolled"—she paused for dramatic effect—"the tiny drunk guy!" She was laughing so hard she could barely speak again. "He had been sleeping standing up in the shed. He rolled out, popped right up, and said, 'Cin'I geta san'wich?' Now this is pretty impressive; you should see me when I get out of bed! I told him, 'NO, you CANNOT have a sandwich, and I'll give you five seconds to get the hell out of here.'"

The group continued to tell funny stories into the night, but it took more than a good laugh for the community to recover from the disappointment of Phil, Jean, and Kenny. The next week, righteous anger replaced meaninglessness, hopelessness, and the cleansing laughter.

Angry Boundaries

During the next weekly liturgy, Joan slammed her fist on the table after the Gospel reading and proclaimed, "Everything we have but don't need is stolen from the poor!" Linda nodded in agreement.

Looking around at Ramona and Frank, an extended community member, I could see that I was not the only one feeling like the difference between the Workers' commitment and my own sat like the proverbial unacknowledged elephant in the room.

"Let's offer our prayers," Joan said. People offered typical intentions: for particular neighbors with troubles and for peace in the world.

This time Joan surprised me by adding a new one: "For our guests, the people who come to the door, the people who stay with us, the children from the after-school, and our extended community—may we be worthy."

Even though the extended community was usually included in the "we," the "we" of her prayer clearly pertained only to Linda and her. With a paradoxical modesty, she asserted both their moral superiority and their humility simultaneously.

In the next few days, Joan prayed aloud again and again to be worthy of helping the people who came to them, but she no longer positioned the extended community as outsiders while offering these intentions. The "we" of the Catholic Workers once again expanded to include the extended community.

Agape opened their boundaries; judgment and anger marked the location of their contracting boundaries. The amount they shrunk corresponded to the distance of the failure. During high points, the "we" of the Catholic Worker was not limited to the community, neighborhood, and movement; it included the whole world. When they failed, this "we" shrunk drastically; during these times, it often excluded their neighbors and guests, sometimes even extended community members.

Melancholy Mysticism

Exactly a month after Phil, Jean, and Kenny left, I walked into the house in time for liturgy and dinner. During liturgy Joan told the group that she had seen Kenny the day before. She had found him across the street, standing in front of the after-school building and looking at the house. "It was cold, so I asked him to come in. But he refused." Her eyes began to tear up. "He wouldn't take food or clothes either." Clearly choked up, she paused for a moment.

"He said, 'I don't want anything. I came to apologize for being weak, for not being able to stay off the drugs. I know I let you down.' He just looked so sad," Joan said, openly crying now. "'I can't go in that house. I'll only let you down. It's a holy house, Joan; I can see and feel it. I'm not sure how much longer I can make it, but—God willing—I'll see you in heaven.'"

She said he gave the Workers fifty dollars; none of us doubted that this was all the money he had. "I was reluctant, but I took his money because he wanted me to. He was sad, but he was proud of himself. He wanted to do what he could do."

The Workers began to pay more attention to the story of Kenny than having anger and frustration over Phil and Jean. There was never a dry eye when they told Kenny's story. Joan often said, "You could touch him, I mean really touch him. We may not have helped Kenny in the way that we wanted to, but we have to remember that things happen in God's time, not ours. We did what we were supposed to do with Kenny, we touched his life, and he touched ours. That was our lesson—we can choose to do the work, but the outcome is up to God. We often don't see enough to understand the effect we have and we need to remember that."

Their structural vulnerability facilitated their emotional vulnerability. Once I commented that nothing was hidden with them because they could not afford to be proud. Joan resounded, "That's definitely true; everything's out in the open with us. Our need is so obvious and we're so vulnerable that many things that would normally be hidden by manners are out in the open for everyone to see. We can't afford to be polite."

New Boundaries

Two years after they had seen Phil and Jean for the last time, someone who had come by for a sandwich told the group that Phil had died. "No matter how much we want to help them, we're just not able to help people who are using. We're just not," added Joan.

Reminded of the trial he represented, I asked them all how they recovered from their experiences with Phil, Jean, and other guests who had let them down. I asked them how they managed to take the risk of inviting a guest into their home again.

"Well, you don't know until you try. Everyone's different. But no more people who are using. We just can't have these people here," said Linda.

Initially the Workers took in whoever asked for help. Even though these three guests' drug addictions and consequent behavior made the Workers' day-to-day lives miserable and pushed the Catholic Worker community to the point of breaking, the Workers ignored the guests' behavior. Then they acknowledged the behavior was a problem but defended the guests' rights to stay according to Catholic Worker theology.

Only when fear for their safety and internal conflict threatened to break the group apart did they ask themselves: Does an effort to build mutual trust and respect with these particular guests represent the potential to bring about the radical transformation of society? They had to decide what it meant to have an open-door policy. Do they allow substance abusers to live with them? If not, when do they break their own rules? With each warning, the group narrowed its strategies, or in other words, they lost potential paths of action.

Struggling with Blueberry

My surprise over Blueberry's presence as a guest in the Worker house grew out of this history. I had seen the emotional turmoil that prompted their policy of refusing guests who abused drugs or alcohol. However, Blueberry seemed to be a reasonable exception to the rule because everyone believed that she had to leave eventually to do jail time—possibly a lot of time.

When Blueberry finally received formal word of the charges against her by mail, she went on a binge and came back so drunk that she could not stand up. She muttered incoherently as Linda helped her up to her room. Ms. Beth furrowed her brows and shook her head. Joan looked defeated. Blueberry, who knew how the Workers felt about her drinking, stayed away the next night and the day after, but not the next.

The afternoon she came back, my after-school partner did not show up, so I volunteered to make some peanut butter and jelly sandwiches. Thomas—a college-aged, self-identified Marxist punk from an upper-middle-class suburban background who had just joined the community—told me there was no bread and offered to get some. I went back to the kitchen while I waited and found Jackie—a new older White guest who wore bright blue eye shadow and an elaborate black wig perched on her head like a hat—doing dishes. I rolled up my sleeves and joined in.

By the time Thomas returned with two loves of bread, my after-school partner still was not there, so Jackie and I made sandwiches. As we worked, Jackie talked about almost joining the convent. She told me that she believed that the sexual abuse claims against the priests were mostly lies and that the people who told them were probably going to hell. Jackie got increasingly worked up, so I was quite relieved to see Blueberry as she stumbled through the kitchen door, until I realized how drunk she was.

"You're trying to kill the cat, and I'm not going to let you!" she yelled, and pointed at us. "You feed that cat too much! You better not feed that cat any more. That cat is getting fat. Its belly is dragging on the ground, and you don't care. I'm telling you I'm watching you, and you better not do it." I bit my lip so I wouldn't laugh, but Jackie managed Blueberry very well by looking grave and nodding her head.

Blueberry turned to the dining room, which was filled with children working on homework. They fell silent as she roared that we were trying to kill the cat. Joan told her to please leave and not to come back until she was sober. Joan let her barely controlled anger go as soon as the last child left. It lasted well into dinner. "She knows she can't come back here like that. We have families with children here. She can't come here falling-down drunk. I told her in no uncertain terms that if she ever came back drunk again, she would not be allowed in the house. This is the line in the sand: no drinking allowed!"

They believed, or at least hoped, she would drink less because they had given her an ultimatum. The plan seemed to be working; in the following days she did not come to the Catholic Worker house unless she was sober.

And then she got good news.

She walked in the door shouting, "Praise Jesus! Praise sweet Jesus! They reduced those charges and said that if Clint didn't show up in court, I'm a free woman. Now Clint, he and I are straight. We got that straightened out between the two of us, and there isn't going to be any Clint in that court. I still have to go to court, but praise Jesus, I'm not going to jail! On the way to see the public defender, I just kept on praying, 'Please help me, Jesus,' 'Jesus is so good!' and 'God is so good!'"

Joan responded with glad exclamations. "Oh, Blueberry! That's wonderful!"

Ms. Beth said nothing but looked at Blueberry through narrowed eyes.

Hearing the commotion, Linda came out of the kitchen saying, "Blueberry, that's great!"

Blueberry moved toward Linda, and I could see she was glassy-eyed and swaying like grass in the wind. As Blueberry's exclamations and swaying grew wilder, everyone else became quieter and stiffer. No one would look at each other, first only at Blueberry, but then only at the floor, the walls, or anywhere but at each other. Slowly we all returned to our work.

In the kitchen I looked at Linda expectantly, waiting for her to comment. Finally she said, "Well, yes . . . well she's just had a little, nothing like a few days ago."

Joan yelled out, louder than necessary, "We're out of bread for sandwiches!" sounding angry.

"I'll go!" called Blueberry. "I'm going to the Pathmark."

"No, you are not! That's a half an hour walk away! Go to the corner store!" yelled Joan.

"But you can get twice as much bread for the same money at Pathmark," said Blueberry, clearly proud of her dedication to getting the best deal for the Catholic Workers' dollar.

"Don't be ridiculous! GO TO THE CORNER STORE!" yelled Joan. Although she yelled like she was angry, it was easy to see she was actually brokenhearted. Blueberry was particularly special to Joan, but she had backed Joan into a corner by coming back drunk.

Blueberry left looking downcast and confused. After she left, it felt as if the tension might suffocate us. No one said anything about Blueberry, and when Blueberry came back significantly more sober, no one said anything to her either.

Blueberry continued to come back drunk. She was always friendly and solicitous to the Workers, especially Joan, but she became increasingly angry and rude with the other guests. They turned a blind eye, and the group's energy appeared to dwindle until Blueberry yelled at some of the children staying in the house.

The Workers realized that they would have to kick her out even though she had nowhere to go. "You see, we *just can't have* people who drink staying with us," said Joan, arguing again with her invisible opponent.

Making Room for Blueberry

Soon after Blueberry left, people from the neighborhood started reporting that they had seen her sleeping in the park. One of her buddies came for a sandwich. "Kids been throwing stones at her," he said, shaking his head.

The Workers cried, wrung their hands, wondered what else they could have done, and reassured each other that she had left them little choice but to kick her out. They heard she was spending her days in front of the liquor store again, so they started bringing hot soup and sandwiches to everyone who hung out there.

And then Blueberry disappeared.

They found her a few months later sitting on a corner a block away from the Catholic Worker house. She had been drinking and had a bright red welt broken open on the side of her forehead. When the Workers asked her what had happened, she told them that her landlady had beaten her. The Workers invited her back to the house again. This time there were no ultimatums, just a request that she go right to her room if she came back drunk.

Almost eight months later, I found Blueberry sitting at the table, in her usual spot, reading a new novel. She had transitioned to more of a community member than a guest. "Hey you, girly," she called to me. With her haircut and clean clothes, she looked like a different person.

"Hey yourself, Blueberry."

"I'm reading this new book. This is a *good* book. I mean it. I do. It's a detective story, and when I read it I'm the detective. You know what I mean? I mean I *become* that detective—that's how good it is. This detective is trying to find her dead sister. Really. A good book, it really is."

I sat with her at the table and looked at the newspaper while she read her book.

"Isn't there a new guest?" I asked, remembering hearing about a new arrival.

"Um-hmm," Blueberry said, shaking her head, "this one is a crazy." She laid her book facedown on the table. "This lady is nuts, absolutely nuts. Makes no sense whatsoever. Hasn't lifted a finger to help since she's been here either. You remember that problem we had with Pete awhile back . . . I don't think we should take those political asylum folks. They stay way too long."

Joan called for Blueberry from the other room. "I'll be right back; Joan needs something," Blueberry told me.

She came back with Joan, who declared that it was time for the kids to arrive for the after-school program. "Which means it's time for me to get the heck out!" Blueberry laughed. "Thank the good Lord I didn't have any of my own," she murmured on her way out.

The children and other community members started to arrive. We helped the children with their homework. Then we packed them up and started preparing for dinner. Ramona was making one of her elaborate feasts. Once the kids were gone, Linda, Thomas, and I left Joan and Ms. Beth at the table to help Ramona with dinner preparations.

A few hours later, we'd almost finished with dinner when Blueberry stumbled drunkenly through the door. She raised her hand in greeting. "Hey, everybody. Looks like a nice dinner. Yup, I'm on my way up."

Everyone called, "Good night, Blueberry," after her.

I asked everyone at the table what they thought about their history with Blueberry.

They were all thoughtful for a moment, and then Linda shrugged and said, "I guess you just never know."

Ms. Beth shook her head and gave an exasperated chuckle.

Joan, as usual, answered at length. A beatific smile spread over her face, and she said, "We don't think about these things in the way that most people do. We believe that God sends us what we need, but that doesn't mean we understand the lesson at the time. Sometimes the most horrible disappointments turn out to be wonderful blessings; other times apparent joys bring nothing but sorrow.

"We try to take each thing as it comes, as a gift from God. Do you know about the Buddhist monks who walk around with empty bowls, equally glad for whatever comes into it? We try to do the same. But it isn't always easy. There's this story about a Buddhist monk who was found crying after the death of his grandchild. His student asked him, 'Master, if all of life is an illusion, why are you crying?' The master replied, 'This is the most difficult illusion.' You see, it isn't always easy, but we work at it."

The Workers pushed themselves hard, and as a result the group was always confronting the limits of what they could handle. Jake, the mentally ill guest, and Jean, Phil, and Kenny, the drug-addicted guests, were too much for the group. Sharing all that they had and living in community with these people threatened their capacity to maintain the group and continue their work. Despite her claim that they took what God sent them, the failure with Jean and Phil was exceptionally painful, and the lesson was etched deep within the group. In response, the group set new limits and redefined what it meant to live up to the Catholic Worker ideal of taking personal responsibility for the poorest of the poor.

Blueberry did not meet that new standard, but in the Catholic Workers' struggle with her she became the even newer standard, the story they told themselves was meant to illustrate the importance of flexibility and openness.

The Catholic Workers often turned to religious ritual to bolster their spirits and elevate their day-to-day struggles to a sacred level, but even religious rituals began to fall flat during this difficult period. Members appeared to be too exhausted and irritated with one another to become fully involved in these rituals. Their mood only shifted when they started telling the story of the tiny drunk. Rather than invoking a sense of mystical awe and reverence, they played tough, unsympathetic, and fed-up characters, attitudes that were the exact opposite of the ones they strove to embody in their work, and it inspired gales of laughter. By sharing humor in misery, they shed the shame of being taken for suckers and not being able to help all of those in desolation around them. The Catholic Workers' ability to release their fear and shame through group confession and humor enabled them to restore solidarity within the group and maintain their storyline about how their day-to-day efforts fit within their broader ideological agenda.

Recovery began at the very center of the group, creating boundaries between the live-in and extended community. Their boundaries widened as they regained their sense of moral authority and righteousness. Eventually the group returned to solidarity seeking, but not without restoring its sense of being special and part of a larger noble cause. A penitent drug addict was an awe-inspiring sign of God's will in the context of others who lie, steal, and prostitute out of the Worker house. Kenny's story was a touching illustration of their capacity to make a difference in someone's life, while Phil's was a story that disappeared from the oral history of the group soon after the group had recovered from him.

By the time Joan explained her mystical take on their problem guests, I had spent enough time at the Catholic Worker house to know that things were rarely as serene as she was making them out to be; taking risks on guests inevitably resulted in tension and disagreement at some point. However, I also had seen that through religious ritual and intense interpersonal relationships, the Workers were able to build and reinforce an emotional involvement in the community, an involvement that is in large part independent of successful outcomes. Their belief that they were "doing God's work" also created space for uncertain outcomes. They could call on a shared belief that "things happen in God's time" to explain failure with a guest as part of a divine plan that was bigger than they were.

––––––

The Catholic Workers hope every attempt to serve will result in a shared sense of solidarity with their neighbors, but they are often disappointed. Disappointments threaten enthusiasm and meaning. When the Catholic Workers extend themselves, they risk feeling shame for having been taken for fools and feeling like they have made meaningless sacrifices. Non-responsive guests put them in an emotional and ideological bind. How can the Workers kick their guests out and still feel like Workers? With no clear paths or expectations for how they should deal with their problem guests, the Workers often argued among themselves. When they set these limits, they had to be able to forgive themselves for falling short of their moral vision of total openness—for turning away those who were ungrateful, those who stole from them, and those who physically threatened them. To recover, the Workers tended to rationalize their perceived failure, return their focus to the group itself, dispel the shame associated with the failure, and rebuild feelings of mutual vulnerability and solidarity that offer the potential for the mystical connections. Laughter, religious ritual, and time facilitated this process of forgiveness. Their mantras became "We can only do what we can do" and "If we only . . . then we have made a difference." They became vigilant against setting objective standards for success.

After each struggle that ended in failure, the Workers redefined what it meant to live up to the Catholic Worker ideal of taking personal responsibility for the poorest of the poor. Despite their continually changing expectations, the community survived as a center of action with a coherent history. They cultivated a mystical humility to counter the urge to gauge their efforts by some measurable outcome. By incorporating humility and disappointment into their understanding of their larger mission, they were able to restrict their sense of loss to particular situations or particular people. This enabled the Workers to continue to take similar risks in the future while feeling that they had learned from their mistakes.[1]

A STOP Story of Collapse and Recovery

STOP's Staff Falls Apart

I waited for Todd to let me in anxiously. I only had been in the field for a short while. My interactions with Todd had gone well, but my interactions with the rest of the staff had been tense, to say the least.

Todd seemed distant and exhausted as he answered the door. I followed him up to STOP's new office space and was overwhelmed with the smell of stale cigarettes and old sweat as we walked through the door. I was surprised to find STOP's office empty. Todd's body language announced he was not open to questions, so I did not ask where everyone else was.

"It would be great if you could help us out by painting the front room," he said, gesturing to the room without meeting my eyes.

"Us" sounded strange when the two of us were the only ones in the office.

I inspected the room and could immediately see why Todd had avoided my gaze. He had made an agreement with the landlord that STOP would clean and paint the new office space in return for a cut in rent. The walls were covered with a thick film of grease that could have accumulated over years of frying food.

I began prepping the walls and soon realized that scrubbing the grease away released a more pungent version of the cigarette and sweat smell. An hour or so later, Todd returned to talk to me as I was laying out drop cloths. "Everyone's gone but me and Lucas," he said. I had heard about

---

1. James explains the saintly disposition in this way: "In the annals of saintliness we find a curious mixture of motives impelling in this direction. Asceticism plays its part; and along with charity pure and simple, we find humility or the desire to disclaim distinction and to grovel on the common level before God" ([1902] 2007, 255).

Lucas but hadn't met him yet. He only worked part-time because he was a high school student.

I looked over my shoulder and saw that he was not looking for a response. His eyebrows were furrowed, and he was glowering. I continued to work as Todd brooded. Eventually he started to explain.

"Laura, the fund-raiser for STOP, didn't get any grants. Didn't even apply for grants. All this time . . . that's what she was hired to do. I guess I should have been checking up on her more. She didn't even get the renewable ones that were supposed to be no-brainers—it's only reapplying for God's sake! Can you believe that we have less money after having hired a fund-raiser than before when we didn't have one?" Todd laughed bitterly.

Todd was referring to some months earlier, when STOP had secured enough resources to hire other employees, and Todd had decided to hire two young White women from the local activist social scene. Laura, a recent college graduate from a nearby liberal arts college and a well-connected activist, was hired as a fund-raiser. Alice, a member of a neighborhood anarchist collective, joined STOP as a part-time community organizer. Todd also hired Benny, a young African American man recently exonerated from death row, to organize the friends and family of people on death row. Beyond these grant-funded employees, Lucas—a White high school student who became involved with the group through his church's youth activities—created his own position as a part-time youth organizer and secured funding through his church to support the position.

"Laura was part-time at first but told me she wasn't getting money because she didn't have enough time, so I made her full-time. I told her we needed money. I tried to make her understand that we *couldn't keep going* without *money*," he said, as if incredulous over her lack of understanding. "It was, it is, crisis time. I told her that I needed her to focus, but she did too much organizing. The steering committee and I were very clear, she was to stop her activism and focus on grant-writing. But she didn't do it, and now we're out of money. That's it. We're out." He held his palms up and tilted his chin up and to the side in a gesture that said, "I told you so."

"A couple of months ago, we received a $250 donation. I told her to process it right away because we were totally broke. Three weeks later, three *weeks* later, I found out she hadn't processed the check." He shook his head in disbelief.

"We told her she was laid off due to 'lack of funds,' but since it was her job to raise funds, she was really being fired." He brooded some more.

"When I told her we had to let her go, she suggested that we all go without pay for a couple of months. Unbelievable, right?" but as he said this, I remembered that many of the neighborhood activists, mutual friends of Todd and Laura, worked without pay.

"I told her, '*No*,' and she flipped out. She said I was 'overstepping the boundaries of my job description' and that I didn't have 'the authority' to fire her. She wanted to speak with the steering committee.

"Can you believe it? After all of this time and she doesn't even know how much authority I have. She doesn't realize I'm *in charge* of the organization! I told her the steering committee was on board with the decision and that they had no desire to speak with her. She left a *seven-page* letter for me on Saturday morning in front of my house, as if I was going to read some seven-page letter from her on a Saturday! Well, she accused me of all sorts of things in the letter, showed up on Monday and informed me she was holding the database hostage until she spoke with the steering committee. Beautiful, right? Height of professionalism . . ."

He laughed bitterly again, shaking his head. "Then it turned into a big screaming mess. I'd had enough. I'd rolled over again and again to please her and the rest of the staff who were so eager to accuse me of being power hungry, but I'd had enough. She yelled and freaked out some more and then stormed out of the office.

"She accuses *me* of being hierarchical, patriarchal, and power hungry. What really gets me about this is that she was always insisting on using a consensus model, that we couldn't try to 'change society and have a traditional power structure,' but it was an excuse to avoid the very limited accountability we have around here. If you look at the radical organizations being run out of the squats doing everything by consensus, they are disorganized, they have no money, people go for long periods of time without being paid, and most of all they aren't really all that effective. Focusing on the internal politics of the group and bearing witness is all well and good, but when there is something that can actually be changed through more traditional types of organizing, there is a moral imperative to focus on the issue over and above group dynamics."

Tension Builds Before the Storm

Three weeks before the morning when Todd told me he was the only employee left, I had waited on the sidewalk outside the door to the office for Todd to let me in. I thought about the warning he had given me about the staff meeting scheduled to start in a half hour. "Be prepared, you might have to 'check in.'" When I looked confused, he added, "You know, telling the group your emotional state and your personal issues before the meeting starts." I had wondered at his apparent distaste for the practice when he was the director. Couldn't he decide to run the meetings in a different way?

The stairs were steep, and I saw Todd's bright white sneakers first as he bounded down the stairs. "Welcome!" he said as he opened the door. "Come on in."

He held the door and gestured for me to climb ahead of him. He told me that Benny, a former death row inmate who worked for the organization, was sick. Lucas, the youth organizer, was in school, so neither of them would be attending the meeting.

"We're meeting in there," he said, once we'd reached the office. He gestured to a large round table that nearly filled a very small kitchen.

"Help yourself to a bagel and some juice."

He told me about restaurants, bars, music—knowledge meant to indicate his privileged position within the activist community.

I changed the subject. "STOP's official goal is a moratorium on the death penalty now. It didn't always used to be that way. Does this upset anyone? Are there people who refuse to give up an abolition stance?"

He sighed, as if my question made him weary. "Yeah . . . there are. We also have people who are satisfied with reforming the death penalty. They say you have to take what you can get, but this is a total sellout. Look, everyone thinks the death penalty should be abolished."

He sounded like he was slipping into a rehearsed speech, and he started to get the wide-eyed look he wore when he began one of his angry tirades. "If we can get a moratorium to investigate errors, inequality, and bias, it basically amounts to abolition. They can't get around that stuff; it's basically abolition." He paused for a moment, clearly frustrated. I thought of the continual balancing act he performed as he tried to manage so many ideological positions within the group. "People against the moratorium, people who will only support abolition, these people tend to be very idealistic and not very practical people. Bearing witness and all that; I'm not against that stuff; I'm not. Look, I've done it myself. But this is what you do when you don't feel like there's anything practical you can do."

He sighed again. "Look, I thought we already talked about this in our first interview."

"You're right. I'm sorry. It must be very difficult to keep all of the potential supporters involved when they have such different opinions."

"Some of the anarchists who get arrested with us have a hard time understanding how we can take money from any pro-capitalist sources.

I have to think about how much it costs to organize and stage these protests, but the radicals don't like to think about the money involved. I tell them, 'Liberal money for radical organizing for revolutionary action.'"

Two women came through the door laughing and talking to each other. One was wearing a loose Indian print camisole with cut-off jeans; the other was wearing a tight faded T-shirt that looked like it was from the 1970s and cut-off track pants; her head was uniformly shaved clipper-cut close. I looked at my watch and noticed they were almost a half hour late. Neither of them looked at Todd or me as they moved through the room toward the kitchen. I glanced at Todd and he looked nervous.

They stopped their laughing conversation abruptly when they saw me. "Looks like we have a visitor," said the woman with the long pale hair.

The other woman looked past me over my shoulder toward the bagels and said, "Must be somebody important since Todd got bagels."

Todd stiffened. "Laura, Alice," he said, looking first at the woman with the long hair and then at the woman with the shaved head, "this is Erika, she's a grad student. She's going to volunteer for a while, while she learns about how we do things around here."

They eyed me suspiciously and sat as Todd introduced me.

I felt myself blush, and Todd looked awkward. Laura did not say anything but smiled at Alice. They made it clear that I was less than welcome. I felt caught off guard—they seemed hostile, and I hadn't expected that. I would have found a way to leave had I come as a potential group member rather than as a researcher.

Laura rested her bare feet on the table next to the bagels.

Alice stretched, yawned, and commented, "I'm beat. It's been hard to get any sleep around the squat these days."

I felt quite certain I was supposed to understand they were radical, "hardcore," and I was not.

Todd did not respond to Alice's comments but launched the meeting by fuming about a recent example of the general tendency for the national anti–death penalty group to corner the market on available grant money.

"The action's at the state level—that's where we're going to stop this thing. It's a waste of time trying to get amendments passed when we can get states to outlaw it. This approach has been the most successful and they know it, but they get all the money and status just because they're the most public face and it's easier to give to one group than all of the state groups. Still, you think they could pass some our way. They even had a piece from our website in their newsletter, but it's not like they're doing anything to help us," Todd said with sardonic laughter.

"You mean they used some of your writing without giving you credit, without citing you?" I asked. The two women looked at each other and looked at me with judgment in their eyes.

Todd looked uncomfortable as he explained, "We don't really care about intellectual property in activist circles."

Afraid I would do more damage, I remained quiet for the rest of the meeting.

As the meeting progressed, Todd danced around every statement that he made. It was as if he were afraid to take up any position, fearing that he could be called out, as I had been, for breaking the apparently demanding and complex activist code that distinguished insider from outsider.

Partway into the meeting, Todd cut a bagel while expressing concern about Benny's health. "I don't know what to do about him. He's so unhealthy we really can't rely on him to show up for scheduled gigs." He stopped speaking for a moment and eyed the toaster on the other side of Alice. He looked at Alice and again looked back at the toaster. Alice saw him looking at the toaster and continued to watch him with a studied blank expression on her face.

Conversation stalled as Todd got up, made his way awkwardly around the large table in the small room, toasted his own bagel, then walked all the way around the table back to his seat. Laura and Alice traded smug looks a couple of times while he toasted his bagel and tried to keep the conversation going.

Soon after he took his seat, Laura asked Alice, "Would you toast my bagel?"

"Sure," responded Alice with a smile. "No problem."

I looked over at Todd, but he was focusing on his bagel as if spreading cream cheese required his complete undivided attention.

It was unclear to me at this point whether or not Todd "deserved" the reproach of his employees; I did not have the background to know if Alice and Laura were responding to past abuses of power or not. However, it was clear Todd wanted to be considered a good activist and included in the activist scene, and Laura and Alice could help or hurt his potential for realizing these goals. This power gave them leverage that they did not hesitate to use.

Although an activist-centered tradition had developed in STOP, the group had no explicit commitment to a particular method, only to the larger goal. The changing political climate and organizing responsibilities split the group. Some staff members wanted to continue to focus on their methods of organizing, but Todd, the director, wanted to focus on influencing traditional politics. Ultimately group members did not resolve their differences, and the existing group split apart. Todd leveraged his institutional authority to maintain his position as leader, while those below him left the organization.

———

Todd may have felt that he's been burned by these particular activists, but over the next few months he continued in his efforts to secure his status in the neighborhood activist scene.

"With this heat wave, the owner has to be making a killing! It's pretty much the best Burmese restaurant in town, and one of the best in the nation. Whenever [known reggae artist] comes to town, he books a back room for the band and his people.

"The owner just put some tables out back since it's been warmer. It's fantastic. Every night I've been going back there, ordering up some beers and appetizers. Every night more people I know keep showing up," he said, as though he just happened to stumble across the hip activist hangout. "It's really *the* place to be these days, and I'm like, 'Hey, good food, good beer, cooler than my furnace of an apartment? I'm there!'"

But Todd's connection to this activist world shifted on a dime after 9/11.

Another Setback

We were sitting in STOP's offices almost a month after 9/11, and only a little more than a month after the staff blowup.

"If I wasn't working to end the death penalty, I might do some other criminal justice type work or maybe environmental work. I don't do that much about the environment now, but I care about it." I nodded in response to Todd as I typed names and addresses into the group's contacts database.

Overnight the death penalty became a non-issue. Politicians, even supporters of the abolitionist movement, moved the issue of the death penalty to the back burner. State politicians focused on developing policy for responding to and detecting terrorism on a state level. They were still unsure how overwhelming the anthrax scare would become. There were even discussions about how long the state legislature would purposely stand idle out of respect.

Rather than worrying about how to keep activists with conflicting ideologies happy, Todd was pressed to find any activists who had not completely shifted their attention to the bombing of Afghanistan and a looming war with Iraq. Even STOP's board members informed Todd that they would be focusing most of their energy on the burgeoning antiwar effort.

Todd decided to shut down organizing efforts until the beginning of the next year, meaning that he wouldn't be going out on speaking engagements or holding the monthly vigils in front of the district attorney's office. "There's nothing in the news about anything but anthrax. I'm not in a place to do any major organizing, and no one's interested right now. I really need to rebuild the organization anyway."

The phone rang, interrupting Todd. The call was from a foundation considering STOP for a grant. Todd explained STOP and its platform politely, emphasizing the class and race bias in the prosecution and sentencing of capital crimes. From Todd's end, it sounded like the interviewer was asking some of the questions that I had heard many people ask STOP members before: "What about alternatives to the death penalty?" "Doesn't it lower the crime rate?" "What about life in prison as an alternative?" and so on. Todd answered these questions effortlessly with rehearsed responses.

Then there was a long pause as Todd listened. He sat up and leaned forward, as if he were steeling himself. "Well, the issues surrounding the death penalty are still unaddressed after September 11th. I was just talking to state senator Smith—he called looking for STOP's support—who told me that the state senate has pretty much shut down to all issues that aren't directly related to September 11th until the end of the year," said Todd.

He waited for another long pause and then said, "Well, no issues other than terrorism, anthrax, and impending war are being given much attention right now."

Another pause. With less energy, Todd said, "No, my perception from handing out flyers on the street is that people don't seem to feel differently about the death penalty after September 11th." Todd hung up the phone looking worn-out and frustrated. He got up and went back to his office without saying anything.

Rebuilding STOP

Eventually Todd began to rebuild STOP's resources. The power his resources gave him became a point of pride, and he distanced himself from the activist scene more and more. In this new era, Todd became far more assertive, angry, and self-assured in his authority. Over the next few months, Todd spent less of his time regaling me with tales of his hopping social life. When he did talk about his social life, he talked more about his new connections in the legal community than the neighborhood activist scene. Increasingly our interactions consisted of Todd instructing me about tasks he wanted me to complete. Almost six months after the organization began to recover, Todd asked me to pick up copies for a mailing. "I need you to stop by the Boulevard copy shop."

His request surprised me; the neighborhood activists boycotted the Boulevard shop because of a race-based conflict at the store the year before.

Todd must have seen my surprise, because he launched into an aggressive defense of his continued patronage. "They've kept our account open when we've run dry many times. Awhile back the governor blocked our funding, and for four months we had no money, but they still let us copy. We do between eight and ten thousand dollars' worth of copying a year."

I must have looked impressed, because he interrupted himself to add, "You know, that really isn't all that much business," emphasizing that I did not know all that much about running an organization like STOP. He went on, "They wait on me right away. That's what they do with their big customers. Everyone knows me there. I can always tell if there's someone new because they'll make me wait in line until the manager sets them straight." His point was plain; the activists from the neighborhood could critique him, but few could boast budgets as big as STOP's, or as big as STOP's used to be.

Eventually Todd renewed funding for STOP's program for prisoners and their families, which enabled him to hire a new organizer for friends and family of people on death row. Todd found two people he felt were reasonably qualified for the job. One was a longtime activist; the other was Marge, a recently retired woman who came to STOP out of her own personal connection to a prisoner on death row. Marge had no ties to the neighborhood activist community; she also had almost no organizing experience. Nevertheless, she had a wealth of office skills, a personal motivation for ending the death penalty, and a modest connection to the Black Christian Leaders, a group of local African American religious leaders. He decided on Marge. "I'd rather take a chance with Marge than be burned again," he said.

Marge may have been old enough to retire, but she did not look it. She laughed when I asked about her retirement. "Retirement? Please! I'm taking care of a three-year-old and a thirteen-year-old and ending the death penalty!"

Just after Todd hired Marge, STOP acquired more office space on the floor above their original offices. The new office's previous tenant spent his ten years in the space frying food and smoking cigarettes. "After one look at the office space, I almost quit on the spot. But then I decided I had to talk Georgia into coming down here with me to clean this place," Marge told me, looking at the space she had recently cleaned and vastly improved with the help of her friend. "People aren't going to treat us like the professionals we are if we don't have a professional place to meet."

Professional, that is how Marge approached her new job as an activist. Marge was enthusiastic, punctual, reliable, and traditionally professional. Like Lucas, Marge primarily focused on growing the movement. She courted the friends and family of people on death row as well as the Black Christian Leaders, a group of well-organized local pastors that brought both people and money to the causes they championed. She would have enthusiastically embraced neighborhood activists if they had filled the streets to stop the death penalty, but they did not occupy a privileged position in her understanding of the political world. So long as Todd or others could defend it as the most efficient way to end the death penalty, Marge focused on changing the law and had few quibbles with any approach to organizing or running the office—just like the post-9/11 Todd.

After sustaining the tension of a split focus between living out their political ideals within the group and achieving concrete political outcomes, a series of changes in material resources and group membership brought about extreme transformations in the daily practices of the group.

————

Marge reinvigorated the organization with her energy—she was filled with at least as much righteous anger as the old pre-9/11 Todd, and she seemed to help bring him back to life. Always talkative, she gave what amounted to a continual sermon on injustice. Marge was angry, but energetic, vehement about the dire conditions of what she referred to as "my community," yet firm in her belief that hardworking people could bring about change. Somehow she managed to tie almost every topic, from carrot cake to meditation, back to social injustice.

One afternoon she told me, "My granddaughters are running me ragged. You know Black youth spend so much of their lives in jail for drugs they didn't bring into this country. That's why the grandmothers are so overworked—the men are in jail." She was eloquent in her critique of oppression, and her critique differed in style, motivation, and consequence from those put forth by the youthful, mostly White activists from the neighborhood. She was also a master at buttering up anyone who might be willing to contribute to STOP, whether it was by painting the new office—which was my job—showing up for a protest, giving money, or volunteering in the smallest way.

Despite Marge's persuasiveness, the decreased attention to the death penalty after September 11th led Todd to revisit previous strategies. When I first talked to Todd, he told me that he benefited from the structure that had been developed at the outset: "We're committed to aggressive non-violent tactics, we work with families of death row inmates, we refuse to advocate life without parole as an alternative to the death penalty, and we absolutely refuse to take a stance on the guilt or innocence of any particular prisoner. The last one is particularly important because it helps us to keep the focus on state-sanctioned killing. It's too easy to get lost in the politics or the different accounts of the people involved. That's a dangerous and slippery slope that we've successfully avoided so far."

Shortly after Todd hired Marge, he was approached about Jack Forest's case, a death row inmate dying of cancer. Many had publicly claimed that Jack had been framed for a murder connected to police involvement in drug trafficking. In a city where police tension with poor African American communities was a long-running problem, Jack's case touched a lot of nerves across the city, but advocating for Forest meant stretching the organization's stance of refusing to take a position on the guilt or innocence of any inmate.

With the near collapse of the organization, Todd willingly walked this fine line. "Technically we're only asking that they stop trying to hide police corruption by stalling the review process so that Jack dies in prison. We're also using this to hook up with the prison reform people who are advocating for proper medical treatment in prison. Besides, a compelling case like this motivates people, captures their attention, gets them angry and off the fence about the death penalty. I've seen Jack's story bring tears to the eyes of people who aren't even against the death penalty."

Phones started ringing. STOP started holding their monthly vigils again, and now many of the signs they brought for people to hold were about Jack Forest. He was pulling more people into the Jack Forest cause, but many of these were lawyers rather than the neighborhood activists who used to be the backbone of the group's larger protest. I remembered

Todd leading demonstrations in jeans and anti–death penalty T-shirts, but he started wearing suits and rarely held signs.

I was riding back from a vigil with Todd when he got a call on his cell phone. "Todd here. Hey, good to hear from you. Yeah, you got tremendous coverage. All over the news and radio yesterday. Fantastic. Yeah, we're on for tomorrow. Ten o'clock. Great. Looking forward to it" went Todd's end of the conversation. He sounded professional, efficient, busy, and in charge.

"She's an amazing professional activist," he told me. "She just got national coverage for medical reform in prisons. She framed it as government waste—absolutely brilliant!"

"What's the difference between professional and career activists?" I asked him.

"Career activists take whatever jobs they can to support themselves and quit if a job gets in the way of their activism. Professional activists make their living as activists. There are a lot more career activists around. Hard to get foundations to support anarchist groups, you know?" He laughed a harsh laugh at his own biting wit. "The career activists are usually the most energized and effective. They tend to have a bias against professional activists. Career activists tend to be very suspicious of people who are being paid."

I knew Todd was defensive about the hierarchical structure of STOP because of the past conflict in the group, but I had not realized he needed to defend his professional status as well. I began to see Todd's stories about his connections and influence and the more current distinction between his behavior toward volunteers and staff members in a new light. In the larger activist world in which he operated, the volunteers had a morally superior position. In a business where success was determined by actors who had access to decision makers and could mobilize large numbers of people, Todd had to know more important people than I did in order to justify not just his power, but his paid status compared to my volunteer status.

Todd went on to make a further distinction between career activists. "There's a big difference between the lifestyle anarchists and the political anarchists. The political anarchists typically don't have much respect for the lifestyle anarchists. The lifestyle ones tend to burn out. At some point they decide they want more from life than living in a filthy squat, and they just disappear one day. One day you realize it's been awhile since you last saw them, and then you know—they've just disappeared. I figure they just go back to the middle-class suburban lifestyles from which they came. The political ones live on little and in those squat conditions so they have time and resources for their causes, their activism." As we parked the car, he added another distinction, the "sometimes" activist. "They are the people who show up for the demonstrations. They're weekend activists."

He suddenly gave me that same worried/caught look that I had seen after his comment about how much work it took to organize volunteers. "*I* don't look down on them. We don't have demonstrations if they don't show up."

We carried the signs and such back upstairs, and I asked Todd where I should put them. He pointed to a spot behind the door. "That's one of the things we talked about at the staff meeting, coming up with a place to store that stuff."

When I turned around, Todd was sitting by one of the shared desks in the general office space, ready to continue our conversation. "The younger people, early twenties, tend to be more radical. They're very concerned about image. There are certain things you can't eat, places you can't go, things you can't do, or you're not 'hardcore'; you're a sellout. But people who stick around until their early thirties, they usually get serious and become very good at what they do.

"The political art collective is a good example. Charlie started the group to make political art for all the lefty causes around here. He got to the point where his group couldn't make art for everyone who wanted it, so he and a few other people wrote grants, got space, and trained people to make their own political art. They just had an exhibit at the opening of the new museum downtown." Todd said this in a tone of awe and respect. "I went to the training for activist groups to learn about sources of funding. The target was liberal, far right of revolutionary groups. But if you're serious, you want to get resources for your cause. There were a lot of mainstream suburban people there, but I saw Charlie when I walked into the room, and I could see he'd made an effort to be a little bit dressed up. That's when I knew he was serious. He went from a young radical guy just doing whatever he wanted to try to make something happen, to being serious."

I laughed and said, "So it goes from doing whatever you want to being a workaholic; that's ironic."

He did not laugh. "No, the younger people act like they do whatever they want, but it's really stressful living up to the standards of the scene. Once you get serious, once you enter that phase, you become more even-keeled. You realize, 'If I stay a workaholic, I'm not going to make it.' So you get a life. I actually make a point of trying to hang out with people who aren't activists now."

He had changed his perspective radically since I had first met him. He used to be so proud of how integrated he had become in the activist scene.

"When I go out and see people from the scene now, they comment about how they haven't seen me around lately. I always think to myself, 'Yeah, because I'm trying to get a life.' They accuse the older people of getting soft, but I just have to be contented with the knowledge that they'll mature and see things my way—if they stick around long enough. But almost all of them will burn out or drop out by the time they're twenty-five. That's why I don't have time for young people who are only concerned with how radical they are. Why should I train them to specialize when they probably won't make it? Lucas's not like that though, even though he's really young. He isn't image conscious. He's more focused on strategizing about the issue. I can count on him. He's serious."

"How do you know if someone can be counted on in the activist community? How do you know that they won't flake out?" I asked him.

"If you're around long enough you just hear certain people's names over and over again. If they stay around long enough, certain groups and people get reputations for being serious. I can give you a list of organizations that get things done, that do good work, and have serious effective people within those organizations. These people get things done because they are connected, enduring, practical, and efficient."

"If you're focused on efficiency and your goal is ending the death penalty, how do you keep people motivated when there hasn't been any concrete progress toward ending the death penalty?" I asked. I thought he might be offended by the question, but I wanted to understand how he reconciled his understanding of what it meant to be a serious activist with their lack of obvious impact. I had seen how demonstrations, media coverage, and meeting with politicians were satisfying for the group, but I did not see how these successes could be interpreted as "efficient."

But he did not seem offended at all. "It's all a matter of strategizing. We set things up so that we can measure success in other ways."

"Like how many people you get to show up for a rally?"

"No, not really. Demonstrations don't really do much but get people who are sympathetic more involved in the day-to-day efforts of ending the death penalty." He said this as though demonstrations were a tiring and unfortunate necessity, indicating that maintaining involvement was generally a secondary concern. "But they're also important for attracting media attention. We measure success by the amount of sympathetic media coverage we receive, and when we get papers to take editorial stances on the death penalty. It's a success if we manage to get hearings on specific issues."

I noted to myself that this corresponded with the Jack Forest campaign.

"Or have bills brought up before the state senate. If we manage to get a new voice in the mix, or we make a new connection to an important constituency, that's a success too. We do have to strategize so that we stay focused on the goal, but keep the feeling of momentum going and avoid the appearance of failing to meet objectives." Todd spent less and less time talking to me about what he did and why as he slowly continued to rebuild STOP's staff.

He had worked with Lucas, a White high school student from a nearby wealthy suburb, to secure funding to hire him as a youth organizer through Lucas's church. Eventually, Todd created a position for a live-in intern office manager and recruited Doreen, a White recent college grad who had created a STOP chapter at her college. During the summer, Marge brought her teenage granddaughter, Christy, to work in the office a few days a week as well.

One Step Back for Every Two Forward

Todd had felt he had been left out in the cold for more than a year, but now he was consumed with developing strategies and networking with important people. He buzzed with energy. He was in the loop—part of a "we" again that was made up of people he saw as important and tactically savvy, people whom he would say "got things done." Todd no longer sat and talked with me about his social life, his personal future, or the future or past glory of the organization; our relationship became increasingly pragmatic as he pushed everyone to complete the ever-increasing amount of organizing work that had to be done for the Forest campaign.

After weeks of conference phone calls, small vigils, trial dates, meetings, and phone calls to potential supporters to publicize the upcoming event, it was finally the day of the big Jack Forest protest. I showed up on that day ready to paint. So far I had painted most of the office; on this day I was planning to finish painting the kitchen.

I parked and ran into Todd on the way in. He was not wearing the lawyer look he had come to favor. Instead he had on a black beret, black T-shirt, black boots, and sunglasses. This was his battle gear, and it was clear that he was already geared up for that afternoon's Jack Forest demonstration. Todd and Marge had planned the demonstration to focus media attention on Jack Forest the day before a judge was supposed to decide whether or not he would receive another trial. (Later Todd found out that the prosecutor's office had requested more time because they said that they had not gotten the electronic documents on time. Todd felt this was an obvious stall tactic to make sure Jack would die in prison so they wouldn't have to face the embarrassment of an exoneration.) He gestured for me to follow him, and he talked excitedly about the protest as I trailed behind him up the stairs. When we reached the office, I could see Marge was wearing what she referred to as her "Afrocentric garb." She greeted me with enthusiasm as usual.

Doreen wandered in wearing a robe with her hair still wet from her shower.

"Are you going to the demonstration?" I asked her.

She surprised me when she answered, "No, I'm not. I'm trying to keep death penalty work between ten and four. I need to work on my boundaries." It surprised me that she considered the protest "work." I had thought of the protests as the show that all the work was for; that it was the rewarding experience after all of the work, but apparently I was wrong.

Todd called me into the kitchen to explain what he wanted me to paint that day. He sat and talked to me like he used to during the down periods. His cynicism was gone, and he was fired up for the events of the day. Rather than feeling powerless and unimportant, he again was in charge of something significant. "Wait until you see the puppet of the district attorney. It's huge and menacing. A local artist also made a huge mural of Jack that we'll have there. We're going to have two exonerated guys, Benny and Warren—the guys just exonerated from death row. They're always big media draws on their own, but two in one place—the press will eat it up. They love that stuff. You've got to have good visuals for the press."

I continued to paint as he talked. "There's a prosecutor who hangs up pictures of death row convicts he's prosecuted in his office with 'death' written across them. We're going to have a large blowup picture of this prosecutor, and when Benny's at the mic, he's going to write 'shame' across it. You need good visuals like that for the media." This was beyond discussing the fine points of strategy. It did not seem to matter whether I was listening or not; Todd just needed an audience so he could spin out his fantasy of the perfect protest moment. He seemed oblivious to the fact that others were working around him as he daydreamed out loud.

During our conversation, Marge interrupted Todd to ask where he thought Karen was. Karen was another volunteer activist from the neighborhood who had remained involved, although less so, after 9/11. She was supposed to find a way to attach the Jack Forest mural to poles in order to make it portable for the demonstration. Todd answered in a distracted way, "I don't know. I told her to show up early. It's going to be a problem if she shows up too late or not at all."

Marge placed a few phone calls trying to locate her. Todd stopped musing about the protest and appeared concerned about Karen's absence. Suddenly he turned to me. "You'll do the job!" he said with equal parts delight and relief. "It's ten feet or so high and made out of canvas. I need you to figure out how to display it for the protest."

Todd seemed to be increasingly comfortable resuming his role of authority, and I increasingly found myself irritated by him. He was so focused on the new coalitions he hoped to forge and the media attention he hoped to gain that he seemed to forget how much he still needed the people within STOP to help with the day-to-day work. Most of the people who comprised this helping class within STOP were the very activists whose attention he had had a difficult time holding since the shift to peace organizing after 9/11.

"I came to paint," I told him. I did not want to refuse, but I did not want to have to go on a wild-goose chase to find the mural and somehow attach it to poles before the protest.

"You've already gotten a lot of painting done," he responded. Marge could see the hesitation on my face that Todd was ignoring.

"Can you do that sort of stuff? I can't," she said, referring to the activity of figuring out how to attach the mural to poles.

"No, not really. I'm not really good at building stuff," I said.

"You'll do fine. It doesn't need to be fancy," said Todd without looking at me. He was not trying to convince me; his attitude suggested it was a fait accompli in his mind.

I bristled as he walked away. I had seen him do this more and more often to others, ignoring their reservations as he pushed forward toward his larger goal. Marge knew he was pushing, but ultimately she needed the mural to be there as well, so she let him push.

She followed me into the kitchen. "It looks so good in here! Would you like to have some lunch?" she asked with a fake highbrow accent.

To me it seemed as though she was attempting to compensate for my interaction with Todd by praising the work I had already done to transform the once-filthy, grease-laden kitchen into a sanitary, if not totally attractive, place to eat and store food. With this positive reinforcement,

Marge left me to paint while she went to organize the next bus trip for friends and family members to see their relatives and friends on death row.

––––––––

Karen never showed up, so I was on my own. Todd told me he would give me a ride to the art collective building where the mural was stored. I could tell he was about to explode, so I agreed. Todd and Marge sat in the front, and I started to climb into the back of Todd's rental car, where I wedged myself in on top of the stacks of posters for the demonstration. Marge asked, "Are you sure you can fit back there?" This was clearly a formality as neither she nor Todd paused long enough for a refusal to be an acceptable option. As Todd looked for parking near the art collective headquarters, I half sat and half leaned and listened to Marge and Todd talk about how great the demonstration was going to be. Marge expressed particular excitement about the likelihood of the Black Christian Leaders showing up.

Frustrated by a lack of parking, Todd suddenly pulled up on the sidewalk. He waited impatiently for me to climb out, then directed me toward a building that looked abandoned from the outside. Marge stayed in the car. As we walked through the unlit and barely finished hallways and stairs, I found it hard to believe that we were in the right place. But I was soon reassured by a series of large brightly painted handprints. When we got to the top, we faced an elaborately painted sign on an easel announcing the space as an art collective museum. Huge, political, brightly colored puppets hung on display around the open industrial loft space. The scale of the large puppets and the caricatured faces lent a surreal feel to the place.

As we wound through the space, we walked past the head of the district attorney puppet. The gruesome figure captured his likeness well. Todd was clearly impressed and so was I. We made our way back to an office where we met a man in a green plaid camp shirt, jeans with high cuffs, and a large hoop in each ear. He introduced himself to me as Charlie. I had never met or seen him before, but I had heard of him; he was an artist and something of a mythic figure in the local activist scene.

"What's up?" Todd asked, suddenly seeming far less anxious than he had been only a moment before. Todd asked for Sam, another artist who had apparently told Todd that she would help Karen with the mural. Charlie responded that Sam was not there and wouldn't be for the rest of the day. Todd looked frustrated and told Charlie what we needed.

"Well, let's see what we can do," said Charlie. Todd and I followed him to a large space, and Todd rolled out the huge mural of Jack Forest. We all stared quietly for a few beats at the hard-edged impressionist picture of the man dying of a terminal illness on death row.

Without looking up, Charlie finally said, "That's sexy."

Todd looked pleased with himself.

Charlie ducked back into a closet and came out with a long bamboo pole. He told us that we would need one on either side and a third one in the back to prop it up. "You'll have to watch it. That thing will turn into a sail," Charlie said. Todd looked confused. "It will catch tons of wind, but you wouldn't want to cut it because that's art, man—definitely art," Charlie explained.

Todd nodded and started to hand the project off to me. But just as he began, Charlie announced that he was leaving, saying he would be back close to two o'clock. The protest started at four. In that one moment I realized two things simultaneously: it was unlikely that we could finish the mural on time, and Charlie was not aware of the specifics of the protest, including time, meaning that Charlie was likely not going to be attending the protest. The look on Todd's face suggested that he shared the same realizations. The neighborhood activists were not helping as Todd had hoped, and now there was little evidence to suggest that they were even planning on attending.

I could see and feel Todd starting to panic. He was focused on building coalitions with the Black Clergy and other race-focused activists, but his previous speech and behavior suggested that he thought that the neighborhood activists would at least be warm bodies at the protest. Even though Todd may have felt personally hurt and frustrated by their shifting attention and loyalties, only now was he fully grasping what this loss of involvement represented in terms of resources.

Todd played it cool with Charlie, not letting on that he was disappointed. He turned to me, and I could tell he was going to push for more. Feeling sorry for him, I buckled before he asked and offered to arrive early to the protest to help carry signs from the center where they stored their props. Todd responded, "Great, that's so great. We could really use that help. It should only take a few trips to get our supplies from the office down to the district attorney's office."

I was bewildered into silence; it seemed to me that he had purposefully misinterpreted my offer to mean a far larger and more time-consuming task than the one for which I had volunteered. Anger flared, but I took a deep breath and told him I would take one trip. He looked relieved that I had acquiesced, and then he looked worn-out.

"Activist volunteers aren't always the most reliable group," I said, trying to make him feel better.

"You're more reliable than most of the people I pay," he said, but it was more as a barb at the staff than a compliment for me.

―――――――

Unlike the Catholic Workers, STOP's leaders did not acknowledge their shame or attempt to rebuild the original group after it fell apart. Instead they drew on their sense of righteous indignation to fuel their new endeavors and to stamp out perceived threats. Indeed, stirring up anger against the opposition became a key tactic as the leaders sought to tap into new potential pockets of political support. Given the potentially deep ideological divides within the increasingly diverse organization—for example, right-to-life activists, civil rights groups, anarchists, prison abolitionists, Catholics, and Quakers—a sense of solidarity was hard-won. Shared anger against an external threat distracted them from the internal focus that historically had proven to be disastrous for the group.

Toward a Theory of How Recovering from Failure Carves Paths to Action

The Role of Failure in the Transformation of Routines

Despite the differences between these groups and the differences in these particular stories of their collapse and recovery, a comparison of the two stories reveals in general how patterns of expectations and strategies absorb threats until the patterns break and change. It is clear that both groups used their emotional histories to assess potential threats. The groups crafted coherent histories through the stories they told themselves about past struggles. These stories became strategies for future interactions. Unanticipated successes, such as the Catholic Workers' spontaneous couch giveaway, required little retooling of the groups' expectations. Such moments required only low-level reflexive awareness to assimilate changes. As a result, these positive changes were not easily articulated. For example, I could not point to the moment when I became comfortable participating in small highly visible demonstrations, or the moment when a particular neighbor became a helper rather than one being helped in the Catholic Worker community.

When the groups' expectations were not met, they felt they had limited control over obstacles they encountered.[2] Unanticipated obstacles undermined the usefulness of particular symbols[3] and initiated feelings of contraction. As with expansion, the feeling of contraction was not a simple reflection of the objective state of the relations between the people who were involved in the interaction; contraction was a sense of moving away from a *particular focus of attention*.[4] It was a feeling of self-consciousness and withdrawal from where the action was, a perception of what an actor was *not* involved in. It felt like being pulled back from entrainment, as though a boundary was drawn around the action, and the actor was positioned outside the boundary.

By looking across these two stories, we see how strong negative emotions created by disruptions could motivate highly reflexive meaning-making that generated new ideas, new solutions, and new strategies to avoid past threats.[5] Specifically, past threats became warnings that bracketed off certain paths to action and marked them as scenarios that were likely to end badly. Thus these moments of destruction were also the moments when new patterns of action emerged.

Periods of absorption preceded the rupture of old patterns and creation of new patterns. The groups absorbed earlier threats to routines by accommodating these threats and adjusting their own behavior. For example, when guests stole from the Workers, the Workers moved their valuable possessions into their rooms rather than asking the guests to leave. Similarly, Todd worked to smooth over his interactions with Laura and Alice, even though the tensions continued to simmer just below the surface.

2. Allahyari notes that frequently volunteers who set out full of enthusiasm begin to struggle when they encounter the moral dilemmas that inevitably arise (2000, 108).

3. While conflict was the primary organizing force in the establishment of meaning and patterns of group action, it is important to note that not all conflict generated meaning-making processes. Only conflict between expectations and outcomes had the capacity to generate new meanings. Social movement groups illustrate this general point particularly well because they often seek out conflict with specific expectations for outcomes. If the expectations are met, the interaction, even though is can be very high conflict, will not generate new meaning. Upcoming chapters illustrate that conflict that is anticipated does not represent the same threat to meaning as conflict that is not anticipated.

4. James describes such feelings of contraction: "He who does a mean deed is by the action itself contracted. . . . For all things proceed out of the same spirit, which is differently named love, justice, temperance, in its different applications, just as the ocean receives different names on the several shores which it washes. In so far as he roves from these ends, a man bereaves himself of power, of auxiliaries. His being shrinks . . . he becomes less and less, a mote, a point, until absolute badness is absolute death" ([1902] 2007, 43–44).

5. As Dewey (1910) pointed out long ago, failure generates new meanings.

Eventually tension built to a breaking point in the Catholic Worker house and STOP, and absorption gave way to rupture, disappointment, and disorder. The apparent triggers that set off these crises would have been absorbed, but the groups' recent histories of absorption made them increasingly vulnerable to threats. For example, without knowledge of the long-term struggle in the Catholic Worker house over the types of guests they could invite into the house, a newcomer might have thought finding Blueberry beaten was the sole cause of the Workers' shift in policy. Similarly, without knowledge about the standing tension between consensus and hierarchical models within STOP, a newcomer might think that the financial crisis and/or Laura caused the radical shift in Todd's perspective on running the organization.

As I said above, the groups held their histories together with moral stories. When the groups reached their limits for absorption, they had to modify their stories or risk collapse.[6] The new stories that arose were based in the groups' efforts to reestablish control over their environment and responses to their environment in order to ensure the best possible outcome within a constraining environment. The most stable stories were "sadder but wiser" stories that cautioned anticipated loss. Neither unanticipated expansion nor anticipated losses would undermine these stories focused on avoiding loss. Thus, symbols imbued with negative meaning persisted long after the initial unmanageable threats that required new stories. In other words, the meanings of symbols associated with strategies to *avoid* future threats were fixed compared to stories based in positive associations because they were not as easily threatened by changes in the environment as were meanings created in moments of expansion.[7] Thus, moments of failure generated avoidance strategies, and these became markers of the limits of shared expectations.[8] Avoidance strategies were more stable than the prescribed strategies or paths for action. Due to their lack of responsiveness to the immediate emotional context, the stories the groups crafted around their experiences of failure became the most stable frames organizing the groups' life.

6. Similarly, Howard finds that actors rejected symbols in order to create breaks in time so as to distance themselves with past identities and avoid the perceived internal limits of these identities (2006, 320).

7. In other words, the basis for meaning is not in any way *in* the symbol, but rather meaning is based entirely in the expectations associated with the symbol, which are based in strategies of action that grow out of actors' emotional histories. Phenomenologists (Husserl [1893–1907] 1991; Schutz 1967), an ethnomethodologist (Garfinkel 1967), and pragmatists (Mead 1934; Dewey 1910) have all pointed to the role of failed expectations in linking symbols and meaning (Summers-Effler 2004).

8. Durkheim ([1912] 1995) refers to such negative boundaries as the negative cult.

In sum, in order to recover, the groups had to reverse the sense of contraction and create new stories. Once the groups' stories collapsed, there was a period of critical plasticity when meaning was unregulated. Small shifts during this period could have powerful implications. Any of the immediate forces within the environment could shape future patterns if they became part of emerging strategies for avoiding similar failures in the future.[9] Major cognitive shifts were always motivated by such eruptions of negative emotion. However, as these stories illustrate, it is impossible to say that either their stories or the emotional consequences of changing external relations drove the formation and transformation of meaning.[10] Old patterns died, and new ones were born in interactions where participants experienced shared strong emotion and dramatic shifts in their focus of attention.[11] Observations over time revealed how their emotional and perceptual dynamics were inherently and fundamentally entwined.

Recovery Requires Emotion Work

The groups absorbed threats but doing so generated anger, fear, and shame—emotions that build up energy and tension in preparation for action to improve an actor's position, either in terms of physical safety or social solidarity.[12] These emotions were the product of *bracing* against obstacles; frustration mobilized energy for action; constraining this momentum in turn *consumed* energy.[13]

---

9. As Dewey suggests, "Emotion is the conscious sign of a break, actual or impending. The discord is the occasion that induces reflection. With the realization, material of reflection is incorporated into objects as their meaning" (1934, 14).

10. The irony of this perspective is that while it would seem that routine expectations are primarily responsible for shaping the structure of our lives, the surprising failures that seem to come out of nowhere actually play a much more prominent role in determining future patterns of action. As Abbott states, "Thus, while we may want to think of them as 'abrupt' and 'chaotic,' and indeed we may discover them because they appear as irregularities in what has hitherto been a stable trajectory or regime, in fact they are the crucial sites of determination in the overall structure of a life course or an organizational career because they change its parameters" (2001b, 249).

11. Husserl ([1893–1907] 1991, 56) and Schutz (1967, 77, 82) argue that memory organizes the perception by tying history to perception through a growing core of accumulated experience. However, the stories in this chapter illustrate that these processes of attention and perception proceed much in the way that Whitehead (1971) describes; reflexive practices allow history to accumulate along particular lines for only so long until significant obstacles lead to collapse, creating an epochal character to perception.

12. See Turner (2002, 81, 135).

13. Dewey notes, "Any attempt to perpetuate beyond its term the enjoyment attending the time of fulfillment and harmony constitutes withdrawal from the world. Hence it marks the lowering and loss of vitality" (1934, 16).

Group members were most likely to become irritated with one another during these periods of absorption. Their absorption of tension paralleled a growing distance or feeling of contraction between actors. The focus on intervening obstacles created or reinforced boundaries between members, generated a sense of distance, and diminished the intensity of the participants' involvement with one another. Failure or frustration turned attention inward, so that multiple actors precipitated out of what was previously one center of action. Internal conflict solidified actors as separate encroaching entities; this separation undermined the groups' potential for experiencing future group-level involvement. As a general rule, the harsher the outcome, the farther the sense of self-consciousness retreated from the risky focus.[14] If left unchecked, both the growing distance and shame over this growing distance amplified negative feelings until they threatened to rip the groups apart.[15]

Through public confession and expressions of grief and shame, the Workers broke down boundaries that blocked expansion. In these moments, they released the following: fear for their safety, anger with guests and neighbors they felt had taken advantage of them, and shame of failing in front of each other that had accrued during absorption. Release was generally marked with awe or laughter.[16] *Awe* and *joy* are also produced by a lack of control and vulnerability. However, awe and joy facilitate *expansion* and the *restoration* of trust and solidarity. By redirecting their loss of control, they released the weight of their helplessness in the face of unrelenting human suffering. For example, the Catholic Workers' story of the tiny drunk transformed the horror of their surroundings to comedy.

In contrast, Todd transformed feelings of rejection into a power struggle, which generated anger that renewed his and the other STOP leaders'

14. Although we could imagine a situation where there would be a crisis big enough to threaten the most basic premise of either group's ideology, such as the assumption that poverty is unjust or that the death penalty should be abolished, I did not see this while I was in the field. The shift and focus that renders the group a field rather than entity generates a sense of contraction, shame, and a sense of self-consciousness that had previously been absent.

15. Scheff (1992) refers to this shame about shame as a shame spiral. Turner states that when shame is "repressed in an effort to protect self from experiencing it," such repression often leads to behavioral pathologies and potentially dissociative behavior (2000, 135).

16. James mentions the role of laughter in religious experience. "Even the momentary expansion of the soul in laughter is, to however slight an extent, a religious exercise" ([1902] 2007, 57). However, the central role of laughter in Catholic Worker recovery contradicts James's assertion that solemnity and gravity in particular characterize the saintly experience. "The divine shall mean for us only such a primal reality as the individual feels impelled to respond to solemnly and gravely, and neither by a curse nor a jest" (49). Scheff (1992) uses accounts of geniuses' predilection for laughter to support his argument that laughter is an important emotional tool for diffusing shame.

Table 3.1   Dynamic of Expansion and Contraction in Coalitions and Entities

Type of Relation	General Process	Expanding	Contracting
Vertical (heroic) relations	Reinforcement of bounded entity	Dominance (encroaching on other) Anger/victory	Submission (encroached upon) Fear/helplessness
Horizontal (saintly) relations	Dissolution of the entity	Transcendence Joy/serendipity	Despondence Loss/grief

energy. But this strategy did not release the shame generated in moments of failure. Whereas grief *destroys* boundaries, anger *hardens* them. Anger could only fuel their activity for so long before the accumulation of tension consumed more energy than their anger generated—their anger devoured as it burned.[17] The leaders could only release this increasing internal tension with a sense of victory over their opposition. Thus while evoking righteous anger restored STOP's leaders' enthusiasm, it left the group vulnerable in other ways.

The groups' patterns of recovery illustrate how emotions are produced by social relations; but also how *evoking* particular emotions *produces* corresponding social relations. For example, the Catholic Workers experienced grief, awe, and joy in agapic moments with guests and neighbors. When agapic efforts ended in failure, they felt frustrated, cynical, and ashamed. Through confessing or by telling heartrending stories, the Workers created the relational conditions that generated *horizontal expansion*, or a feeling of solidarity. Todd and STOP's other leaders experienced victory and dominance when they competed for and won attention space over their opponents. When they lost attention space, they felt expendable. By telling stories about political influence to those who had less, the leaders, Todd in particular, created the relational conditions that generated *vertical expansion*, or a feeling of power.

Recovery in both groups could only begin from the point to which the groups had contracted. Subgroup recovery could undermine the involvement of the larger group, which meant that ironically the recovery process could push individual actors farther apart from one another. The rare moments in the Catholic Worker community when confessors did *not* forgive resulted in sharp contraction and more resilient boundaries

17. Turner explains how individuals consume emotional and physical energy when repressing unpleasant emotions such as anger, fear, guilt, and shame (2000, 114).

between members. Similarly, Todd and the other STOP leaders' displays of power renewed their enthusiasm, but only at the cost of excluding others or making others feel less powerful. In both cases, subgroups enjoyed vertical expansion at the cost of horizontal expansion that would have included other group members.

Shift in Focus and Emotional Recovery from Collapse

Like a rat coming up against a dead end in a maze, when the groups encountered unmoving obstacles, they had to shift both their *focus* and redirect their *paths of action* if they were to continue.[18] As noted above, the Catholic Workers' and STOP's recovery efforts changed social relations within the groups. Their efforts changed social relations because they shifted the groups' focuses of attention. Refocusing attention to reestablish assumptions of stability actually created a sense of stability. In other words, actors find the conditions that enable them to feel stable. The groups' focus of attention identified the appropriate *field of action* and the *source of action* within it.[19] The groups' focus of attention was, at its most basic, either *inward* facing or *outward* facing. For example, in response to failure, the Catholic Workers became more internally focused while STOP became more externally focused. The ways in which participants focused attention—whether on the group itself, their opponent, or injustice—influenced the emotional tone and intensity of involvement within the group. Once habits of attention were established, the habits constrained future perception by determining which environmental factors were relevant and meaningful.[20] By refocusing attention on a field of action where they could successfully avoid obstacles, the groups were able to reestablish a sense of control over their environment.

A comparison of these groups suggests more generally that focusing attention to establish or reestablish a sense of control over our environment and ourselves enables us to detect stability in both the objects we perceive and ourselves.[21] Stability is a sense of time, in particular a sense

18. One of Collins's most important theoretical contributions is his emphasis on focus of attention in interaction (2004, 23–24). By clarifying the role of focus, Collins fills out Goffman's framing perspective (1974). I suggest that we can think of frames as the edges of an actor's attention.

19. We can think of such fundamental interaction expectations as White's concept of style (1992, 17–18, 166–69). Rigid expectations are disconnected enough from tangible embodiment that they can be very clear on an abstract level but are often unclear about how they should be embodied in terms of social relations or tangible social space.

20. See Kelso (1995, 184).

21. See Schutz (1967, 47, 51), Husserl ([1893–1907] 1991, 55), and White (1992, 77, 214). Schutz states that tension between thoughts—in other words, reflexive awareness—and the sense of duration is the basis of meaningful awareness (1962, 69).

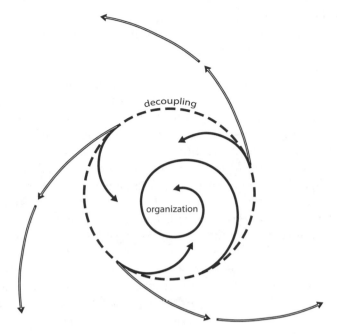

Figure 3.1 Emergence of a pattern.

of duration and a sense of continuity. The referencing of history is motivated by the intention to act. In order to initiate action,[22] we must base our perceptions in a historical framing of a scene that allows us to believe that our actions will matter in that scene. The drawing on history to organize purposeful action creates a sense of continuity across social scenes that we could otherwise experience as random and unconnected. Thus a sense of continuity and duration are crucial for creating a sense of control over our environment enabling purposeful action.

A comparison of these groups also suggests that, like time, space is inherent in the act of attention, not in objective external reality. Intervening objects between us and our focus creates a sense of distance

22. By "action," I am referring to behavior purposefully undertaken in response to unanticipated change in an actor's environment. In other words, "action" is emergent problem-solving in response to uncertain or unexpected conditions. Goffman defines action as "activities that are consequential, problematic, and undertaken for what is felt to be their own sake (1967, 185). Apter would call this behavior intense paratelic activity: activity of high intensity undertaken for its own sake, such as a sporting event (2007, 39). My definition of action is similar to these two in that I identify "action" as more activity that is intense than activity during predictable times. However my definition differs from Goffman's definition and Apter's description of intense paratelic activity in that "action" can also arise when engaged in ends-driven behavior.

between us and our focus that is absent if the space was unobstructed.[23] In other words, confining attention so that few obstacles lay between us and our focus creates a sense of closeness and intensity. For example, focusing attention on the groups' boundaries generated feelings of pride, importance, and immediacy (a feeling of "I *am*"). Focusing attention on obstacles beyond the groups' boundaries created a sense of shared righteous anger or of gearing up for a conflict as a team.[24] A more distant focus could create multiple embedded foci, which allowed actors to have a sense of themselves as actors within actors.[25] The sense of involvement in a coalition emerged when actors' attention was trained on embedded dynamics. In a coalition, the group felt like a field of action for constituent entities *and* a center of organization that facilitated action with respect to more distant obstacles. This is to say the groups' sense of their location relative to meaningful obstacles shaped their emotional styles, foci, and stories.[26]

A comparison of these two cases suggests a paradoxical relationship between the distance to their explicit goals and the distance of their day-to-day focus. Ironically, the farther a group is from success, the more local the focus. The closer a group is to perceived success, the more distant the focus. In other words, the more radical the goal, the more likely a group will be focused on the political implications of their personal lifestyle decisions. The more mundane their goal, the more likely they will view their personal interactions as a means to an end. For example, the Workers had an apparently far-off goal of the radical transformation of society, which indirectly kept their focus close to the boundaries of the group. STOP was comparatively closer to success and potentially far more powerful beyond the boundaries of their group. Although STOP's goal appeared to be much closer, the group's day-to-day focus was distant compared to

23. See Merleau-Ponty (1962, 56).
24. Durkheim ([1912] 1995) and Simmel (1964) both point out how focusing on distant conflict helps to maintain feelings of solidarity within groups.
25. Abbott uses the example of urban development efforts that require coordination across a number of sectors to illustrate how competition within sectors can be related to success for the coalition (2005b, 247). We can think of entities that are focused on the entity itself as examples of White's concept of an arena, where the focus is on solidarity and purity is valued. The primary process associated with an arena is selection, thus reinforcing boundaries between insiders and outsiders. A coalition fits with White's concept of a council, where the focus is on power and where prestige is valued. The primary process associated with a council is mobilizing alliances or connecting across boundaries to grow networks (1992, 32). See Bandy and Smith (2005)
26. Bergson argues that observing action from different distances creates different emotional and psychic tones ([1988] 2005, 14).

the Workers; the site of action always appeared to be just beyond their current site of involvement.[27]

This paradoxical relationship between proximity of goals and shifts of focus in response to obstacles suggests that rather than considering whether a movement is an abeyance or not, we might gain analytic leverage by thinking broadly about the conditions under which movements will develop different styles of strategies.[28] Similarly, rather than thinking about particular strategies as liberal, radical, or cultural, we could think of them as particular types of relationships between efforts to bring about social change and the field in which their attention is focused. The fact that more prosperous Catholic Worker houses engage in farther-reaching and larger-scale activity (which requires consistency in labor and resources) supports this argument.[29]

Forbidden Emotions Are Managed with Emotional Slingshotting

Assumptions about how interaction should unfold within the groups were at the heart of the groups' efforts to stabilize. The groups relied on shared expectations for interactions to lubricate their interactions during their mundane day-to-day activity. Sustaining habits that smoothed interactions helped to minimize internal conflict so they could focus on working effectively as a collective. Thus the groups' day-to-day expectations for interaction were key to their capacity to achieve both their proxy and ultimate goals.[30]

The groups' shared expectations for interaction were made up of both prohibitions on and expectations for particular emotions. *Prohibited* emotions reflected the aspects of the groups' environments over which historically they had *little control*. For example, anger was a

27. To put the groups' focus in Eliasoph and Lichterman's terms: STOP focused on group boundaries, or what their relationship with the wider world should be while involved in the group; the Catholic Workers focused on group bonds, or what members' mutual responsibilities should be while involved in the group (2003, 739).

28. See Taylor (1989) and Tarrow (1991).

29. However, there could be a selection effect where would-be Catholic Workers select particular houses or form particular strategies in houses based on preexisting preference. There is also a possibility that because the groups tend to be so small, with ten or more people constituting a large Catholic Worker house, the personal histories of the actors play a much larger role in the development of a style than in groups that allow for less direct personal influence. We would need to see how these dynamics emerged over time to determine whether they support or add new dimensions to the argument made here.

30. See Nash (1996, 97) for discussion of ways in which doable rituals can come to represent larger ideological goals.

forbidden emotion for the Catholic Worker community. STOP had triumph as a ready antidote to anger, but it was nearly impossible for the Catholic Workers to experience triumph when they could not control whether their work resulted in positive outcomes for guests and neighbors. Similarly, grief was a forbidden emotion for STOP. Mystical awe and agape were the Catholic Workers' antidotes to grief, but STOP had little capacity to experience mystical awe and agape when they could not draw on any specific religious discourse without losing parts of their base.[31]

Both groups recovered from the threat of forbidden emotions and the day-to-day mundane drains of routine work through managing their emotions.[32] In particular, the groups harnessed the power of their negative emotions and emotional vacuums more generally to recover from the continued threat of forbidden emotions.[33] They did this by transmuting dangerous negative emotions into negative emotions that they had the capacity to release.[34] Using negative emotions that they could manage allowed them to slingshot from dangerous emotions to their complementary positive emotions.[35] This slingshotting process also energized the group by reestablishing a shared focus of attention and emotional intensity.

For example, by telling tragic tales, the Workers redirected anger and frustration, for which they had no release, into grief. The Workers told stories about abandoned children, the injuries of children working in the sugarcane fields, and grandmothers and their children sleeping on

31. When the groups focused on *what* had to be done, action was instrumental, and their expectations for involvement were relatively easy to articulate. The groups very rarely articulated their shared expectations for *how* the groups would interact, even when these expectations were violated. Mere exposure to a dynamic was not enough to understand the emotional logic; newcomers had to take up a similar position relative to the focus of attention in order to experience similar emotions. As Gibson points out, "We tend to think of direct stimuli from the terrestrial environment as being like words and pictures instead of realizing that words and pictures are at best man-made substitutes for these direct stimuli. Language and art yield second-hand perceptions. These second-hand perceptions no doubt work backward on direct perception, but knowledge about the world rests on acquaintance with the world, in the last analysis, and this is our first problem" (1966, 29).

32. Haidt argues that emotional intelligence involves not only going toward positive emotional experiences but managing inevitable negative emotional experiences (2006, 18).

33. If negative emotions can be harnessed, they can be a particularly powerful tool for emotion management because reactions to negative conditions are more intense than reactions to positive conditions, and a history of surviving negative experiences strengthens the capacity to maintain positive expectations in the face of challenges (Haidt 2006, 29, 139).

34. "There are only two ways in which it is possible to get rid of anger, worry, fear, despair, or other undesirable affections. One is that an opposite affection should overpoweringly break over us, and the other is by getting so exhausted with the struggle that we have to stop—so we drop down, give up, and DON'T CARE any longer. Our emotional brain-centers strike work, and we lapse into a temporary apathy" (emphasis in original; James [1902] 2007, 194–95).

35. See the discussion about the Plutchik emotion wheel and opposite emotions in chapter 2.

benches in the cold. The Workers often talked about feeling inadequate for not participating in Plowshares actions, civil disobedience that could land them in prison for years. They grieved their moral failings, even when confessing to people who claimed to have the same ideological commitments but risked far less than the Workers. Telling tragic tales and publicly calling attention to personal weakness and failures may have appeared self-destructive to outsiders, but their grief and self-effacing behavior lowered boundaries, reinforced intimacy, generated emotional intensity, and reestablished members' focus on the group.[36] Their facility with religious rituals and mystical stories enabled them to release the emotional vacuums created by grief and humility.[37] Rather than depressing the group, grief and humility could also create a hunger for humor. By emphasizing different aspects of stories, dark humor transformed tragedy into absurdity.

When STOP's staff lost control over their environment, they felt either sorrow or helplessness. By telling stories of injustice, they redirected dangerous feelings of sorrow and helplessness into horror. Their horror stories emphasized either a specific injustice or an impending but preventable tragedy. The group used anger to keep dangerous emotions at bay and preserve emotional distance. Members of STOP were well practiced in generating righteous anger and knew how to be a good audience for a well-performed rant. The staff created excitement by envisioning both past success and the splendor of future protests where they would be recognized as a political force with which to be reckoned.

The groups' well-practiced capacity to work up righteous anger allowed them to release the emotional vacuums created by the sense of impending horror or threat. Evoking anger helped them to avoid focusing on the meaninglessness, sadness, guilt, shame, boredom, and potential ideological conflict that continually threatened STOP. Preaching to the choir, sharing political rants, reliving the past glory of conflict, and imagining future conflict all renewed the group's feelings of righteous anger and power while reinforcing their solidarity with one another.[38] Much as

36. James describes the power of religious confession: "There is a state of mind, known to religious men, but to no others, in which the will to assert ourselves and hold our own has been displaced by a willingness to close our mouths and be as nothing in the floods and waterspouts of God. In this state of mind, what we most dreaded has become the habitation of our safety, and the hour of our moral death has turned into our spiritual birthday. The time for tension in our soul is over, and that of happy relaxation, of calm deep breathing, of an eternal present, with no discordant future to be anxious about, has arrived. Fear is not held in abeyance as it is by mere authority, it is positively expunged and washed away" ([1902] 2007, 55–56).

37. See Osa (1996, 79).

38. Drawing on Durkheim, Collins suggests that when networks are diffuse and cosmopolitan, they will be less likely to experience righteous anger when sacred symbols are transgressed (2004,

in sports, the shared position against the opposition made them a team.[39] By engendering a sense of crisis, STOP's leaders created opportunities for recovery that were independent of the group's success in meeting external challenges.

The capacity to transmute dangerous negative emotions into manageable negative emotions enabled the groups to become somewhat emotionally independent from their immediate social context, which allowed them to maintain stability during threatening times. Each group's emotion management techniques served as emotional Band-Aids; they held the groups together by temporarily releasing emotional tensions that threatened them.[40]

However, this slingshotting process consumed energy, especially the energy of the leaders who staged the recovery efforts. These efforts could also fail in dramatic ways; thus the emotional slingshotting was analogous to playing with emotional fire.

Emotional Logic Is Embodied

No matter how obvious the connection between abstract ideology and concrete goals seemed to the groups, their ideological commitments had to be translated to be meaningful in the groups' into day-to-day activities.[41] The groups' ideological commitments played some role in guiding their emotional styles. For example, they established some general shared

127). However, in creating a front-stage performance of righteous anger, STOP uses the emotion in reverse, to create rather than reflect a moment of high social density and local focus. By temporarily pulling the group into the focus of action by situating the group as a shared position relative to the opposition, the interaction overshadowed histories of divergent positions or even conflict.

39. Lawler argues that social expectations are emotion-based when groups engage in common activities or tasks (group as entity), and that expectations for interaction will be less emotion-based when individuals play unique roles in group activity (group as coalition) (2002, 14). The analysis here suggests that the most basic expectations for how to go about doing group work are always emotion-based, but there are important distinctions between the emotional dynamics of entities and coalitions. Involvement in a coalition may feel more instrumental and "rational," but this may be a product of the type of emotion work coalitions do, particularly the sanctioning of internally focused collective emotion management within the group. Conflict focuses a group's attention not on the group itself, but on the opponent in the external environment. This external focus draws the group's attention away from differences between group members that could potentially undermine the group's solidarity. Engaging in conflict as a group creates a feeling of being on a team across ideologically diverse perspectives.

40. As James points out, "Given a certain amount of love, indignation, generosity, magnanimity, admiration, loyalty, or enthusiasm of self surrender, the result is always the same. That whole raft of cowardly obstructions, which in tame persons and dull moods are sovereign impediments to action, sinks away at once" ([1902] 2007, 147).

41. See Williams and Blackburn (1996, 170) for discussion of the distinction between formal and operative ideology.

meanings and narrowed the range of symbols that the groups could draw on.[42] However, the groups' histories of environmental conditions shaped the ways in which they made sense of the world most directly. Indeed, these stories illustrate how a group can *fail* to maintain involvement and support from even ideologically sympathetic newcomers and outsiders.[43]

Abstract ideological commitments clearly shaped the groups' focus[44] and primed them for certain types of responses rather than others.[45] However, the groups' immediate environmental conditions determined whether their expectations could be met or if their intentions could be carried out.[46] Changes in the social environment, not the ideology itself, afforded opportunities for making new connections between ideology and day-to-day goals.[47] Their expectations for the most basic group activities were grounded in emotion, and the symbols tied most closely to their emotional experiences were local, not the abstract ideological ones that were publicly available.[48] For these groups, ideology was more like a language through which actors express themselves rather than the meaning itself.[49]

One might think that insiders could instruct newcomers and outsiders about the local emotional expectations,[50] but both groups routinely

42. See Osa (1996, 72).

43. See Sikkink and Regnerus (1996, 148, 164) for illustration of the wiggle room left between larger ideological commitments and day-to-day practice, and how under certain structural conditions this wiggle room can be leveraged to motivate action that ultimately directly undermines larger ideological commitments.

44. See Goffman (1986) and Snow et al. (1986).

45. See Clark (1997), Eliasoph (1998, 346), Damasio (1994), and Gopnik and Meltzoff (1997).

46. Bourdieu (1984) makes the point that despite strong relationships between taste and class, people feel like taste is an individual expression, a choice that reflects personal orientations. The stories in this chapter illustrate how emotional tastes arose within groups in a patterned way, yet the groups similarly felt that their tastes were direct manifestations of value connections.

47. Wuthnow and Witten (1988, 65); Oliver and Johnston (2000).

48. See Bergson ([1988] 2005, 99).

49. Certainly language constrains the meaning actors can conceive of or express, but it remains only a tool for the more basic processes driving meaning-making. Gibson argues, "Discrimination has to precede association for language to be of any use. The ability to name and to predicate fixes the gains of perceiving but it does not explain perceiving. It fosters the education of attention to the facts of the world but cannot substitute for it" (1966, 321).

50. Social scientists have long noted that much of the coordination of action required to carry off interactions, as well as our motivation for many of our actions, operate below the level of conscious awareness (cf. Bourdieu 2000; Clark 1997; Ekman 1992; Hatfield, Cacioppo, and Rapson 1994; Katz 2001; Polanyi 1962; Turner and Stets 2005; Weber ([1951] 1978). Weber explains how we use social knowledge to proceed much of the time without conscious thought. "In the great majority of cases actual action goes on in a state of inarticulate half-consciousness or actual unconsciousness of its subjective meaning. The actor is more likely to 'be aware' of it in a vague sense than he is to 'know' what he is doing or be explicitly self-conscious about it. In most cases his action is

failed to clearly state the emotional logics underlying their day-to-day expectations,[51] even when newcomers and outsiders asked for this information directly.[52] The groups could tell their stories, the post facto explanations that tied their evolving *emotional logics* to their histories, but the emotional logics themselves were, at their heart, not discursive.[53] Rather, the emotional logic guiding their day-to-day interactions was *embodied*.[54] With experience, members grew increasingly sensitive to their environment by responding to increasingly subtle cues about how and when to look. In doing so, participants learned how to manage themselves and coordinate action in the group by focusing their attention to produce particular relationships between themselves in their environment.[55] They

---

governed by impulse or habit" ([1951] 1978, 21). Jonathan Turner explains the brain dynamics that account for *how* much of human behavior is guided by processes operating below conscious awareness. "Individuals are often at a loss, cognitively, to understand why they make certain decisions or behave in certain ways: the answer is that subcortical, emotional memory systems are mixed in with cortically controlled ones. Thus, rationality is often a mix of emotional valences, some capable of being articulated to the self if need be and others remaining outside of full self-awareness" (2000, 61). Damasio breaks these cognitive brain processes into two basic mechanisms: attention and memory. Attention is required to make sense of any environment since every moment contains more stimuli than we can process. Memory is key for making sense of the stimuli we attend to because it provides both duration and durability, both of which are crucial for meaning-making (1994, 197).

51. Polanyi explains that the more basic information is to our understanding of the world, the more difficult it is to articulate: "The capacity for deriving from a latent knowledge of a situation a variety of appropriate routes or alternative modes of behaviour amounts to a rudimentary logical operation. It prefigures the use of an articulate interpretative framework on which we rely as a representation of complex situation, drawing from it ever new inferences regarding further aspects of that situation" ([1958] 1962, 74). Similarly, Bourdieu states, "If the implications of inclusion in a field are destined to remain implicit, this is precisely because there is nothing of the conscious, deliberate commitment, or the voluntary contract, about it. The original investment has no origin, because it always precedes itself and, when we deliberate on entry into the game, the die is already more or less cast" ([1997] 2000, 11).

52. See Gopnik and Meltzoff (1997, 22).

53. It was precisely because emotional styles were so fundamental to the groups' experiences of the world that neither group was able to articulate expectations for emotional style to newcomers or outsiders. Schutz refers to internal experiences that are close to the private core of the person, for example, corporal sensations and emotions, as "essentially actual" experiences (1967, 52–53). He suggests that even though these experiences are crucial for guiding action, and thus future experiences, they can only be reflected upon in a vague way, if at all. Therefore, they are not retrievable, subject to conscious thought, or easily communicated to outsiders. Schutz (1967) assumes that individuals are the authors of these temporal core experiences, but the stories above illustrate that this process can be centered in groups as well. Assuming that emotion, rather than cognition, is the primary motivation organizing perception makes sense of the pragmatist argument that the source that motivates reflexivity is a reflexive blind spot (Mead 1934; Wiley 1994). Turner notes that conscious internal conversation is too slow-moving to account for most of the perceptual processing required for daily life (Turner 2002). This is why, as Tilly points out, we must not rely on after-the-fact explanations to explain social processes (2001, 41).

54. Wacquant similarly describes how the embodied logic of boxing could not be conveyed without taking up the position of a boxer (2004, 101).

55. We often have a sense that culture is fluid and structure is stable, but if structure is made up of relational conditions that appear to be at least relatively independent of the mediating effects

were like chefs who simultaneously lose pain sensitivity to heat but increase their capacity to discern temperature. Their histories fine-tuned their attention, enabling them to perceive with a subtlety previously unavailable to them.[56]

The central role of local emotional experience in organizing these groups' day-to-day actions did not, however, mean that ideology was irrelevant. Their ideological commitments primed action by establishing general perspectives on solutions and responsibilities and by focusing attention. Where the groups focused their attention determined what the groups experienced as external constraints or resources. However, the fact that in both groups the same ideology was invoked to support contradictory expectations reveals how they drew on their ideologies to signify rather than produce their emotional styles.[57]

Because newcomers usually needed to have experience occupying positions similar to insiders in order to understand the emotional style of the group, intimacy did not grow steadily. Rather, its evolved unevenly over many fits and starts of attraction and repulsion. First, regulars had to establish that a newcomer was not a danger. After this was determined, newcomers were often popular with the regulars. New people not only brought optimism and energy into the groups; they were a wonderful audience. Newcomers were always impressed with the more established people, and even the most democratically inclined members couldn't resist soaking up admiration from the newcomers. Eventually, however, the regulars either began to feel increasingly drained by the performance standards they initially set for themselves, or the newcomers stayed long enough to witness the regulars running up against obstacles and failing. When keeping up performances became draining, growing intimacy slowly ground to a halt. And when newcomers witnessed

---

of ideas and assumptions—for example, a sharp blade bearing down on us or a lack of food—these conditions only have lasting consequences (and therefore stability) through physical and cognitive remnants. Alternately, eating disorders—a condition where history plays a more prominent role in capacity to eat than access to food—are a tragic illustration of the resilience of meaning compared to immediate relational conditions. See Bordo (1995) and Bartky (1990).

56. Gibson argues, "The data of sense are *given*, by definition. The perceptual systems, however, are clearly amenable to learning. It would be expected that an individual, after practice, could orient more exactly, listen more carefully, touch more acutely, smell and taste more precisely, and look more perceptively than he could before practice" (italics in original; 1966, 51). By learning how and when to focus their attention, the groups learned to detect subtle shifts in particular relational conditions, regardless of whether or not they remembered or were able to recount the specific moments that were crucial for developing their greater sensitivities (Gibson 1966, 275, 276).

57. In *With the Boys* (1987), Fine details the dynamics by which groups develop and diffuse culture.

failures and frustrations, the regulars felt exposed and vulnerable and responded with defensive and hiding strategies that halted the progression of intimacy.

In cases of failure, the regulars would attempt to act as though failures and frustrations were "no big deal." Although such performances prevented newcomers from seeing the insiders as vulnerable, performing resilience exacerbated the contraction they felt in response to the failure. Failure heightened self-consciousness, and acting as though a failure did not matter required the insiders to pull back *even farther* in order to manage the performance, which increased reflexive awareness, created feelings of contraction, and undermined the potential for experiences of expansion with the newcomers and among themselves. The groups had to recover if the newcomers were to continue with the groups. These internal recoveries followed a similar pattern to the group-level recovery processes detailed above. Members could use symbols associated with the drain as warnings for what would create shame and negative reactions in the future and to recognize which narrowed paths to involvement undermined the flexibility of the relationships between group members. Members could also diffuse mounting shame through confession or laughter; in which case, the threat to intimacy ultimately became the stage for creating much more intense intimacy.

Recovery Concludes with the Modification of Stories

As Mead describes, by taking up the perspective of the other and becoming a thing-like object to itself, actors gain the capacity to anticipate the reactions that their actions will draw out of the other (1934: 46, 77). When obstacles constrain the flow of action, they communicate structural information about the boundaries of the actor and its environment.[58] An obstacle creates boundaries that reflect the action's ambient energy back to its source, giving it its first distant thing-like perspective on itself.[59] As the above stories illustrate, this notion of the "other" need not be limited to other people or even groups. Any block to action can reflect energy back to the actor that will allow the actor to anticipate the future effects of an obstacle. New obstacles communicate new informa-

58. Gibson states that "the solid environment is a 'support' for behavior. It is rigid. . . . Rigidity gives geometrical permanence to places and constancy of shape and size to things" (1966, 9).
59. This is similar to the focus of Gestalt psychologists (Koffka 1922; Wertheimer [1945] 1982), but rather than focusing on how perception of an "out there" works, the focus is on how the perception of an interior "in here" works.

tion about the nature of the actor back to the actor.[60] Anticipation is the foundation for reflexive and conscious strategizing.[61]

Memory is crucial for an entity's capacity to become and remain "thing-like" to itself. Memory, or historical referencing, enables anticipation of future obstacles based on the history of the entity. Reflexive awareness, the process of creating a coherent history through referencing the past in habitual ways, enables the actors to have a sense of themselves in relationship to an environment unfolding over time. Memory need not manifest as a neurological process located in a biological individual. Organizations, governments, and libraries continually update textual memories. Oral traditions create the memory of a family, group, neighborhood, and so on, through the repeated telling of stories.

As described above, these groups stitched their histories together with stories that connected and made sense of past sequences of action. Accordingly, after failure, the groups had to translate the changing meanings of particular symbols into a reflexive understanding of why the failure happened and how the groups could avoid similar outcomes in the future. New understandings required new accounts about the relationship between practice and ideology. Generally, these stories were not literal accounts of what transpired. Rather, they were myths that served as moral warnings of the outcomes that befall transgressors.[62] Once the groups established their stories of their failures, the failures provided substance for stories of caution; recounting these stories affirmed proscriptions against certain actions and established group boundaries.[63] This meaning-work allowed the groups' goals and foci to evolve so that they were able to perform different actions with the same moral motivation.

60. Polanyi describes how perceptions become increasingly narrow over time: "Indeed, any modification of an anticipatory framework, whether conceptual, perceptual or appetitive, is an irreversible heuristic act, which transforms our ways of thinking, seeing and appreciating in the hope of attuning our understanding, perception or sensuality more closely to what is true and right" ([1958] 1962, 106). In that narrowing, we lose the flexibility that he suggests is a requirement for continued adaptation to a changing environment: "Owing to the unceasing changes which at every moment manifestly renew the state of things throughout the world, our anticipations must always meet things that are to some extent novel and unprecedented. Thus we find ourselves relying jointly on our anticipations and on our capacity ever to re-adapt these to novel and unprecedented situations. This is true in the exercise of skills, in the shaping of our perception and even in the satisfaction of appetites; every time our existing framework deals with an event anticipated by it, it has to modify itself to some extent accordingly" ([1958] 1962, 103).

61. Strategies for action, or what White refers to as control efforts, emerge in this reflexive moment (1992, 12).

62. See Durkheim on the negative cult ([1912] 1995, 304).

63. White explains the role of stories in reestablishing control projects after failure (1992, 13). Stories can block action (309), but they can also create opportunities for fresh action (13).

As I noted in chapter 2, the feeling of expansion requires initial boundaries to provide a sense of origin, experiences that inculcate feelings of growth and the perception of change over time. In this chapter, the stories reveal how the feeling of contraction similarly requires a sense of origin, leaving, and change over time. That is to say, the most basic emotional experiences of expansion and contraction are based in a sense of being anchored temporally. Actors anchor themselves in time by referencing their own history to anticipate the future. When the groups habitually referenced their stories, the expectations that shaped their perception lagged behind the groups' immediate contexts, which decoupled them from their environment. This decoupling enabled the groups to exert efforts to control their environment.

The above stories of collapse and recovery in the Catholic Worker community and STOP reveal how attention is generated at the intersection of space and time.[64] If time is a stream, the actors' sense of history is created only by looking backward, when they turn back against the flow in order to anticipate the future.[65] Without such, they would perceive a fluid and unfolding environment. In other words, the primary forces of organization are temporal. Although we tend to perceive the unfolding environment in terms of space, the capacity to perceive the adjacent relationships that comprise a sense of space is a product of history. Our perception of space is better thought of as a product of and constraint on organization rather than a cause of organization.

Referencing histories to form expectations creates the possibility for "internal" dynamics. Such referencing assumes a sense of an internal space that can be controlled in order to anticipate and respond to environmental conditions.[66] Strategies to anticipate environmental conditions—in other words, actors' own sense of their capacity to create stability in a field of action—reinforce the actors' sense of their own interior in relationship to an exterior environment. Memory creates a sense of duration; anticipation and action in response to memory create the persistence of both the actor and the acted upon.

The indirectness of the relationship between the immediate context and the groups' patterns of action creates the capacity to filter the influence of their immediate context. Thus, the sequential orientation of the groups' stories generates their capacity to give meaning to the unfolding context. By decoupling the actor from its immediate future contexts,

64. Gibson refers to this distinction as adjacent and sequential order (1966, 41).
65. See Schutz (1967, 47).
66. See Bergson ([1988] 2005, 133–34, 217, 219) and Emirbayer and Mische (1998).

Table 3.2   Expectations as Orienting Processes

Type or Orientating Process	Embodied	Narrative
Goal	Focusing attention	Creating meaningful symbols
Technical apparatus	Temporal and spatial	Discursive
Reflexivity	Limited	Extensive
Conditions when dominant	Settled times	Unsettled times

the process of updating histories to anticipate the future actually creates an actor who uses reflexive awareness to carry out purposeful action in response to a future obstacle. Thus, evolving stories create actors as much as actors create their stories.

Leaders Are Created and Sustained in Recovery

Leaders were made and reaffirmed in the recovery of the groups following collapse. To recover, leaders had to pull themselves up by their emotional bootstraps, evoke the emotions associated with success and expansion, and craft the stories that made sense of the groups' failure.[67] The saints had to be more *humble* and *closer to the divine* than those around them. The heroes had to be *braver* and *more powerful* than those around them. Both Todd and Joan had a flair for the dramatic; they invested energy to generate highly dramatic and successful rituals that were the scenes for expansion and recovery.[68] They also had active imaginations with which they envisioned tremendous future success. A good follower or participant would get wrapped up in their fantasies.

Both of the groups rode emotional roller coasters, but the leaders rode more extreme ones, benefiting the most from success but also losing the

67. The description of the role of leaders in emotional recovery here is similar to Weber's notion of charisma ([1914] 1978, 1111).

68. Durkheim describes the experience of the charismatic leader: "His language becomes high-flown in a way that would be ridiculous in ordinary circumstances; his gestures take on an overbearing quality; his very thought becomes impatient of limits and slips easily into every kind of extreme. This is because he feels filled to overflowing, as though with a phenomenal oversupply of forces that spill over and tend to spread around him. Sometimes he even feels possessed by a moral force greater than he, of which he is only the interpreter. This is the hallmark of what has often been called the demon of oratorical inspiration. This extraordinary surplus of forces is quite real and comes to him from the very group he is addressing. The feelings he arouses as he speaks return to him enlarged and amplified, reinforcing his own to the same degree" (Durkheim [1912] 1995, 212).

most and feeling the most drained and stuck when the group failed.[69] They had all of their proverbial eggs—in this case, identity, expectations, and interaction tools and strategies—in one interaction basket. They stood to gain more when they were able to pull a group back from the edge of disintegration, but they also stood to lose more if the group disintegrated. Charismatic leaders were like emotional batteries.[70] These emotional batteries keep the scenes together through maintaining the focus of attention and the positive emotions associated with this focus. By compelling attention, the leaders became a "sacred object" of the group.

Not everyone could, or wanted to, give as much as the leaders did to these groups. Therefore, in some aspects, hierarchy was rather inevitable; certain people emerge as more central when they are involved more frequently or in a deeper way. However, differences in status and power can also follow from larger structural inequality, such as race, gender, and class distinctions. When expansion encompassed the group, the internal differences within the group were minimized; even players on the bench won when the team won. Because of their ability to create a sense of "we" in the face of such internal power imbalances, the leaders could temporarily mask the threat that power imbalances could present.

Although charismatic leaders have the capacity to stimulate horizontal expansion within their groups, either as mystic or captain of the team, they also have the power to claim vertical power over group members. If leaders took advantage of their position of power granted by the followers, there was a feeling of betrayal. Using charismatic authority to exert vertical power was a form of unfaithfulness, a breach of trust. Leaders who appeared more invested in gaining or preserving personal vertical expansion rather than horizontal expansion were felt to be "sellouts," in which case the leaders found themselves reviled rather than revered. As was the case with STOP, lower-level members could become attuned to slippage between horizontal and vertical types of power.

Conclusion

Both the Catholic Worker community and STOP encountered events that threatened to destroy them. There were no guarantees that they would recover; they could have collapsed for good, as so many social movement

---

69. In Hallett's (2003) terms, during moments of recovery leaders drew on and developed the legitimacy to invoke and create local organizational culture.

70. See Collins (2004, 124).

groups do, and members could have become involved with other groups. In order to survive failure and collapse, the groups had to reestablish involvement or attract new involvement. How the groups recovered determined their focus of attention and emotional styles.

Recovery was not a return to equilibrium; rather, it released the forces that threatened to destroy continued involvement. Their negative experiences served as emotional warning signals, so evolving strategies became ancestors of earlier struggles and failures. Both groups built strategies by seeking some interactions and avoiding others. Their avoidant strategies became the most entrenched strategies, thus they provided the foundation for their organization. The groups' emerging strategies for action and their abstract ideological commitments were connected through stories after the fact. The Catholic Workers' and STOP's evolving strategies created distance between the emotional histories that generated these strategies and any particular action. Stories protected established patterns by obscuring this distance.

Although both groups may have *felt* that their goals were a direct reflection of their ideology, at their root their day-to-day goals were emotional.[71] As the next chapter illustrates, the points on which the groups were likely to be the most intractable were not necessarily the ones that were the product of their ideological commitment, but rather the ones that were forged in the fire of failure. That is not to say, however, that their ideological commitments did not shape action; indeed, they surely narrowed the scope of conceivable paths to recovery for both groups. As the next chapter illustrates, the importance of emotional histories for group life often made it difficult for ideologically compatible newcomers to accurately predict the sorts of actions that would set off strong negative reactions within the groups.

71. See Goodwin and Jasper (2006) and Goodwin, Jasper, and Polletta (2001).

FOUR

Evolving Emotional Histories Shape Styles of Persistence

In order to be more than an aggregate of individuals, the groups had to coordinate collective action and achieve some sort of stability. Each group attempted to achieve stability by anticipating threats, both internal and external. The groups' past threats shaped future options for responding to changes in their environments. Their expectations for future failures transformed obstacles associated with past failure into more stable obstructions, and these obstructions became the basis for the groups' routine logic for action.[1] Thus, the very act of reflecting in order to stabilize changed what was reflected upon.

The groups could not anticipate threats without assuming stable conditions between members, the groups and their environment, and the groups and their own histories. However, none of these assumptions bore out. Members changed with time, so the relationships between one another had to change as well. Their environments also changed, so the relationship between the groups and their environments had to change. Finally, the groups themselves did not remain

---

1. Like the Gestalt psychologists pointed out, actors use negative space, in this case signs of impending interactions that actors associate with past failures, to create meaning out of relatively sparse information (Koffka 1922; Wertheimer [1945] 1982).

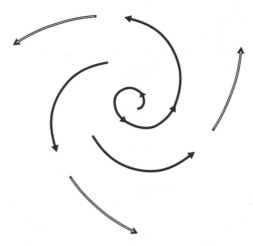

Figure 4.1 Collapse of a pattern.

the same across their history. Just as our bodies change every day, despite the fact that we usually do not notice the change until we look back on pictures from years before, so, too, groups continually change.

The groups achieved some stability by controlling their own behaviors in anticipation of internal and external threats, but the groups' efforts to achieve and maintain stability were based on impossible assumptions. Their attempts were failing propositions. The very effort to control themselves and their environment through reflexive awareness prepared the way for miscommunication. Thus their future collapse was written into the very fabric of the groups' efforts to stabilize.

Since conditions change, techniques only work for short periods of time. Thus, to persist, the groups had to either delay this collapse or learn to recover quickly and easily. The first approach, delaying collapse, facilitated persistence by slowing down the trajectory of pattern formation, stabilization, and collapse. The second approach, recovering quickly and easily, reduced vulnerability to ultimate collapse by focusing on recovery from frequent smaller collapses.

The Catholic Worker community and STOP illustrated two types of persistence: speeding up to reduce windows of threat, and slowing down to prolong stability. The Catholic Workers persisted by hastening collapse and recovery, which increased internal flexibility and decreased the influence of their surrounding environment. Their rapid fluctuation between emergence and collapse created a feeling of timelessness. STOP persisted by extending the distance between their mundane internal responsibilities and their external focus of attention, which forestalled collapse. STOP's increasingly external focus was exciting for the leaders, who were always at the center of the action, but time passed slowly for the office staff at the slow-moving center.

A Catholic Worker Story of Persistence

Trouble Fitting In

"This is what I'm going to say when I get a chance to speak: 'This is another case of corporate greed sucking the lifeblood out of the people,'" said Nick, a White man in his early sixties with a slight southern accent who had contacted the Worker house a month before, out of the blue, to start a chess club for neighborhood kids. He was planning to attend a protest against the building of a chain restaurant the next day, and he practiced a speech he had prepared.

Not looking at us but at an imagined crowd behind us, he continued. "They'll tell you they're bringing jobs to the community, and there will be a handful of minimum-wage jobs created by this corporate monster, but the real money is being siphoned out to the military-industrial complex. They kill us with their poison disguised as food and make us pay for it."

Nick orchestrated the speech so that he traced a large "m" in the air whenever he said a word that began with "m": minimum, monster, military, and so on.

He wore an eager expression as he shifted his attention back to the group. "I'm going to write the speech up before I leave so everything will go perfectly."

He was so excited to share his speech, but I was the only one giving him my attention. Linda and Joan turned away from him as soon as he started. They usually loved talking about injustice and protest, but they clearly were not interested; they actually seemed irritated.

"I've decided to get arrested at the Good Friday protest," Nick said, changing the subject but still looking for a reaction.

Joan and Linda seemed more interested in this. They usually attended this protest, and Joan had been arrested for civil disobedience at it a few years before.

"Do you think it would be good if I went limp when I'm arrested? I can imagine myself being dragged away by the police. I've been thinking about what I'm going to say for this one as well," and he launched into another speech.

Again, Linda and Joan turned away and looked annoyed. The look on Nick's face conveyed confusion and injury as his speech trailed off.

Joan looked at him and said, "The first time I was arrested there, I refused to give my name. They kept me there for three hours at the station trying to get me to give them my name. Finally the officers went to get one of the higher-ranking officers. He told me, 'I don't know who you think you are, but [famous activist] gave us his name when he was arrested here.'"

Then she laughed at herself. "You should have seen me carrying on. It was me against the system, but I was being a complete idiot, so I told him my name."

Nick looked confused but appeared to force himself to join in the laughter.

Later Nick continued a conversation he had been having with Ramona about Cuba while she worked on one of her feasts in the kitchen.

"I think some of the older boys would really enjoy reading *Motorcycle Diaries*. I think they'll be able to relate to Che, and they'll find it interesting, especially the motorcycle part. If I can help raise their radical consciousness and leave them with the morals they need to overthrow capitalism, I wouldn't care how they acted those beliefs out. I'd leave that up to them."

Ms. Beth pursed her lips and looked up and off to the corner away from Nick.

Linda rolled her eyes as she entered the room behind Nick and walked through to the kitchen but didn't say anything.

Joan's mouth was set in a straight line as she looked at the table and shook her head in disagreement as Nick spoke. When she spoke, it sounded as though she was trying very hard to be patient.

"That's very dangerous. I can't see how it would be productive for these kids when they don't have an outlet for that anger. They already struggle with anger. This will only make them more rebellious, and we're trying to do everything we can to keep these kids out of jail."

She sounded like she barely had enough air to finish the statement, a quality her voice took on when she got upset. "I see our vision as providing stability and order for kids who have very little stability in their lives, not trying to incite behavior that will only create more problems for them." She continued to shake her head.

I moved to the kitchen to chop vegetables for Ramona, and Linda followed me and told me about a paper she was writing for a course.

"I'm writing about what's going on in the world, like I usually do, but it just gets me so upset. But I guess that's what activists do to keep their

energy up, right? They make themselves angry," she said this with deri-
sive humor. "It's so self-destructive. How do they sustain that?" she asked
rhetorically as she left the room.

A few weeks later, Joan seemed depressed over dinner. She launched
into a long pleading defense of their decision to not invite neighbors to
their regular Wednesday community dinner and liturgy.

Linda looked frustrated and rolled her eyes.

Toward the end of Joan's explanation, she revealed that Nick had
asked them why they did not include neighbors in these dinners.

I knew immediately that whether he had meant to or not, he could not
have come up with a better question to take the wind out of their sails.

I was not surprised to see the Workers' less-than-warm response to him
over the next few weeks.

The Workers Struggle with Extended Community Support

Despite their frustrations with Nick, the community would never send
him away. Their political and religious commitments demanded an open-
door policy. Furthermore, extended community support represented not
only resources for their neighbors and guests, but also for the house. They
were hardly in a position to turn down help or donations.

Similar problems had arisen with a major financial supporter of the
house. The Workers had met Rebecca through a regional feminist Catholic group. Since that time, Rebecca had been a regular donor.

The Workers had hosted a meeting of the feminist group one evening,
and during discussion over dinner, Joan had used the phrase "pocket-
book activists" in a clearly derogatory way a few times.

It was difficult not to cringe as Rebecca's face registered a stronger
emotional reaction each time Joan said the phrase.

A few days later, the Workers received a letter from her.

"I'm tired of you all implying that you're morally superior to those of
us who have jobs and earn money. Don't you know that you only exist
because working people give you money?" the letter said.

Linda was livid. "As if we don't work! We work all the time. It never
stops. People knock on our door all times of the day and night."

"This is ridiculous. Some of my best friends have jobs. I had a job for
years. We don't act morally superior," said Joan.

I pressed them on this. "But don't you live the way you do because you
believe it's the right thing to do?"

Joan and Linda looked surprised.

Ms. Beth nodded her head, and Frank, an extended community member who worked, said, "Of course you do."

Neither Ms. Beth nor Frank looked accusatory, but both Linda and Joan looked stricken anyway.

"But we know that we rely on the support of donations from people who work," explained Joan.

"But you believe that if everyone lived like this, you wouldn't need to rely on their donations, don't you?" I asked.

Reluctantly Joan and Linda agreed. They clearly believed that what I was saying was true; they probably talked about it behind closed doors, maybe with extended community members who lived in voluntary poverty as well, but I could see they were reluctant to agree to this position in front of me.

For Joan and Linda, the world was chaotic and uncontrollable. They worked hard to maintain their belief that they only could control their own flexibility, trusting that openness allowed for the work and will of God.

Rebecca, on the other hand, came from a tradition based in the belief that change was brought about by well-organized, politically savvy people. In Rebecca's world, morality did not dictate sacrifice, but a willingness to work for the right side.

Rebecca's perspective that coordinated collective action was necessary for substantial change rendered the Workers' personal sacrifice meaningless. On the other hand, the Workers' perspective undermined Rebecca's understanding of herself as a "good guy" who was on the side of justice. She sacrificed much of her time and personal resources in order to bring about change, and she resented being lumped in with the problem rather than the cure.

Their conflict with Rebecca reminded me of an earlier discussion I had had with them. Joan and Linda had said that conflict between community members and the community's supporters were some of the most draining interactions.

They had told me, "People think it's the neighborhood people that are tough, but it's the supposed supporters that cause problems . . . that are the real drain."

Nick Moves In

Nick moved into the community a few months later and learned that he did not need to seek anger—it found him easily enough.

The other members of the community would openly grieve or laugh over the harsh conditions and their helplessness. In contrast, Nick's fiery passion faded to cynicism, and he grew increasingly weary with each passing day.

He told me how the constant noise and waste was making him cynical. "I've come face-to-face with the meanness and brutality this environment breeds. Every night I fall asleep to the sounds of fighting—adults fighting, children fighting, adults and children fighting. There's something about the night. Either people fight more, or I'm just still enough to hear it then. In the morning, I see the guys drinking on the corner waiting for the bar to open."

During this discussion Joan came into the room.

She heard the last comments and said, "Mother Teresa said that serving the poor was 'serving her Beloved in His most disturbing form.' When you see how bad it is, it can make you cynical or compassionate, but it always changes you."

Joan misted up as she spoke.

Nick looked like he thought he was agreeing with her point when he responded by referring to a book about discipleship and saying that the way of the disciple included suffering. "I've decided to accept that suffering." He sounded resigned.

"Joy is the surest indicator of the presence of God," responded Joan.

Nick did not look moved.

Joan changed the subject and told me that Blueberry was sleeping in the park again. Blueberry's hearing (for her arrest when she threatened her boyfriend with a box-cutter) was supposed to be the next day.

"She didn't turn up when her sister was supposed to meet her here," she said with mild disgust.

"What courtroom is she going to be in and at what time?" Nick asked.

"I'm not sure." Joan shrugged and turned to her newspaper.

"I thought she left the information with you shortly after the hearing was scheduled," Nick persisted, sounding increasingly annoyed.

Joan sighed, dug around in a stack of papers, and gave a slip to Nick. "Unless I hear from Blueberry that she's going to be there, there's no way I'm going down there. If she can't make her appointments with her sister who gives her phone cards and treats, she certainly won't show up for a hearing. I can't see dragging myself down there just to be told that the trial's going to be put off."

"I suppose if you're going to be practical about it . . . ," Nick responded with a sarcastic edge; his body language suggesting that he thought Joan was logical but overly callous. He continued to sound and look put off, but Joan ignored him.

Ms. Beth walked through the door, and Joan exclaimed, "Ms. Beth! You just missed your best friend!" She was referring to a usually drunk man who liked to flirt with Ms. Beth when he stopped by for sandwiches.

Ms. Beth shook her head and chuckled, and Joan burst out laughing.

Under his breath, Nick said bitterly, "Oh yes, humor runs high at the Catholic Worker."

He was right; the Catholic Workers were just as likely to laugh as to cry. Despite the fact that the Workers had to continually struggle against the threat of anger, the group's ready laughter was one of the first things I noticed about them.

Anger in the House

On an afternoon a few weeks earlier, I had greeted an elderly couple at the door of the Worker house, a White woman who seemed spaced out and a very thin, tall Black man. He swayed slightly and told me his name was Nate and that the woman's name was Minnie.

Joan must have heard Nate say Minnie's name from the dining room, because she yelled out in an angry tone, "Minnie, please come in here."

Linda looked like she was taking a deep breath as she gestured to a seat. Minnie sat stiffly on the edge of her chair and looked straight ahead.

"Hello, *Minnie*, do you have anything to say to me?" Joan asked.

Silence stretched for a minute, as Minnie looked obstinately ahead, ignoring Joan.

Finally Joan exploded, "You should be asking for forgiveness! I will not tolerate being talked to like that. If you can't apologize, you won't be welcome here!"

"I apologize," said Minnie, clearly apologizing in form only and still not looking at Joan.

"Erika, can you give Minnie a sandwich?" Joan said in disgusted dismissal.

Linda followed me into the kitchen. "Minnie's a *nasty* drunk. Last time she was here, Joan said something about being Catholic, not to Minnie, but Minnie heard it. She told Joan to 'shove it,'" Linda said, laughing. "Oooo, Joan did *not* like that."

I gave Minnie the sandwich and saw her to the door.

When I returned to the room, Joan was muttering, "'Shove it. *Shove it!*' Who does she think she is?!"

Before I had come to the Worker house, I would have been astounded by Joan's anger with this woman who was clearly heavily addicted, intermittently homeless, and probably mentally ill, but since spending time with the group, I grew increasingly sympathetic toward Joan's anger as I found myself having to swallow my own frustration over and over again.

Joan remained angry the whole evening and repeatedly told the story of Minnie's initial offense and her reluctant apology.

Nick's Transition

Nick lived in the house for only a few weeks before he decided he had had enough. He moved out and cut his involvement back to the chess club and the community liturgy and dinner.

Not long after Nick moved out, Father Ted, a priest from a parish in a wealthy suburb, showed up to say Mass. He came to the Worker house two or three times a year to "let his hair down" and generally opted for group discussion rather than a formal homily.

Nick spoke first after Fr. Ted finished reading the Gospel. "This gospel reminds us that we should anticipate hardship and suffering because it's the way of the Cross. We should expect to suffer for justice."

Joan nodded her head in agreement. "Lately I've been thinking that way more myself. I've been thinking: maybe I should get used to the hard parts because they're inevitable," she said, sounding defeated.

Fr. Ted calmly countered this sentiment, "The Cross doesn't make sense without the Resurrection, or else we're just a masochistic people."

Nick looked like he was concentrating hard and trying to make sense of what Fr. Ted had said.

Joan smiled and nodded with her eyes closed, as if Fr. Ted had reminded her of something important.

I could not figure out why Fr. Ted's comment was resonating with Joan.

After a moment, I turned to her. "You often quote Teilhard,[2] 'Joy is the most infallible sign of the presence of God.' I don't understand how that fits with what you said about 'the way of the Cross.' " She looked thoughtful but did not answer right away.

Fr. Ted looked at me and then shifted his gaze around the group as he spoke. "We must understand that suffering and joy are not opposite ends

2. Pierre Teilhard de Chardin.

of the same continuum.[3] They are intermingled, and we cannot have one without the other."

Joan nodded and spoke with her eyes closed, as if she were reminding herself. "A lesson I have a hard time remembering sometimes. We have to be open to the pain of injustice before we can move beyond it. Anger can carry you, but only as far as violence will take you. Only deep conviction in your own worth, the justness of your cause, compassion for others, and courage will allow you to be open and forgiving, not just toward yourself for having tolerated the injustice, but toward those who inflicted the injustice."

Occasionally Joan transformed into a great orator, and this was one of those moments. In moments like this one, the Catholic Workers' lifestyle, which might otherwise have seemed like masochistic sacrifice, made sense in an otherwise crazy world. This night they did not seem like a small pocket of people on the political and religious fringe; rather, they belonged to a lineage that stretched through time.

———

Over time Nick gradually increased his involvement in the community again. His hair grew longer, his clothes more threadbare, and his attitude more relaxed. He routinely participated in acts of civil disobedience but usually said very little about doing so.

Linda told me, with obvious admiration and humility, that Nick had begun to walk everywhere, even though he lived eight miles from the Worker house.

One afternoon Nick and I were waiting for our after-school partners to show up. Attendance at the after-school program had dropped off as the school year drew to a close.

Eventually Nick announced with a grin, "If they don't come to us, we can go to them. What do you say we go get 'em?"

Both of our after-school partners lived in the same house, so we walked together to retrieve the children.

Nick hummed as we went. "I think it's safe to say that this is one very nice afternoon," he commented.

We turned the corner and saw the brothers of our partners wrestling by the steps to the house.

3. "What empire is comparable to that of a soul who, from this sublime summit to which God has raised her, sees all the things of earth beneath her feet, and is captivated by no one of them? How ashamed she is of her former attachments! How amazed at her blindness! What lively pity she feels for those whom she recognizes still shrouded in the darkness!" (James [1902] 2007, 363).

Nick grinned at them. "Hi, guys, how you doing? Beautiful day, isn't it?"

We knocked at the screen door, and when his partner came to the door, she said, "Oh, after-school. We don't have homework."

"How about you come over, and we can read together and play chess," Nick answered.

"OK."

As we waited for the girls to return, Nick tried to teach the boys "bean toss," which consisted of picking up a seed that had recently fallen out of the tree and attempting to hit it with a thin stick to see how far he could make it go.

"We used to play this when I was a kid," he explained with an encouraging look.

The boys looked at him like they thought he was crazy.

Nick shrugged, laughing. "Well, I guess maybe you had to be there."

The girls finally came out with books. As we started to leave, it became clear that the boys were coming with us too.

"Joan's going to be irritated that we've got extras," I warned Nick.

"Well, I suppose that's true, but I say 'the more the merrier.' Go with the flow, right?" he said and laughed.

Angry Nick had become unflappable Nick. He initially had assumed that feelings of righteous anger motivated and sustained the community. He had not realized that the Workers did not have to go looking for anger; it came looking for them. Indeed, anger did not refresh the group; it was a continual threat that the Worker community had to manage in order to maintain individual involvement. Nick had experienced for himself the wear of anger as the brutality of the neighborhood burned his righteous anger down into caustic cynicism. However, with time he, too, had begun smiling in the face of personal aggression, hopelessness, and chaotic conditions.

Laughter Is the Best Medicine

A few months later, after the war on Iraq officially began, Joan told me they were considering spending the weekend going to peace protests, but they decided the best way to work for peace was to help the children in the neighborhood.

She told the group, "A friend of the house called us to tell us that she had begun knitting mittens and hats for all of the kids in the neighborhood when the war broke out. Knitting mittens—what a revolutionary idea!"

"Knitting mittens" became group-speak for how they saw themselves resisting the war.

The war escalated, and they talked about knitting mittens more frequently, as if they needed more frequent reminders of the link between their local efforts and the global situation. Eventually a sense of futility began to settle over the group in response to the escalating war.

One Wednesday Father David, a priest who came to say Mass at the Worker house every so often, used peace as his theme for a community liturgy. When it was time for less formal group reflection, Fr. David suggested the group share ideas about working for peace.

Joan responded first, "I'm so very upset, just sickened, to see people from the neighborhood painting an American flag on the side of a building on the next block."

She was loud, and it felt almost like she was yelling at us, even though she knew the group agreed with her.

"These people have had almost none of the American dream. They have no idea where their interests lie. They are aligning themselves with the people who keep them poor, people who would gladly send our neighbors to war so that they can be certain they keep their wealth!"

She was bright red and running out of breath as she spoke.

"Absolutely, absolutely," Frank, an extended community member, added.

Nick nodded.

"It's ridiculous. I mean, I know they watch TV and the news, but really, how can they be so gullible. Come on," said Linda.

Ms. Beth looked as though she had pulled back slightly from the group. As usual, she did not say anything verbally, but her body language suggested that she was not in total agreement with Joan, Linda, and Frank.

Fr. David, who was usually happy-go-lucky, appeared to be thrown off balance. In past discussions, Fr. David had indicated that his politics were aligned with the Workers, but he had identified primarily with their theology.

Joan shifted uncomfortably in her seat, visibly itching for a fight.

"We can't allow our anger with the U.S. to blind us to the horrors Hussein perpetrated against his own people!" Joan said.

Linda and Frank took immediate exception with Joan's argument.

"His crimes were ignored until they were useful as propaganda for attacking. Somehow everyone seems to have forgotten that we *gave* him the weapons explicitly for these purposes," said Frank as he hit the table for emphasis.

Linda made noises of agreement as he spoke.

"We gave him the weapons, and we've done horrible things as a country. What does that have to do with letting him brutalize his people? *He* was the one who used the weapons against his people! Haven't you seen the pictures of the Kurds and what he did to them? The man is a monster!" Joan focused her anger at Frank and Linda. "What are we supposed to do about him? Are we supposed to just let him do this to his people and do nothing about it?!"

Everyone looked slightly shocked. Joan had questioned pacifism, which meant she had questioned one of the fundamental tenets of Catholic Worker theology.

"Nonviolent resistance *does* work and *has* worked, but it takes the *ultimate* sacrifice. You have to be ready to risk *everything*," responded Frank, who shook as he spoke, as if his control was hanging by a thin thread.

He paused to collect himself.

"There are Americans going over to Iraq, as we speak, to put themselves in the line of fire. They are going to meet the brutality of the U.S. war machine with pacifist resistance."

"Then why aren't *we* over there right now?!" Joan threw back.

Her accusation seemed to echo in the silent room for an endless moment.

What could anyone say in response? This was a time of reckoning for them as peace activists, and they were falling short.

On one level, they believed in the importance of "knitting mittens," but on another they would like to think they would be the ones who would risk their personal safety, even their lives, to end war. But here they were, at home. They were humbled.

There was an uncomfortable brooding silence until Fr. David rallied and ended the discussion by instructing the group to sing "Peace Is Flowing Like a River."

After communion, he directed the group to hold hands and sing the Lord's Prayer and had the group sing again "Peace Is Flowing Like a River."

The group felt more stable by the time we were done singing.

Fr. David saved dinner with his self-deprecating comments and contagious laughter at his own jokes.

"Not only can't I cook; I'm the wimpiest, pickiest eater you'll ever meet. I'll tell you how pathetic I am: here I am making a grand ole pig out of myself over these rice and beans. Ya-um! Hope you don't want any Ms. Beth, because you'll have to arm-wrestle me for them."

Fr. David winked at Ms. Beth.

Ms. Beth chuckled, raised her eyebrows, and told him in mock serious-ness, "Those are all yours."

"Good. Now, like I was saying, here I am making a pig of myself, and you know what? If there were any other choices, I'd never have tried the rice and beans—that's how ridiculously picky I am!"

We could not help but to laugh along with him.

Next he started on gold bullion. "I've always wondered why our eco-nomic system is based on gold bullion. It seems perfectly useless to me. What sort of use do I have for it? Paperweight? Self-defense, oh that's right, we're pacifists . . ." and everyone burst out laughing.

"Seriously, I'm afraid that one day everyone's going to realize the use-lessness of gold bullion all at once, and then we'll have a worldwide economic collapse."

He pointed his fork at us. "And when that happens, you remember to tell everyone you heard it here first."

Everyone, except for Frank and Fr. David, who was playing the straight man perfectly, was laughing so hard we couldn't speak. People were cry-ing, hitting the table, and practically falling out of their chairs.

Frank, who always took things very seriously, looked concerned. He tried multiple times to jump into Fr. David's monologue on gold. "You see, it's useful for computer parts, necessary really, and it's the one metal that's found lumped together. It doesn't require processing like other metals . . ." He trailed off, looking confused as he realized people had begun laughing at him.

His confusion only made the group laugh harder, especially Linda, who was coming unglued. And we all laughed harder at how hard she was laughing.

Nick put a hand on Frank's arm in comfort but could not stop laugh-ing himself.

My stomach was hurting, and I could barely speak, but I had to put Frank out of his misery. "It's not really about gold."

"But it really is useful," he said with a look of earnest confusion.

I laughed harder as I realized I could not figure out how to explain it to him. Finally I said, "Oh, Frank, we're just laughing to laugh."

He seemed to get it then and joined in instantly.

Suddenly a stiff breeze moved through the room carrying a strong smell of chocolate. "Anybody else smell that? I smell chocolate," said Ms. Beth, and the group began to wind down from laughing.

"Oh yeah. That's definitely chocolate," said Frank, as he closed his eyes, clearly luxuriating in the smell.

Joan, still chuckling, said, "Blueberry's brother just sent her some chocolate. The box is right behind you. She said it's to share. Why don't you pass it around? We're welcome to it."

I handed the box to Fr. David, who studied the box carefully and said, "This is important business, you know," and made his selection.

"Oh yes," said Nick, playing up the seriousness of the matter at hand as he selected a chocolate for himself.

Linda wiped her eyes, stood, and took orders for refills on coffee. "Who wants decaf or regular?" she asked.

"That reminds me," said Frank. "I'm going to bring by a big bag of that equal exchange coffee as a donation to the house. It really is *so* important now, especially now." He bobbed his whole body up and down and slapped the table to punctuate his conviction. "The World Bank is starving, I mean it—they're starving the Columbian coffee growers."

Fr. David looked concerned, and Nick nodded in enthusiastic agreement as he chewed his chocolate. Joan responded in a conversational tone, "Speaking of equal exchange, we should be talking about equal exchange chocolate. Did you know that they use child slave labor to pick the beans, and the children who pick them will not see enough money to even taste the chocolate?"

Like Frank, her critique of injustice seemed genuine, but she did not really sound all that angry. It sounded more like she felt that she couldn't let the moment pass without saying something about this injustice.

Without thinking, I commented, "You could've at least waited until we'd eaten the chocolate before you brought that up."

Everyone erupted in full belly laughter, laughing again until they cried.

Joan choked out, "Yeah, I guess my timing wasn't so great on that one." And the laughing started all over again.

"Oh help, I can't take it anymore. My stomach hurts," Linda pleaded.

The chocolate was passed around again, and they helped themselves to another piece as they wound down.

For a moment I observed the interaction from the outside, remembering Nick's journey into this community where grief and laughter played surprising roles in buoying heartrending involvement.

I later would come to think of this chocolate discussion and laughter as quintessentially representative of my experience in the community, a community that has a sense of humor about eating a borderline homeless woman's chocolate while talking about the child slave labor involved in producing it, yet continuing to enjoy the chocolate anyway.

They did not laugh because they were heartless; they laughed in humility before, and in defiance of, the magnitude of their challenge to live a morally consistent life in the face of overwhelming suffering.

Epilogue

About a year later, the group sat around the table with Ramona and a friend she had brought for the first time. He was an Episcopal priest who had agreed to lead the liturgy that evening. He had an activist look about him that made me think he might fit in, but when he started the liturgy out by saying, "We the righteous," I knew it was not going to go well.

Although their facial expressions did not change, I could feel Joan, Linda, Blueberry, and Ms. Beth pulling back and putting up their guards.

Nick smiled and looked curious.

The priest blundered again when he said that he wanted a lot of children. "People like us, who can give children a good upbringing, should have as many children as we can."

I winced. I could feel the community members' response. People like who? People who came face-to-face with their moral failings every day? People who were often humbled by their neighbors' generosity? I figured that Linda and Joan would burn over this remark, and the looks on their faces suggested I was right.

Nick looked at the priest, raised his eyebrows, and tilted his head, as if to say, "Well, that's one way to look at it."

The priest gave a traditional homily rather than the typical conversation about the readings that usually served as the homily on Wednesdays. He talked about how Mary Magdalene was able to see Jesus when the other apostles could not. "She saw him through her grief. But the others were blinded by their fear, anger, and concern for the practical."

His voice cracked. I was sure I was mistaken when I thought he looked like he was fighting back tears, but he started to cry.

Despite the fact that the community tended to like a good cry, no one but Ramona looked particularly moved. This time it felt awkward. The more awkward things became, the harder he cried.

Nick, who was sitting next to him, kept smiling at him and patting his arm, saying, "You're all right. You're doing just fine."

As I remembered Joan's frequent comment, "There are two kinds of Catholic Workers, new and grumpy," I thought about how this visiting priest was lucky that Nick was still relatively new.

143

A STOP Story of Persistence

I arrived early one morning only a few days before STOP's staff dissolved. Todd explained the upcoming Abolition Week events to me. He asked me to make small stop signs for the participants to hold during the demonstrations.

I jokingly said, "Great. I like coloring."

"Actually no, these signs look pretty professional."

I followed him to the front room of the office, and he cleared a space on a table where the materials were laid out.

"Glue the stop signs to the poster board. Cut them out and staple them to the paint mixing sticks once they're dry. Believe me; they look pretty professional when they're done." A sign that someone else had already started caught his eye, and he frowned. The two pieces of paper had come unglued and were curling up into a sticky mess. I bit my lip so I would not laugh. "Try to roll the signs in the opposite direction. They seem to be curling."

On his way out of the room, he noticed the glue was nearly gone and sighed deeply. "I'm going downstairs to the dollar store to get some glue. I'll be right back."

A few minutes later, he handed me the glue and thanked me for my help. He turned to head back to the other part of the office, saying he had "pressing work to do."

"Me too," I said in another feeble attempt at humor.

He stopped, looked at me in confusion, then closed his eyes and nodded briefly as he got it, then turned and walked away.

He came back about an hour later to check on me. His posture suggested that he was ready to pivot and head back out the door, but I had the sense that he wanted to talk. I asked him if he grew up in the area. One question led to another, and he eventually leaned against the doorjamb and seemed to settle in. He told me about his father and mother and started chatting about his family.

Todd often talked to me quite a lot when I was the only other person in the office with him. He would tell me about local and state politics, but mostly about his social adventures within the neighborhood activist scene.

————

Shortly after STOP took up Jack Forest's cause, Todd hired Doreen, a recent college graduate who had previously volunteered at STOP, as a live-in office intern. She would live in the front room of the office and earn a small stipend for managing STOP's office work.

Two days after Doreen started working with STOP, Todd asked me to finish painting the kitchen and headed back to his office. Doreen sat down on the kitchen floor to talk to me as I worked. After a moment she sprung up.

"I've got something to show you," she said with a huge grin on her face.

I followed her to the bathroom, the only room in the office that I had not painted yet and the one I was least looking forward to. The paint was old, dirty, and gray. The grout was moldy and the tiles cracked. It was grimy in a way that made one feel dirty just for having seen it.

Doreen threw open the door with flourish. The walls were bright purple, and the trim was bright orange. Tiny mirrors from a disco ball were arranged in patterns on the wall. The grout was still stained with mold, and the floor tiles were cracked, but the paint transformed the room.

"It's beautiful!"

Doreen smiled with pride.

Marge came up behind us. "Isn't it amazing? Isn't she something? I would never think to do that in a million years. She's an artist."

I went back to my own boring white paint project in the kitchen. "Todd never tells me when I'm going to be painting, so I'm never wearing painting clothes when he asks," I complained, mostly to myself.

Marge laughed. "That's because he's a man. They never know what they're going to be doing next."

Doreen sat down on the floor near me as I got ready to clean the walls in the kitchen. "So, what's your dissertation about?"

I was surprised she was asking me, but she listened carefully as I told her. She asked a few questions and then said, "I would like to do something like that; well, not exactly like that. I don't think I'd like research. I mean I want to do something where I feel like I'm doing something that matters but not full-time activism. It makes me too sad. It consumes you, takes over your life, you know? I just find the whole thing so sad."

Conflicting Expectations

At 9:15 in the morning a week later, Doreen was still in the front room that served as her bedroom and private quarters.

"It takes forever for her to get up and get going," Todd grumbled to no one in particular.

They were expecting their new stove to be delivered that morning, and there was a vigil during the Jack Forest trial in the afternoon.

I went into the kitchen to get some water before I sat down to enter more contacts into their database and found a little note on the water pitcher: "Please refill me if you use me." It was in Doreen's handwriting and signed with a peace symbol.

Doreen came out of her room with a robe on and a towel on her head while I was still filling the pitcher.

"Wow, that's *so* great that you're refilling it. Really great. You know it makes it so much nicer for other people when they're thirsty and the pitcher is full. It's really thoughtful, you know?" She was carrying on so much that I started to feel uncomfortable, but I understood that Todd was her real audience. Lucas walked into the main office area, and she made her point about refilling the pitcher to me again, so I figured that he had been guilty of not refilling in the past as well. "A lot of people don't do that. They don't refill it after using it, even after I put the sign on it. I really appreciate your filling it."

Neither of them seemed to notice Doreen.

"Are you going to the vigil this afternoon?" I asked, attempting to change the subject.

Her response surprised me. "I don't think I will. I need to work on my boundaries." Boundaries that separated her further from the action seemed like they would only make it worse. Now that Doreen was no longer attending vigils and protests, she was cut off from almost all of the potential excitement associated with working for STOP.

Doreen went back into her room, emerged ten minutes later, and announced that she would be back around lunchtime.

"We need to have someone here for the stove," Todd called after her.

They were expecting the stove to arrive before we were supposed to leave, but only minutes from when we had to leave to be on time for the vigil neither the stove nor Doreen had arrived. Todd was anxious but attempted to play it cool, whereas Marge was annoyed. "Where is she? She knows that we need to leave by now."

"She'll be back," said Todd.

"They're going to charge us for a second delivery if we're not here to get it, and we can't be late for the vigil. It's unprofessional. People will be waiting for us," replied Marge.

When Doreen showed up, the group had only five minutes to get to the vigil—they would definitely be late.

"Hey, why are you guys still here? You're going to be late," she said.

"We were waiting for YOU. We're getting the stove today. Remember? We've been waiting for YOU," said Todd.

"Oh, sorry about that," said Doreen, fleeing back to her room.

Tension Builds

A few weeks later, Doreen was the only one at the office when I arrived. Since she was alone, I took the opportunity to ask her about how things were going. "Are you going to stay for the whole six months?" I asked her.

"I'm not going to make it through the summer," she told me. "I'm an only child. It's really difficult for me to live with all of these people. It's their office, but it's my home, you know? People leave their messes all over. I'm cleaning the kitchen and the bathroom because I'm the one living here, and no one seems to notice. I've tried to talk with people about it, but Todd and Lucas don't get it. It's like they're irritated that I'm trying to talk with them about what's happening here, like we're only supposed to talk about the death penalty or something.

"Todd keeps coming into my room and waking me up at nine with a long list of things for me to do that day that I'll never get done. He's making me crazy. This is his thing, his life, totally. He can work on it until eight or nine at night every night, but I don't want to. It just isn't my thing the way it's his. I care about other things. I want to be able to do other things. I've tried to talk to him about the way he's so demanding, always ordering me around, but he won't listen. It's like he won't hear me.

"I was thinking about leaving to work for a flower farm in England, but I'm staying to give it one more try. I want to fulfill my responsibility, you know?"

———

Marge answered the door when I arrived a few days later. "Today's the day! I have been waiting forever and an age to meet with the Black Clergy—they have the power and the resources. If we can get them behind this, there is nothing that we can't do!" she said.

As I walked into the office, I saw Doreen looking aggressively worn-out and sad, like she was desperate for someone to notice. Considering the general aversion to sorrow, I did not think she stood much of a chance.

She asked if I would mind taking a look at her résumé. "I'm applying for a job with the prison society and a few positions at jewelry stores." I looked over the résumé and made a few comments.

Marge was getting antsy. "We have to get this newsletter for the friends and family out today. We've decided the winners of the poetry contest, and we need to let everyone know. We've got to get moving on this stuff."

Marge's urgency stood in stark contrast to Doreen's lethargy. Marge felt a sense of momentum, but Doreen shared in none of this excitement. Doreen spent her days paying the bills, scheduling appointments, answering phone calls. Regardless of the group's growth and effect, Doreen's job would remain pretty much the same, except she might get busier.

———

The situation deteriorated quickly. A couple of weeks later, I was waiting in Todd's office to talk with him about my schedule when Doreen came in and waited to talk with me, looking woe-begotten again.

"I just want to be around people who appreciate me, who notice I'm alive. I don't like to interrupt, but if I don't, they won't even notice I'm here. I tried to talk to Todd and Lucas about how I'm feeling, and they treat me like I'm selfish, like I should know there are more important things going on. I'm miserable."

Todd popped his head in. "I'll talk to you about your schedule later. Can you type up the rest of the poems? Doreen, we need you for the staff meeting upstairs." This time I was not invited to the staff meeting. Doreen rolled her eyes and left.

I could not find the poetry file, so I started copying a stack of flyers until the copier jammed beyond repair. With nothing left to do, I cleaned up the office and waited for them to return.

An hour later the staff returned, with Doreen leading the way and looking sad again. I asked her if she was OK, and she gave me a meaningful look.

Lucas planted himself at the computer. I was somewhat confused about what to do since I was supposed to be using it once someone pointed me toward the poetry files. I thought maybe he was going to help find the poems, but when I asked him, he said, "Hmm" in a distracted way and that was it.

Doreen looked at me and asked, "Erika, are you waiting to use the computer?" in an overly loud voice.

Feeling increasingly uncomfortable, I answered, "I can wait."

She gave me a look that said this happened all the time. But if she was making a point, no one else seemed to get it.

"I need help unjamming the copier. I thought if it needed to be forced, I should let one of you do it," I told the room, but no one responded. Not sure what to do, I wandered back into Todd's office where the copier was, hoping that someone would come along to fix it at some point.

A few minutes later, Lucas and Marge came into his office but ignored me as I stood next to the copier. Doreen came in and started to move her bike. Lucas stopped what he was saying to Marge, looked at Doreen, and said, "Sorry to ask you to move it, but it's so small in here already." Doreen did not respond.

Todd came into the center office looking flustered and started talking to Lucas about files.

Doreen interrupted to ask for the checkbook. "It's out on the table," Todd replied, visibly irritated. She stiffened and turned on her heel. She came back in, insistent and upset.

"It's not there, Todd."

"Look again, I know it's there," he responded. She came back moments later and asked again, openly insulted by his lack of concern. The tension was thick, but Todd just pushed right ahead ignoring it.

As he finished fixing the copier, I commented, "You probably thought you were going to be an activist, but as the head of a nonprofit you have to be an expert on everything, don't you?"

He instantly changed tones and nodded his head in solidarity and agreement. "I hate the fact that I have to be the genius about everything, even the copy machine fixer." As he was saying this, he handed the previously stuck chewed-up paper to Doreen.

"We need heavier paper."

"I bought that paper because it said it was multipurpose," she said, sniffing.

Again he plowed ahead. "Heavier paper won't jam, so we need that."

"What type? If you write it down, I'll get it."

Todd was getting exasperated, but he checked a ream of paper to see what pound paper they had to get.

Doreen followed me out of the office to the kitchen. She told me that she was planning to buy a van and go to Arkansas to mine her own quartz crystals for making jewelry. "They're really cheap, and they're the best crystals. I heard about it while I was out traveling in California." She talked more about her interest in sociology and the possibility of going to graduate school. She looked meaningfully in Todd's direction and said, "I want to know why it makes *some* people want to vomit to do things the traditional way," implying that Todd was not one of these people.

———

Tension in the office continued to increase as members were pulled in different directions and the differences in influence between staff members continued to grow.

Todd temporarily managed some of the tension between Doreen and himself by giving some of the tasks that would have fallen to her to me and other volunteers.

"Here you go," said Todd, handing me a list of numbers on his way out the door. It was two days before the big Jack Forest protest. Only moments before, Todd had instructed me to cold-call people from their list of donors; I was supposed to persuade them to attend the protest.

"You'll be great at it," said Marge. "This is an important job. We really need to get people out for this. I think people will be *glad* to know about it. They *want* to do what's right; we just have to give them the chance." Despite her attempt to bolster me, I'd just seen the rest of the staff's aggressive efforts to pass the job off until it landed at my feet—the bottom of the pecking order. The behavior indicated what I'd already known to be true: this assignment was far from desirable.

Doreen sat on her feet as she leaned over a desk to work on a business letter for the organization. Marge leaned back in her chair and took a paperback novel out of her purse.

Vivian—a volunteer who'd been involved with STOP since the beginning and was a part of the local activist scene—was working on some paperwork for the friends and family trip.

Time stretched out as I moved at a snail's pace through the list of numbers. The few live people I managed to reach generally hung up on me. More often than not I reached voice mail, and I felt foolish with the other staff members listening in as I repeatedly delivered my rehearsed speech about the upcoming protest.

I looked at the list to see how many names were left; there were a lot. Then I looked at my watch to see how much longer I was obligated to stay at STOP; I had plenty of time to make all of the required calls. I braced myself, called the next number, and thought about the series of choices in my life that had brought me to telemarketing as I waited for someone to pick up.

"What? Who? I'm sorry I'm busy," said the next person I reached before they hung up on me.

"I don't think they're all going to know about Jack Forest. You should explain about his situation. It's really compelling. His story moves people—it will really bring them out," Doreen commented.

Marge countered, "I have experience in this, and you should keep it short. If you go on too long, people will just tune you out. Just the facts. I thought you did fine."

"You should be a little more fired up, you know?" Vivian added, without moving her eyes from the work in front of her.

I nodded vaguely in response to their comments and swallowed my irritation. I made a few more calls, increasingly anxious as I waited for rejections from the people I called and critiques from my audience.

My tension mounted as I worked my way down the list. As though she could sense my increasing hostility, Marge looked up from her reading and said, "People shouldn't be irritated. You're just asking them." Again I nodded and went back to calling.

Doreen stood up and stretched. "I'll be back. I got to get a tackle box for my jewelry-making stuff." I felt chained to my task and bitter that Marge was reading, and Todd and Doreen could leave so easily.

"You should really sell it more. Don't say so much, but sell it more, you know?" Vivian commented a few calls later.

"What? What's STOP? I'm sorry, I'm not interested," said the next person who answered. The next few people had no idea what STOP was, and a couple argued in support of the death penalty.

"It's hard to believe that some of these people are on the list of donors considering they're *for* the death penalty," I said, feeling dangerously close to losing my cool. Out of the corner of my eye, I could see Marge monitoring me out of the corner of hers.

"Well, here's your opportunity to make a compelling case for Jack, change a few people's minds," Vivian responded, still not looking up from her work.

I gave Vivian a frustrated look that Marge caught.

Suddenly Marge slammed her book down, looking disgusted. "You know, we wouldn't need to do this if the DA wasn't so intent on killing innocent people! But he has to. Yes, he *has* to. He has a *reputation* to uphold. You see he's keeping us *safe*. Safe from a terminally ill man on death row who committed no crime! Who, now I ask you, who is going to keep us safe from the crooked cops and the bloodthirsty DA?"

As long as Marge was providing an excuse for me to avoid my next call, I was willing to give her my full attention. Vivian finally looked up from her lists and turned to face her as well.

"We need to get out there. We need to wake people up. Two-thirds of the people voted for that DA. They don't know about the injustice. I refuse to believe they don't care. The DA's office just scares the hell out of them, and they vote out of fear," Marge roared with the familiar anger that paradoxically energized and soothed STOP's staff.

My frustration ebbed, and I returned to calling with renewed vigor.

It did not last for long. After a few more awkward phone calls, I was resentful again.

As I neared the end of the list, Doreen returned.

Todd rushed into the room just behind her, shrugging into a checked sport coat as he shouldered open the door. A short African American man, who looked like he was in his late twenties, entered behind Todd.

"Hey, everyone, I'd like you to meet Ronald," Todd said as he offered Ronald a chair.

Marge jumped up to shake his hand, saying, "I'm so honored to meet you. You're my hero." It took me a moment to place him, but I realized he was one of the people who had been released from death row who worked with the group.

"Thank you," Ronald said, looking slightly uncomfortable with his celebrity status. "I'm honored to meet you, too. You do important work."

Like Marge, I found myself awestruck. I couldn't fathom having my freedom taken away for so many years, much less facing death for a crime I did not commit.

Todd, however, sounded completely relaxed as he chatted with Ronald about another man who was about to be released from death row. I began to enter names from a petition into their database and thought about how Todd knew many people on death row, most of the people who had been exonerated, and all of the other public leaders of the movement. In fact, he spent much of his time interacting with these highly visible people.

After about twenty minutes, Todd looked at his watch and stood abruptly. "Shoot! We'd better get going if we're going to make it on time."

"Oh yeah, we'd better," agreed Ronald as he jumped up and followed Todd out the door.

Marge looked annoyed as she watched the door close behind them. "Do we have any idea about where he's going or when he's going to be back?"

This was a rhetorical question; if she did not know, she knew that none of the rest of us would.

Vivian showed no sign of registering Marge's comment, but Doreen sighed. "So, we still haven't set a time for the staff meeting?"

Marge shook her head as she turned back to her desk, saying to herself, "I have energy, but Todd's a whirlwind, a whirlwind."

The Breaking Point

The next week Doreen was obviously upset at the staff meeting, but everyone ignored it. Finally Doreen lost it. "I'm tired of running everyone's errands, answering the phone, and answering the door. Can't everyone take care of their own stuff once in a while? I'm tired of being maid and servant around here. I didn't go to four years of college to do this sort of work."

Everyone bristled. Marge shifted her weight, tilted her head, widened her eyes, and stuck her chin out in contempt.

Lucas said, "I haven't been to college. What are you trying to say?"

"Look, the job description was clear. It isn't a glamorous job, but you agreed to do it," said Todd.

An hour later I was driving with Lucas and Todd to the monthly vigil. Todd said to Lucas, "Yeah, that wasn't cool what she did in the meeting today. Not cool at all. Marge hasn't been to college, neither have you. Are you both supposed to wait on her? It's not a glamorous job. The job description was clear, and she was certainly eager to take it," Todd continued.

"Is the job description in writing?" Lucas asked.

"It sure is, and she saw it."

"Well, good, then we don't have to negotiate about that. We need to think about how we can use her to benefit the organization at this point," said Lucas.

"Absolutely. We don't have time for this crap. Lives are on the line. I don't have time for this petty bullshit," said Todd.

Lucas suggested to Todd that they should consider sending the White staff members to a race-awareness class offered by another neighborhood activist group. "It's a good place to network; besides, I don't know where Doreen stands on these issues."

"Yeah, I think there's some race and class stuff going on there."

———

A month later Doreen decided to leave. Although Marge said that she should stay and try to work it out, neither Todd nor Lucas put up much resistance. With two weeks left, they all but ignored Doreen as they went about their business and began to prepare for her absence.

One afternoon Doreen came in and slumped to the floor next to Marge's desk. "Are you feeling OK?" I asked her.

"My stomach hurts," she answered. "I'm really anxious now. I'm leaving, and that's good, but I don't have anywhere to go. I really need to figure out how I'm going to get that van so I can start traveling. You know, so I can start mining crystals," she explained.[4]

Marge and I nodded.

"I feel really terrible because it feels like Todd's ready for me to go now. He treats me as though I don't do any work, as though I just get in the way of the work that needs to be done. But I do lots of work. I work all of the time."

"He's just thinking ahead. Moving on to when you're not going to be around," responded Marge.

"It just makes me feel like crap that this is his organization, I'm living here, and he doesn't care that I'm here. I don't feel welcome, you know? And this is where I live. That's why my stomach hurts."

Marge walked me to my car when it was time for me to leave. "Women are just more sensitive. Todd doesn't mean it personally. He's just all about business, all about ending the death penalty. He needs to do this, to move forward so that he's not left high and dry when she's gone. She shouldn't be sensitive about this. But I'm going to talk to Todd about it because I want everything to be open. That's what I like where I work, open communication."

I left, uncertain that Marge was going to get what she wanted.

———

STOP's Internet service went down on the afternoon the staff was going to take Doreen out to lunch for her last day. Todd argued for over an hour with the phone company as he was passed from person to person. The group grew weary and hungry waiting for him.

"He needs to grow up and stop being so self-centered. He should know better than to indulge his moral outrage while we all sit around the of-

---

4. Bourdieu describes the bodily reaction of the dominated: "The practical recognition through which the dominated, often unwittingly, contribute to their own domination by tacitly accepting, in advance, the limits imposed on them, often take the form of bodily emotion (shame, timidity, anxiety, guilt) . . . it is betrayed in visible manifestations, such as blushing, inarticulacy, clumsiness, trembling, all ways of submitting, however reluctantly, to the dominant judgment . . ." (2000, 169).

fice for two hours not getting any work done and feeling hungry," Marge complained, but he was wrapped up in his phone conversation so he did not hear.

Finally he gave up, slammed the phone, and started walking out of the office. "Let's get this show on the road," he said, without looking at or waiting for anyone.

"Looks like we'll need two cars," Lucas pointed out in the parking lot. "How about boys and girls?" he joked.

Marge and Doreen jumped on this opportunity. Marge was clearly done playing go-between with Todd and Doreen.

"He needs to stop being so insensitive and self-centered. He spreads his emotional crap around like it's no big deal, but it's not so easy for women to work around it. He has serious problems with women," Marge said.

"Have you noticed he can only work with women who have way more power or who are way older?" Doreen asked. "Lucas said Todd has gender issues, but I'm not sure Lucas is much better."

"He's better. Well, at least a little," responded Marge.

———

Doreen left with hard feelings on all sides. Marge started focusing more of her energy and time organizing events with the Black Clergy. I felt as though I were on an irreversible slide toward the margins of the group.

Almost a year later, on one of my last days with the group, Marge answered the door to let me in and simultaneously handed me guidelines for visiting prisoners on death row that she wanted me to copy.

"People have to follow these rules or that's it! I'm not taking them back again. People leave their trash all over the bus, they wear bobby pins and underwire bras, and forget their IDs. And who do they expect to straighten everything out? Me."

Christy sat at the desk next to Marge's, her head propped on her hand. She lazily lifted her other hand in greeting when she saw me.

I followed Marge back to the office space Todd now shared with Lucas. She showed me the copy machine they had purchased a couple of days before, which everyone understood to be a major indicator of success and stability. Gone were the days of not building complicated structures.

"Todd said he'd give me a quick training, but we have things to do."

She located the "on" switch and left me to figure out the rest.

A few moments later, Todd rushed into the room while he was sliding into a sport coat.

"Hi," I said.

He looked distracted. "Oh, hi. Having any luck with the double-sided copies?" he asked pointedly.

"I haven't tried."

"It's going to be too heavy single-sided."

Marge heard this and called out, "Todd, it's only going to be three pages!"

I followed Todd back out into the general office space, only to so see both Todd's and Marge's backs just before the door closed behind them.

Christy rolled her eyes at me as she lethargically labeled envelopes. "They're going to a staff meeting at the deli. I never get to go anywhere. Someday I want to work in a real office. What's a real office like?"

I answered, "In my experience, it's a lot like this."

She did not look too impressed. "Then I'm going to have to find something else to do. What do you think of doing nails?"

The copy machine jammed soon after they left. I tried to fix it, but it felt like pulling the paper out might break the machine, so I sat and stamped envelopes while Christy stapled and folded the copies I had made.

A little over an hour later, Marge flew into the room looking aggravated, muttering, "Women get right back to work, but that's so like men to go get a cup of coffee."

Todd followed close on her heels saying, "I didn't get a cup of coffee."

I told her that we did not have the registration and guidelines copied; she looked flustered, annoyed, and embarrassed.

I went back to where Todd was bending over the copier. He seemed none too happy about the jammed machine, especially when I added that I did not want to be the one to force it, if it had to be forced.

I followed Todd back out into the general office space.

Christy rolled her eyes at me as she lethargically continued labeling envelopes.

Marge suddenly stood up, shaking the stamped mailings she held in her hand. "You used the stamps on my desk." I looked confused. "Those were postcard stamps!"

"Oh, I'm so sorry." I winced.

She murmured, "That's OK," and turned back to her desk and sat back down.

I went back to make the rest of the copies. When I brought the rest of the copying out to the main room, I saw Marge refolding the first set. She looked at me and said, "We need to go through and refold all of these. They're going to charge us more if they're all bunched up like this."

I was starting to get annoyed too, and for a moment I was tempted to point out that Christy had folded the copies, but I looked over at Christy and saw her looking up at the ceiling, obviously waiting for me to get her in trouble, so I said nothing.

Todd looked over Marge's desk as he walked by, stopped suddenly, and gave a sharp, exasperated-sounding sigh. "The prison won't let stapled letters through."

"They're going to the *families*," Marge responded.

Todd sat at the computer opposite from Marge so that his back was to her.

The copier went into standby mode when I had left the room. As soon as I turned it back on, the power went out.

"Arrgh!" Todd yelled, and stalked out of the office.

I leaned against the wall while I waited for him to return and turn off his computer.

Once the copier was up and going again, Marge called, "Keep bringing them out here in small bunches so that I can get them ready."

Every time I handed her a stack, she made a big show about saying how helpful and great I was. "What a help you've been. Hasn't she been, Todd? So wonderful. Thank you."

When I indicated I was ready to leave, Marge indicated that I'd stayed over my scheduled time and said, "I'm going to bring you back a little something from my trip."

"Yeah, thanks. I really appreciate it, too," Todd said.

He got up and followed me out. I gave him a questioning look. "I've got to go get stamps," he explained without looking me in the eye.

―――――――

My regular time with STOP drew to a close, but I continued to drop by every few weeks.

Todd called me up and asked if I would volunteer again.

I said I would for a few weeks, and then asked him how things were going with the staff.

"Let's just say that we're learning that it doesn't work so well to have a student intern in charge of the office."

He came close to blaming the most recent intern for the latest problems, but then backed off and made it sound like they were larger organizational mistakes.

"Now that we're truly statewide, it's more important than ever that our office run smoothly. I've hired a full-time organizer with experience so I can make sure the organization is well oiled."

When I showed up a few days later, Edward, the new organizer, let me in. I realized that I'd met him months before when he had temporarily joined the staff for the final weeks of the Jack Forest campaign. Edward remembered me with some prompting. He was friendly, but so serious and unsmiling. When I'd first met him, I assumed that his gloominess had to be humor, but I realized that he was entirely serious.

He asked me if I'd be willing to do some data entry and then went to make phone calls. He came back about a half hour later and chatted with me about a few mutual acquaintances. Then I asked him what his position at STOP entailed.

"I'm doing chapter formation, organizing, and coordination across the state. We're growing like crazy. I'm seeing about the details on major events. This leaves Todd time to meet with politicians, lawyers, and board members. He finds potential funding, writes funding proposals, and generally makes things go. But mostly he just goes crazy. We all have our things, and we try to stay out of each other's way, but mostly we stay out of Todd's way while he goes crazy."

A week later Edward looked even more worried and distracted than usual when he let me in.

He showed me a press release he'd just prepared.

"I just picked up the copies at the printer, but there's no second page. I can't figure it out. Maybe we didn't include it or maybe they screwed up. I was going to ask you to help me stuff the folders. But I need to figure this out. It isn't good," he said with furrowed brows.

Todd came in from outside, and Edward filled him in. "I don't know if we ever had the second page of that story. We're missing a lot of their press clippings because we lost two of our binders."

Todd was clearly trying to walk a fine line as he indicated to Edward that he was taking this as a big deal, but at the same time letting Edward know that it wasn't a big enough deal to keep them from stuffing the press kits.

Although Edward still looked worried as he reluctantly agreed to stuff the kits as is, Todd appeared more relaxed than I had seen him in years.

As we stuffed the folders, I asked him about the presentation the local chapter of STOP had just hosted. The presentation was designed to educate the public on a bill that would appear soon before the state senate. This bill would prevent executions of people who were mentally handicapped according to clinical standards.

He gave a generally dissatisfied shrug. "I don't even know why we did it. I mean, of course, education is worthwhile, but only thirty-five people showed up. And I don't see how it will lead to any further organizing around the moratorium. It *is* an important bill, and we do have to apply some pressure to make sure it's a good bill; otherwise they make it so loose that they'll be able to kill the mentally handicapped by slipping them by the standards. I'm worried that all of the talk about this bill is going to distract from the thrust of the movement. They're [state senators] going to feel like they've thrown us a crumb, which will make it more difficult to get support for the bigger issue."

Edward kept interjecting apologies as he talked, saying that he was afraid he was coming off as a cynical, negative person. "It's just difficult when we haven't seen any real progress. We point to victories and get fired up about our strategies, but at the end of the day they're still executing people in this state. There are people who've been working on this movement for the last twenty years, and Illinois is all we have to show for it."

"So how do you keep going?" I asked.

He gave a sardonic look and humorless laugh. "Diet Vanilla Coke," he said as he held up the bottle in his hand to show me.

Toward a Theory of How Evolving Emotional Histories Shape Styles of Persistence

In order to persist over time, the groups had to contend not only with continual environmental threats, but also with their own efforts to stabilize. As disturbances and threats accumulated over the groups' histories, relationships became routinized and formed what felt like firm structures.[5] Expectations became increasingly elaborate, tighter, more local, and more rigid. As a result, the groups became less flexible, which threatened

---

5. Work by DiMaggio and Powell (1983) and Wilson (1995) argues that organizations tend to take on the form of the institutions they rely on for resources. A comparison of the group structures within the Catholic Worker community and STOP provides a compelling illustration of this claim. Initially STOP lacked financial or political resources; it relied entirely on activist involvement. STOP came closest to having an "authentic" activist feel during these early days. As the group secured grants, it developed a hierarchical nonprofit structure much like its patrons. Finally, as Todd's social and political capital increased, the group developed a political feel, with Todd as the candidate and everyone else working to support his campaign. Alternately, the Workers refused grant money; they sought support from individuals and families. Just as STOP's structure reflected the sources they courted for resources, the structure of the Catholic Worker community reflected the source of their financial support—at some points they operated as independent individuals and at others they operated as a family.

their access to the resources they needed to sustain themselves. Eventually, continued stability required the groups to consume their own energy, so that maintaining stability required more energy than it gave them. This left the groups increasingly vulnerable to collapse.[6] For example, the Workers relied on outside donations.[7] Although their personal rejection of both money and elaborate planning helped them to avoid draining expectations, their attitude about money created a multitude of conflicts between the Workers and financial supporters of the house.

Similarly, newcomers were not in a position to see how the Workers' prohibitions on planning and righteous anger helped them to avoid draining emotional dynamics, or how their ready dark humor and laughter created momentum and helped them to deal with uncertainty and chaos, which, in turn, fostered the potential for interactions that were deeply satisfying. The Workers' hard or lighthearted reactions exacerbated the newcomers' apparent anguish over frustrations and unanticipated moral dilemmas. On the other hand, newcomers who were idealistic, proud, or ambitious often made the Workers feel pressured and judged.

STOP's leaders' focus on their political influence helped to stabilize the group, but their disinterest and occasional disdain for internally focused activity ultimately undermined their capacity to maintain good working relationships with their office staff and volunteers. The leaders' emotional techniques failed to draw in the lower-level members, who were responsible for managing STOP's mundane internal tasks. As a result, lower-level group members frequently left the group after relatively short periods of involvement.

For both groups, newcomers and outsiders did not share the local emotional history that gave rise to internal expectations for how interactions should unfold. Newcomers and outsiders often found the groups' expectations for interaction confusing and even alienating.[8] Similarly, outsiders and newcomers inadvertently pricked the groups' sore spots and threatened the members' capacity to meet the expectations that sustained the group.[9] This tension between relying on outsiders yet un-

6. See Douglas ([1966] 2002, 152) and Ulanowicz (1997, 59).

7. One of the three types of communism that Weber describes is "the communism based on love and charity in a religious community." He notes that such groups are in such direct conflict with rational and traditional approaches that they can only be sustained with the help of external support from patrons ([1951] 1978, 153).

8. Not only did the groups' emotion management techniques drain and alienate newcomers; the newcomers' lack of experience rendered them more sensitive to drains that the groups routinely managed. They tended to overreact to changes in their environment because they missed early clues to shifts in context that were important and obvious to those more experienced.

9. Simmel describes how such identification with a group arises: "Herewith the enormous service

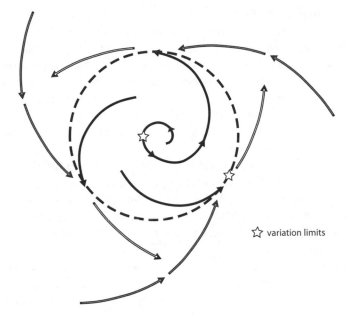

☆ variation limits

Figure 4.2   Maintenance of a pattern.

intentionally alienating them illustrates how a group's efforts to achieve stability eventually undercut it.

The stories in this chapter illustrate how social organization is a fundamentally historical process. From this perspective, if we want to understand how groups survive over time, we have to pay attention to the evolution of emotional patterns in response to their changing contexts.

Histories of Repulsions Drive the Evolution of Groups

As the earlier chapters illustrate, if we look at groups over time, there is no stable thing that can be pointed to as "the group." Rather, the stories

is manifest which honor renders to the self-maintenance of the group, for what I call the honor of the group, represented by the honor of the individual, proves, on close examination, to be nothing else than the stability, the unity, and the durable character of the group. Honor demands of the individual those kinds of conduct which promote these ends of his society. Since conformity to this demand acquires, on the one hand, an ideal worth, so ideal and so powerful at the same time that honor is preferred to life; since the preservation of honor, on the other hand, has very sensible pleasurable effects upon the individual, and its loss produces equally keen pains, it comes about that honor constitutes an extraordinarily close bond between the whole group and its elements. Accordingly honor is one of the most thorough means of maintaining the existence and specific significance of the group" (1898, 682–83).

above illustrated that STOP and the Catholic Worker were better thought of as change-oriented pockets of organization formed in response to obstacles, or slower-moving constraining dynamics[10] that were stable enough for a single thread of history to develop across time. Goffman writes that personal identity is a product of the assumption that individuals could be differentiated from all others, and this assumed difference would become the candy floss to which a single continuous record of social facts could be attached (1986, 57). We can think of groups in much the same way. Quite literally, the groups were the process of referencing and updating their histories of obstacles to anticipate future action.[11] Individual processes influence, but do not determine, the group-level process, just as external and material issues influence, but do not determine, the group-level process. This combination of openness and independence from any one social force enables groups to be important sites for innovations.[12]

What we generally think of as "groups" periodically move between different patterns of organization: entities that are sources of action within fields of action, contentious fields of action, or coalitions of instrumental relations focused on distant goals. This is to say that at different moments, a group operates as an entity, coalition, or field. For example, at

10. Looking to how emotional histories are embedded in stories thus provides tools for anticipating how groups' collective representations shift across time, reconstituting boundaries and criteria for success (Eliasoph and Lichterman 2003; Polletta 2006; Taylor and Rupp 2002). In a chapter on social movement groups, Fine and Sandstrom suggest that social movements generate two distinct styles of groups: inward-looking ones focused on small working groups and outward-looking ones that operate as a headquarters with an extended membership that only gets together on occasions for particular events (1993). We could anticipate that inward-focused groups might have trajectories similar to the characteristics of the Catholic Worker community, including a relatively fast feel, fuzziness about the group's sense of history, and difficulty coordinating with other groups. On the other hand, outward-focused groups may share some of STOP's characteristics, such as a slower sense of time for those working at the center than for those working at the margins, clear status distinctions, and an emphasis on coordinating and networking with other groups. These types of groups would be more likely to continue to seek stability through rigidity and continue to slow because the tentative stability of dissimilar positions and perspectives creates a tendency to protect against the potential for any disturbance (Simmel 1898, 831–32). We could anticipate that as diversity increased, such groups' responses to obstacles would ironically become increasingly conservative.

11. Phenomenologists have argued that an observer creates the persistence of both themselves and the observed within a particular temporal field by drawing on memory to focus their attention and anticipate action (Husserl [1893–1907] 1991, 55; Merleau-Ponty 1962, 34–35, 478; Schutz 1962, 42, 51). Attention creates a field out of which meaningful experiences are possible. Husserl points out that if one listens to a melody as an intentional act, then the experience of the entirety of the melody is the act of perception. However, if we are listening to a tone within the melody, then the experience of the tone is perception while it lasts, at which point it becomes retained for as long as it remains meaningful in some way ([1893–1907] 1991, 40). These acts of perception then shape future acts of attention.

12. For example, Fine and Harrington note that the tactical innovations associated with the civil rights movement were developed by small groups responding to local conditions (2004, 346).

times the Worker house and STOP were entities acting as unified centers of action. At other times, they were made up of multiple centers, each working to dominate or force the others out. And at still other times, they were composed of multiple centers working together to exert force against a distant obstacle.

Observation of these two groups over time provides a picture of groups as cycling centers of action that evolve through these phases of organization in response to the continual reconciling of culture and immediate context across the duration of a pattern. The groups' histories of moving through such phase transformations created the rhythms of their involvement.

As the earlier chapters illustrate, the groups focused their attention in anticipation of future environmental conditions. They did not passively experience the environment; in fact, the capacity to actively engage the environment gave shape and meaning to their environments. After each collapse, new attraction had to be reestablished if the groups were to survive failure. Recovery was not a return to equilibrium; it was an adequate release from the forces that threatened to destroy continued involvement. If involvement reemerged, modified cycles were ancestors of earlier patterns; the collapse remained as a "not" tagging in the new pattern, a warning that established a wider field of potential transgressions to anticipate and avoid. Each storm they weathered reduced flexibility and created a tighter relationship to history. Patterns of action stabilized when anticipation shunted action into increasingly well-worn paths; in other words, patterns emerged from within the group in response to its local history of collapse.[13] The longer the history, the tighter the loop. Thus the groups' ideological commitments and successes pulled them into involvement, but stability was the product of their histories of failures, both survived and anticipated.

The stories illustrate how obstacles did not always lead to the collapse of action and meanings. Disturbances were absorbed until a threshold was reached; beyond this threshold, patterns of action and the meaning

13. Understanding the area of the group that will be the least responsive to change (thus aspects of group involvement that were most likely to create points of friction in response to a continually shifting environment) requires knowledge of the location of a group's outside frame, the most basic and stable expectations for focus and emotional tone that the group draws on to negotiate and make sense of their environment. We should not make the mistake of assuming that this always will be physically farther away, because imagination can anchor one's experience far away from one's physical environment. For example, STOP's slowest-moving frame was at the physical center of the group and focused on the internal maintenance of the group. This is why the analogy of the organism, with the image of firm exterior and fluid internal processes, is not adequate for the understanding of social organization. Indeed, STOP illustrates how organization can be the exact opposite.

of symbols shifted like phase transitions, changing the entire layout of the cycle of involvement. This disconnect between the groups' stories that informed their strategies for negotiating their environment and the unfolding context in which they enacted the strategies scored the social landscape by dragging history through these emerging contexts. By referencing history, they carved paths that constrained the flow of action. Chapter 3 illustrates how these paths were sensitive to external factors. This chapter illustrates that as these paths developed history, they became increasingly sensitive to internal factors as well. Thus as organization proceeded, the groups encountered increasing numbers of obstacles, further narrowing the available paths to action and increasing vulnerability to external obstacles. Eventually, like a dam that ruptures, paths collapsed, freeing up action to flow into new streams. Thus, groups' stories about themselves evolved in fits and starts.[14]

The moments between the creation of a path and its collapse marked the duration of both the pattern of action and the meanings that sustained it. These were the periods when expectations and strategies looped back and constrained unfolding action; the loops only shaped future loops in limited ways: by locating the next loop's origins in a specific social and physical space, by bringing particular physical material to that moment, and by carrying a certain amount of momentum from past movement.

Over time internal organization became more rigid and less responsive to environmental fluctuations, so that the centers of action maintained status as entities and their position in the field at the cost of depleting energy—more energy was consumed preserving stability than the groups were able to pull in from their environment. These periods of stability were like stretching rubber bands; potential energy built as the tolls of absorbing environmental disturbances mounted. Eventually, tensions building from within pulled the groups toward collapse. There appeared to be a readiness for, if not a motivation toward, destruction, freedom, and release.[15] Both success and collapse released the tension of these emotional vacuums, but only collapse destroyed past patterns and, thereby,

14. Whereas Bergson ([1912] 1999, 26) has described the unfolding of consciousness as the unrolling of a coil across time, Whitehead describes experience as accumulating along certain lines until it reaches its limits, and this creates the experience of duration (1978, 47). Drawing upon Mead's notion of a "specious present," Abbott illustrates how shifting the conditions that link the past and present creates turning points in the conditional, relational history that actors invoke across time (2001b, 228). Zerubavel similarly describes the flow of time as uneven (1981, 111).

15. This may be similar to the dynamic that Freud ([1920] 1990) refers to as the death instinct.

released some of the pull of history as well.[16] Failure was "the kinetic phase which mark[ed] the release of energies that are restrained in ordered intervals of rest" (Dewey 1959, 189). Chapter 3 illustrates how the drama of collapse could propel future organization and stability if the groups reestablished involvement.[17]

The tension of impending and actual collapse can preserve organization throughout the cycle of involvement by maintaining or repeatedly reestablishing a shared focus of attention and a pull toward involvement.[18] Or collapse can propel constituent elements out of a center with a strength that rivals the peak of attraction into involvement. Thus, collapse opens up new possibilities for involvement,[19] but it is volatile. This volatility could fuel intense new involvement, if a group is able to attract that new involvement under new conditions before members are taken up in a different pattern of action. These moments present genuine risks for the continued persistence of a group, especially if members are involved in other more compelling centers of action.

This chapter, which generally describes how stability is born of an attempt to anticipate and avoid past threats, also illustrates how groups experience milder moments of relative attraction and repulsion throughout any given day. The absorption of mild disturbances, mini collapses, and reemergence could follow one another, creating a meta-stability of organization. Thus, stability itself is made up of oscillating patterns of involvement.[20] The repetition of more routine adjustments during the

16. The longer the duration of local history embedded in an interaction, the more abstract and concretized the context of the interaction feels. The longer history gives more weight to established patterns and expectations. In other words, longer durations undercut the sense of emergence in interactions.

17. Dewey describes this: "Contrast of lack and fullness, of struggle and achievement, of adjustment after consummated irregularity, form the drama in which action, feeling, and meaning are one. The outcome is balance and counterbalance. These are not static nor are they mechanical. They express power that is intense because they are measured through overcoming resistance" (Dewey 1959, 16).

18. Simmel similarly argues, "These also plainly need the stimulus of difference in order to retain and protect their unity. Now this difference may reside either within the relationship itself, in the different characteristics of its temporal divisions, or in the difference which appears between the relationship as a whole and, on the other hand, experiences and emotions quite outside of it" (1898, 47).

19. When organization narrowed to the point that internal dynamics seriously constrained the potential for experience of expansion, imagined or real threats may be the strongest forces holding a center of action together as an actor in a field. As organization neared collapse, the pull toward involvement temporarily increased, reflexivity diminished, and organization decreased slightly as energy was mobilized to defend against extreme threats to established patterns.

20. Dewey describes this process, stating, "Direct experience comes from nature and man interacting with each other. In this interaction, human energy gathers, is released, dammed up, frustrated and victorious. There are rhythmic beats of want and fulfillment, pulses of doing and being withheld from doing" (1939, 15).

stability part of their cycles of involvement creates the emotional rhythms of everyday life.[21]

This comparison of the long-term evolution of emotional dynamics suggests how groups' histories of challenges, collapse, and recovery shift their foci of attention, emotional styles, and speed of interaction. These, in turn, establish the momentum and direction of the evolution of strategies within groups and thus the influence of the future conditions they encounter. Fine (1979) notes the importance of studying interaction for understanding culture as a process. Indeed, studying interactions over time illustrates culture as a temporal process and suggests how and when particular elements of local cultural processes become central to the persistence and transformation of cultural forms.

Although social theory is generally predicated on an assumption of stable motivations for action, we cannot say that actors are solely motivated by emotional, rational, self-consistent, or self-destructive drives. Nor can we simply argue that actors are motivated by all of these drives. In order to understand an actor's motivations in any particular moment, social scientists need to understand the evolution of an actor's cycle of organization, the speed and rhythm of the actor's cycle of organization, and when a moment falls within the larger cycles organizing an actor's action.[22] The stories throughout this volume suggest that at any one moment in a particular field of action, an actor will be motivated by different drives.[23]

The moments when new strategies are born are the ones that are the closest to being driven by rational choice motivations. However, once strategies are formed, they stand in for direct positive and negative experiences of the environment. The capacity for memory and generalization precipitate a second-order desire for stability. Thus, as soon as an actor begins to act according to reflexive strategies, the desire for expansion is balanced against the desire to affirm an actor's understanding of both its environment and itself. In other words, during the most stable periods of action, the actor is motivated by a drive toward self-consistency.

21. Although these overarching rhythms may unfold over months or even years, insiders will see cycles of organization, collapse, and recovery that happen over weeks, days, or even hours. Outsiders and newcomers often can only pick up on the more dramatic cycles where the persistence of the group as a center of action is at stake.

22. Weber's types of action ([1914] 1978) motivate behavior at different times, and we can see that they are cyclically bound to each other. From the perspective of cyclically organized action, the question should not be whether or not action is driven by one type or another; the question is about when certain types of action are likely.

23. As Dewey has pointed out, in a gender-exclusive fashion, "the rhythm of loss of integration with environment and recovery of union not only persists in man but becomes conscious with him; its conditions are the material out of which he forms purposes" (1934, 17).

The Experience of Time Shifts with the Cycle of Organization

Organization, expansion, stability, and reemergence focused the groups' attention in different ways, and these differences shaped their perception of time. Encounters with obstacles demanded focus and involvement; more mundane moments required less intense involvement. Fast-moving and uncertain scenes generated feelings of expansion and absorbed attention, creating a sense of timelessness that felt elongated. As with the risks that generated feelings of expansion, extreme threats that ended in collapse absorbed attention and felt timeless, so that the final moments before collapse might have felt like the longest hour, day, or fifteen minutes ever. By narrowing focus so that neither the past nor the future was particularly meaningful, expansion and destruction were both experienced as sacred moments out of time, despite the fact that they were organized in different ways. These moments were risky, and as Goffman points out, uncertain or risky moments bring an actor into a special relationship with time (1967, 261), so that seconds and minutes stretch out as moments of uncertainty, piggybacking on each other, and all time becomes eventful. On the other hand, time slowed during periods of stability, when involvement in these groups was grounded in reflexivity and historical referencing.[24]

Movement through the cycle of expansion, contraction, stability, collapse, and reemergence created an uneven sense of time.[25] *Internal tensions*—such as periodic tensions between opportunities for expansion and the need for food, sleep, work, or quiet—and *external constraints*, such as limited resources, push actors through the cycle of organization. When actors confront these obstacles at regular intervals, patterns of emotional and temporal experiences emerge. In other words, patterns of obstacles generate emotional and temporal rhythms. Thus, as Abbott points out, the experience of duration is encoded in the constraints of social organization in that moment (2001b, 235). As Lefebvre notes, rhythm is a sense of time that has a momentum that compels regulated involvement through

24. The intermittent historical focus slows the experience of time as it unfolds, but speeds it up during reflection because absorbing involvement is less frequent. As James explains, "A time filled with varied and interesting experiences seems short in passing, but long as we look back. On the other hand, a tract of time empty of experiences seems long in passing, but in retrospect short" (1890, 150).

25. Lefebvre notes that the distinction between regular periods of breaks, resumptions, and intervals created a differentiated time, a qualified duration (2004, 78). Similarly, Jasper notes, "History seems to move faster at some times than at others, not just species evolution but also political history may be a series of 'punctuated equilibria'" (1997, 22).

non-rational means (2004, 9).[26] Indeed, the groups' emotional rhythms had the capacity to draw involvement into synchronization over time. By doing so, the groups' emotional rhythms reached forward and backward in time (Husserl [1893–1907] 1991), and in and out in space (Rappaport 1999, 228), to create the sense that the group was a bounded entity that endured across time. Thus, the groups' experiences of unexpected obstacles, and the intense focus and strong emotions that they generated, created the groups' sense of their overall duration, as well as the duration of particular periods or eras within the groups (for example. the "Phil and Jean era" in the Worker house and the "Doreen era" in STOP).

We can imagine a continuum with quick durations and tight, intense involvement on one end, and longer durations and loose, cool involvement at the other end.[27] As discussed in chapter 3, a group's focus is shaped by its experience of control. The group's history of control determines the frequency and regularity at which epochs of stability turn over. That is to say, the tempo and rhythm of involvement in a group varied with its experiences of control across time.[28] The distance of a group's focus of attention and its emotional history—that is, the style of its control projects—determines the strength and frequency of the disruptions it encounters, and thus the intensity, tempo, and rhythm of the group's involvement.[29]

26. Lefebvre describes how obstacles create rhythmic patterns thusly, "Everywhere where there is interaction between space, time and an expenditure of energy, there is **rhythm** (bold in the original). Therefore: a) repetition (of movements, gestures, action, situations, differences); b) interferences of linear processes and cyclical processes; c) birth growth, peak, then decline and end" (bold in the original; 2004, 15).

27. I use "speed" to refer to a relative relationship between the groups that comes closer to being captured by objective clock time—do the groups generally consider the future to mean five minutes or five months? Does a lot happen in five minutes, or does very little happen in five days? These questions cannot be answered objectively. There are an infinite number of events happening in every moment; only our attention can explain the duration of our experiences, and our experiences are always grounded in history (Husserl [1893–1907] 1991, 25; Whitehead 1978).

28. Control was a sense of being over and against outside conditions, thus their sense of control was predicated on their experience of both the internal status of themselves as an object in relation to their environment, and objects in the environments as objects in relation to them as actors (White 1992, 11). The groups' experiences of control were not just registered cognitively; they were also registered and remembered bodily. By "bodily," I mean any of the senses that we use to filter our environment in order to create meaningful information for ourselves. We anticipate and imagine with far more than our conscious reflexive minds that we too often assume are at the center of the action (Lizardo 2004; Wacquant 2004). For example, emotional and mystical experiences are often more accurately communicated in literature than in academic texts (McRoberts 2004), but an apparent gap between religious experience, especially mystical experience, and academic discussions of these experiences remains.

29. Kanter argues that groups seeking to preserve community while providing a service will require multiple and incompatible forms of organization. She suggests that this dynamic forces groups to narrow their focus (1972, 149). This book supports her argument, but additionally illustrates how tension also generates cycles of action as a group moves between competing demands. Negotiat-

The Catholic Workers' more frequent encounters with obstacles generated intensity and a much faster tempo of involvement than experienced in STOP. On the other hand, the increasingly longer durations between STOP's encounters with obstacles reduced their intensity and generated an increasingly broad and slow involvement. Thus, the Catholic Workers' cycles of involvement were much faster than STOP's.[30] In the case of STOP, success in creating change beyond their borders pulled their focus away from the group, while continual limits of the Catholic Workers to influence their environment in perceptible ways pulled their focus in toward the center of the group. By shifting its focus away from its center, STOP approached the slower speed of the obstacles in their environment, namely, the political world, and became increasingly rigid.[31] The Catholic Workers, on the other hand, would intermittently take on overwhelming projects and then recover by tightening their focus to speed their involvement back up.[32]

The speed of involvement affected the groups' experience of time as well as the stability of their expectations for interaction, emotional tone, and meaning. The Workers' faster cycles supported flexibility in the face of environmental changes. Their more fluid style enabled them

---

ing these transitions while maintaining efforts toward self-consistency (Robinson and Smith-Lovin 1992) is the backbone of the groups' emotion work.

30. For example, the dynamics in chapters 2 and 3 unfold over successively longer periods of time (chapter 2 illustrates the micro-dynamics of expansion that pull actors into involvement; chapter 3 illustrates recovery following contraction and the pull away from involvement). However, the dynamic in chapter 4, the cycle of involvement, unfolds over yet a longer time in STOP but not in the Catholic Worker house. James suggests that the mystical awe that the Catholic Worker community often relied upon to recover from failure can only be sustained for brief durations. Therefore we could anticipate that in general groups that buoy themselves emotionally with mystical states will develop faster cycles of involvement than groups that use righteous anger to recover from drains ([1902] 2007, 73).

31. Being at the slower unmoving center or periphery is less intense than the faster involvement of uncertainty. Faster tempos of organization indicate involvement closer to uncertain action. If "success" is defined as a sense of influence, thus power and control, we can see how achieving influence but not the stated goal could be emotionally unsatisfying.

32. Simmel long ago noted these two general approaches through which groups preserve themselves. "The group may be preserved, (1) by conserving with the utmost tenacity its firmness and rigidity of form, so that the group may meet approaching dangers with substantial resistance, and may preserve the relation of its elements through all change of external conditions; (2) by the highest possible variability of its form, so that adaptation of form may be quickly accomplished in response to change of external conditions, so that the form of the group may adjust itself to any demand of circumstances" (1898, 831). Allen and Starr similarly note that actors adapt to obstacles by speeding up or slowing down (1982, 67). The stories in this volume illustrate how slowing down makes a group more rigid and capable of defending itself within the same field as the obstacle, and speeding up makes the group more flexible so that the obstacle has less influence on the group. Thus they add to Simmel's and Allen and Starr's work by explaining how and why groups develop either of these two styles of preservation.

to maintain stability of meaning, particularly for those inside the group, but led to very little consistency in action.[33] STOP's slower emotional cycles made them more rigid, so they were able to absorb the influence of environmental changes for longer periods of time before their patterns of action changed. This allowed them to stabilize their patterns of action, but the meaning of this action for both those inside and outside STOP was less stable.[34]

Faster speeds and slower speeds generated different risks for maintaining involvement. For example, the Workers risked implosion. Binding ties could also become claustrophobic. Worker involvement was so narrow and intense that single random spikes in environmental fluctuation, like illness or the loss of one patron, could tip and destroy the pattern altogether. However, the Workers could risk more frequent internal conflict and collapse than STOP could because they were physically bound together.

STOP's slow speed meant low intensity for those who were involved, so low that even small environmental fluctuations undermined the involvement. Although breadth helped ensure that each particular STOP worker was replaceable, small distractions (beautiful weather, other groups' meetings, or even a good conversation) pulled STOP's employees and volunteers away from mundane tasks. Their relatively loose coalition structure put them at lesser risk of fracturing under sudden pressure, but at greater risk of losing any particular member to other actions.[35]

33. See Borer (1996, 137) for discussion of the power of religiously motivated political action that is not dependent on achieving noticeable outcomes.

34. James describes the wearing out that was visible among STOP's members in his description of action that is motivated by a moral rather than religious commitment. "The moralist must hold his breath and keep his muscles tense; and so long as this athletic attitude is possible all goes well—morality suffices. But the athletic attitude tends ever to break down, and it inevitably does break down even in the most stalwart when the organism begins to decay, or when morbid fears invade the mind. To suggest personal will and effort to one all sicklied o'er with the sense of irremediable impotence is to suggest the most impossible of things. . . . And whenever we feel this, such a sense of the vanity and provisionality of our voluntary career comes over us that all our morality appears but as a plaster hiding a sore it can never cure, and all our well-doing as the hollowest substitute for that well-BEING that our lives ought to be grounded in, but alas! are not" (emphasis in original; [1902] 2007, 55).

35. Simmel has described this balance: "On the other hand, the persistence of the group depends on the fact that the organ thus differentiated does not attain *absolute* independence. Rather must the idea remain ever operative (although by no means always conscious) that the organ is in fact only a corporealized abstraction of the reciprocal action within the group itself. The group remains always the foundation. Its powers, developments, purposes, only receive a peculiarly practical form in the organs. The latter only exhibit the mode in which the directly reciprocating primary elements of the group may work out their latent energies most completely and efficiently. So soon as the differentiation of the organ releases it from dependence upon the aggregate movements of the group, its preservative action may be turned into a destructive influence. I suggest two types of grounds for

Common sense suggests that ideological commitments and espoused goals might serve as good proxies for the distance of a social movement group's focus of attention. The above comparison of these two groups suggests that a group's focus of attention will follow its experience of control, not its hopeful goal.[36] For example, a researcher could be tempted to assume that a group organized around a particular zoning battle would have a closer focus of attention than a group generally committed to promoting a national socialist government. However, when goals are very distant and abstract, there seems to be a *paradoxical effect*. For example, despite the fact that the Catholic Workers' project would appear to be longer and thus their focus would be farther into the future, if not physically farther, the immediate uncertainty of their day-to-day lives highlighted the many obstacles between them and their ultimate goals. When they could not feed a family who asked for help, it was difficult for them to imagine the series of concrete actions required to achieve the revolution they envisioned.[37] STOP, alternately, had a history of internal conflict that discouraged a close focus. Improving political conditions also enabled them to envision a clear course of action to reach their goals. Both of these factors supported a distant focus and a slower tempo. Thus, the above stories provide a perspective where the unfolding history of paths to action, in particular the emotional implications of timing, determined action more directly than symbolic representation of local histories or a group's abstract ideological agenda. Yet it also is clear that these groups created their stories of themselves in relation to their ideological commitments, and these stories constrained their actions during routine times.

By paying attention to the ways in which local conditions shaped the groups' sense of control and the distance of their focus, we could imagine scenarios where the Catholic Workers might slow down and become less intense. This might happen, for example, if a large number of people joined the community or if the group suddenly became responsible for managing a large amount of resources. Similarly, we could imagine scenarios where STOP became much faster and more intense. A complete loss of funding and traditional political connections might have returned

---

this: First, when the organ gains too vigorous independent life, and does not place the emphasis of its importance upon the worth of its service to the group, but upon its value to itself, the persistence of the organ may come into conflict with the persistence of the group" (1898, 694–95).

36. Lichterman (1995) illustrates the limits of ideological convergence for understanding whether and how social movement groups can collaborate. As Simmel notes, the local logics that sustain a group tend to be only indirectly related to the group's explicit goals (1964, 35).

37. This may be a good definition of faith—a non-rational expectation that cannot be tied to a series of concrete actions.

STOP's focus to the process rather than the ends of organizing. The comparison of these two groups suggests how we could imagine a more general relationship between the speed and intensity of group involvement and a social movement group's environment: in other words, the conditions under which a group working for a particular cause would be able to anticipate long-term strategies and the conditions under which it would only be able to anticipate the following month, week, or even day.

Implications of the Speed and Rhythm of Involvement for Getting into a Group

The centers of these two groups not only moved at different speeds; they had different rhythmic qualities. Over time the groups' histories of obstacles created the tempo and rhythm of their involvement.[38] For example, the Catholic Workers' inconsistent resources and chaotic environment created comparatively unpredictable cycles of involvement. Stability in unpredictable circumstances looked more erratic, like putting out fires rather than engaging in predictable involvement. STOP's regularly scheduled vigils, office work, and meetings created a slow steady pulse of expansion and drain. Relatively consistent alignment between external forces produced periods of involvement with a rhythmic pulsing quality.

The groups' rhythms were the temporal orientations that were the higher-order contexts within which the groups negotiated symbolic meanings (Schutz 1962, 73–74, 76). Goffman uses the analogy of traffic laws to explain the flow of events that pass by during interactions (1967, 12, 9). Like merging onto an expressway,[39] actors must know more than how to drive the car and how to stay within the appropriate lines; actors must get up to the appropriate speed.[40] Being in sync or out of sync is the basis for much social organization.[41]

38. In ecology the length of time required to return to relative stability after a disturbance suggests either a system that operates near unstable equilibria, even at its most stable, or a weak repulsion from a nearby unstable system (Ludwig, Walker, and Holling 2002, 47).

39. Not all social action requires joining in an already established flow; sometimes new action takes off (White 1992, 315, 245; Goffman 1974, 251–60).

40. Just as the term implies, coordination requires timing (Berger and Luckmann 1967; Goffman 1967; Zerubavel 1981). Ultimately actors must accurately identify an opening in the flow of traffic. If one identifies an opening but merges at the wrong speed, there is at least a chance that an accident will be avoided. Whereas being off about an opening *is*, by definition, an accident (Fine 1990).

41. See Zerubavel (1981, 65), Fine (1990), Flaherty (2003), and Abbott (2005b, 254–55). Zerubavel points out that the creation of alternative self-subsistent worlds allows cloistered religious communities to pull themselves out of sync with the larger environment. Such distinctions strengthen divisions between insiders and outsiders (Lamont and Molnar 2002). Fine explains how organizations mediate workers' experience of the relationship between time and task, and in doing so shape workers' behavioral and emotional responses to their contexts (1990, 110).

The capacity to catch the rhythm of involvement and maintain the expected flow was far more fundamental in determining the success of an interaction than familiarity with the discursive content of an interaction. While the appropriate speed did not guarantee coordination, enduring successful coordination was impossible without getting up to the appropriate speed. These stories illustrate that threats to rhythm of involvement were far more emotionally significant than ideological transgressions. In fact, the above stories suggest that incompatible expectations for the speed of action marked the groups' most basic and emotionally charged boundaries (Goffman 1967, 11–12, 33).

For the past twenty years, the concept of framing has played the central role in cultural approaches to social movements. Most of this work has been based on Snow and Benford's work (1988) that draws on aspects of Goffman's frame analysis (1974).[42] All of the processes explained in this literature are highly cognitive and reflexive moves that explain ideological transformations and alliances—that is, how social movement participants or potential participants think about the world. However, the above stories suggest that *when* we look, whether into the future or the past, is more basic than the substance of *what* we look at. Thus cuing speed would be fundamental to any type of the more cognitive frame alignment processes (Zerubavel 1981, 66–67; Abbott 2005a, 254).

Simmel suggests that the immortality of a group depends upon its slowness and gradualness (1898, 662). This chapter reveals that this is true insofar as an observer will perceive a group as enduring when either a group's patterns of action or meaning change slowly and gradually from the observer's perspective. However, the stories also reveal how the perception of the speed of action varies with the location of the observer. For example, the differences in my experience can just as easily be explained by my different position within the two groups as it can be by the dynamics of the groups themselves. From a focus that produces the group as an entity, such as the focus at the Worker house, the center is fast and absorbing. Permeable boundaries slightly further out move more slowly and are less entraining. Beyond their boundaries, solid thing-like objects limit the group's paths to action within their unfolding environment. Farther yet are pockets of organization so distant that they appear not to exist. Since

42. Frame bridging involves linking two ideologically similar but practically unconnected frames. Frame amplification is calling attention to already existing values and placing more emphasis on them. Frame extension involves social movement organizations broadening their target issues to attract potential adherents. Finally, frame transformation refers to putting an entirely new spin on an existing framing of a situation so that it is perceived to have a totally different meaning. This type of frame alignment is similar to a conversion experience (Snow et al. 1986).

the Worker house was so centered in a physical space, merely being there physically pulled me into much of the entraining action.

In coalitions the action is rarely as fast as it is in entities. The center moves slowly. The fastest action is at the boundary of the coalition; this is where the members can potentially create new connections. Coalition members focus attention beyond the unfolding interaction, often physically beyond, where all of the action appears to be. New connections generate a first-order sense of expansion between the coalition member and the external actor and a second-order sense of expansion between coalition members for involvement in expanding the coalition. From the center, the action appears to be moving away. From the fast-moving rim, the center appears to be standing still. Ethnographers talk about gaining access to a field site as "getting in," suggesting that the center is where the action can be found. However, the most intense action is only at the center in scenes that are operating as entities. In coalitions, the center is slow, and the action is at the margins.

If social scientists are interested in the dynamics that motivate the formation of the symbolic, reflexive, and conscious meanings that people are literally able to tell us about, we should focus on understanding the emotional dynamics that shape actors' focus of attention and rhythm of involvement. As the above stories illustrate, the rhythm and tempo of actors' unfolding histories shape perception and action more directly than symbolic representation of local histories, much less abstract ideological agendas. Indeed, the emotional consequences of actors' history of control over their environment largely shape the patterns and ranges of particular actors' temporal focus of attention, in other words, the formation and collapse of social organization. The perspective offered here helps us to understand apparently irrational rigidity, or how a threat is easily absorbed at one time but is experienced as catastrophic at another. It also shifts our focus from arguments about the causal authority of either cognition or emotion to asking questions such as: How do different tempos for action emerge and change? What happens when actors fail to recognize or are not able to adjust to the appropriate speed for action?

Emotional Trajectories: The Acceleration or Deceleration
of Emotional Dynamics

Over time the Catholic Workers' and STOP's histories of challenges and their responses became the *trajectories* of their involvement, while the unfolding cycles of involvement generated the *tempo* of their emotional rhythms.[43] Both groups continued to respond to obstacles as they had in the past, by either speeding up or slowing down, until a particular duration of activity in the two groups ended by slowly dying out or collapsing. These groups' trajectories of involvement reflected their experiences of control over time, or in other words, their histories of control. Chapter 3 illustrates how the groups' foci of attention reflected their past limits of control. An increasing sense of control drew STOP's attention farther from it, and a diminishing sense of control pulled the Workers' attention closer to it.

The Workers' involvement moved through frequent cycles. At points, it followed a trajectory of broadening its influence and slowing down until it collapsed; at other points, it followed a trajectory of narrowing, speeding up, and intensifying until either its insularity threatened to cut it off from necessary resources, or the emotional intensity of interactions within the group threatened to burn it out. The Workers' self-correction often resulted in the group swinging from one trajectory to the other. The shorter duration of any one of the Workers' trajectories meant that involvement was faster, and there was a narrower range of action over time.

STOP's involvement slowed down, and its intensity diminished as its history of increasing control continued to draw its attention farther away from its physical center. Thus, if STOP were to continue on the course it set, it would either collapse and regain some intensity of involvement by reorganizing at a faster speed, or it would slowly die out as the intensity required to maintain involvement continued to drop off.[44]

A comparison of these groups suggests that if we want to find the tempo and trajectory of involvement in such groups, we should look at their histories of obstacles and how the groups' sense of control over their environment has shaped how far their attention extends into their immediate environment, and how far their attention extends into both the past and future.[45] The stories throughout all of the previous chapters

43. Zerubavel explains that "*the temporal regularity of our everyday life world is definitely among the major background expectancies which are at the basis of the 'normalcy' of our social environment*" (1981, 21; emphasis in the original). Bourdieu ties control of temporal dynamics to the construction of legitimate power: "Recognition of legitimacy is . . . rooted in the immediate agreement between the incorporated structure, turned into practical schemes, such as those which organize temporal rhythms . . ." (2000, 177).

44. James Wilson lists three causes of organization change: increase in resources, loss of resources, and uncertainty in the flow of resources (1995, 209–10). As the stories above reveal, STOP experienced all of them within the group's first few years. Prior to 9/11, STOP experienced an unanticipated influx of resources when they successfully secured grant money. The group also experienced periods of scarce recourses, particularly after 9/11. Finally, uncertainty in the flow of their resources created a boom/bust type of atmosphere.

45. Nippert-Eng notes that "mental, categorical boundaries are reflected in the boundaries we place around time and space" (1995, 289).

support Gibson's assertion that senses are trained through experience, so that actors with differing histories will have differing sensory experiences[46] in the exact same environment and, in this case, different emotions. By learning how and when to focus their attention, these groups learned to detect subtle shifts in particular relational conditions, regardless of whether or not they were able to remember or articulate the specific moments that were crucial for developing these greater sensitivities. Absent a direct observation of a group's entire history, a shorter observation of their emotional dynamics, the particular emotions at play, and how and when they shift in response to environmental fluctuation over time would offer a revealing window into the speed and trajectory of involvement in such a group.

As discussed in chapter 2, emotion can be thought of as social proprioception, a sensory experience of an actor's social relation to other actors in the particular social field. Emotion indicated the groups' positions, orientations, and movements in relation to a center of action. The immediate relational conditions may determine whether an environment affords the potential for intense involvement or even the potential for experiencing particular emotions, but groups' longer-term and immediate emotional histories shape how they will respond to these affordances.[47]

The order and intensity of emotions convey much about a history of relations between a group and its environment. The groups' evolving styles exhibited hysteresis, a phenomenon in which the response of a physical system to an external influence depends not only on the present magnitude of that influence but also on the previous history of the system. This dynamic has been identified in basic individual-level perceptual dynamics, and it can be seen here that it operates at the group level as well. For example, the groups experienced different emotional outcomes when an expectation of success was followed by failure, rather than when an expectation for failure was followed by failure.[48]

Knowledge of the groups' trajectories of involvement is also crucial for identifying the limits of the groups' ranges of involvement. Only knowl-

46. Gibson suggests that proprioception, or the sense of an actor's orientation in relation to the environment, is only possible over time—or in other words, in acts of perception that depend on a sense of duration. In fact, many stimuli can only be detected in a pattern across multiple senses, thus they are only possible through the training of attention over time (1966, 38, 270). Schutz likewise states that the unity of the act is the span or breadth of the project and that this unity is not determined by the act as an external object separate from the observer but through the observer's direction of attention (1962, 63).

47. As Husserl suggests, "Every change has its rate or acceleration of change (to use an image) with respect to the same duration" ([1893–1907] 1991, 78).

48. To put the argument in ethnomethodological terms, emotions not only have adjacent indexicality; they have historical indexicality.

edge of a group's emotional trajectory, whether they had been slowing down or speeding up, would reveal whether a particular failure marked the inside or outside boundary of a group's range of attention; in other words, whether a group collapsed because it became too intense and narrow or because it became too bland and broad. If a group slowed down after a failure, it would be reasonable to consider that the failure marked the perceived inside limit of the group's focus of attention, or the closest they could focus their attention and endure. If a group sped up in response, the failure may have marked the outside limit of the group's focus of attention, or the farthest they could focus without losing the minimum intensity required to hold the group together. Indeed, beyond shaping how attractive or satisfying a group would find particular emotional affordances, their history would determine whether they would even notice them.

Expectations for Focus of Attention and Emotional Tone Can Reinforce Patterns of Persistent Inequality

These stories illustrate how actors' differing positions in relation to their groups' histories can generate conflicting perceptions of situations. Differing positions in relation to patterns of persistent inequality can unintentionally reproduce enduring patterns of inequality. For example, the Catholic Workers understood themselves to be deeply committed to addressing racial and ethnic inequality. They talked routinely about the incarceration rates of African American males, police profiling, and the rates of poverty among racial and ethnic minorities. They participated in public actions against racial discrimination. However, in spite of the Workers' critiques of racial and ethnic inequality, they insisted that "color-blindness" was possible in interaction.

The Workers' radically local focus allowed race to disappear as a meaningful category, despite its implications for the people with whom they lived and served. Their "color-blind" approach indeed blinded them to their guests' and neighbors' personal histories of racial injustice in interactions and to many of the ways in which larger patterns of racial and ethnic inequality were shaped by such personal histories.[49] For example, Joan talked about her frustration with a friend of theirs from the neighborhood who taught her kids that they should avoid White people because White people would not respect them. Linda complained that their parish offered retreats specifically for African American prisoners,

49. Becker similarly finds, "Personalism, here, bracketed off the hard issues of structural inequality and group-based interests that must be confronted head-on if our society is to achieve political, not just residential or social, integration" (1998, 470).

saying that doing so only highlighted differences when everyone should be recognizing what they had in common.[50]

Likewise, STOP's focus on distant dynamics contributed to their inability to see the gender inequality unfolding right in front of them. STOP, with its external goals of political influence and increased membership, placed a premium on unique networks and information. High-status members focused more of their time and energy on the more exciting activities, while the lower-status members did the bulk of the draining mundane work. Without access to the excitement at the outer boundaries of the group, involvement eventually wore thin for those in the middle of the group. Marge, Todd, and others could feel like conquering heroes when they secured new support or beat an opponent in a political battle, but those focused entirely on the center of the group, the mundane office activity that supported the leaders, eventually burnt out.

Because of the division of labor within STOP, the group's external focus supported emotional expectations that privileged the men on the staff over the women.[51] Particular styles of interaction that appeared to be gender neutral put the women staff, who were primarily responsible for the routine draining tasks associated with running the office, at a serious emotional disadvantage. When the entire staff was gathered, women generally performed the expected interaction and emotion styles, but when they were alone, they openly defied these patterns. When they were backstage, their talk with each other was openly emotional, solidarity seeking, and filled with laughter. On the occasions when Todd would talk to the women staff members about problems with his kids or a girlfriend, the women would help him save face and offer emotional support, all the while covering his breach of the general expectations that staff members would not seek emotional support from each other.[52]

---

50. Diana Hayes, a scholar of African American Catholicism, suggests that "all too often persons of faith have been silent, as hard-won gains towards racial equality are being nullified and labeled preferential treatment" (1998, 5). This story about the Catholic Workers suggests how, beyond remaining silent, well-intentioned persons acting on their faith may inadvertently *contribute* to this nullification. This work here illustrates how maintaining a tight focus on personal responsibility and morality can undermine the ability to see the consequence of systematic and institutionalized racial inequality for any particular person.

51. Weber notes "the influence of women only tended to intensify those aspects of the religion that were emotional or hysterical" ([1951] 1978, 153). The implied essentialist understanding of gender and the term "hysterical" are clearly offensive to modern sensibilities. However, his gender distinction would make sense in so far as gender dynamics keep women's focus comparatively closer than men's. That is to say, if the men were trained to maintain a more distant focus than women, we could anticipate that women might have negotiated and amplified emotional dynamics with relative ease compared to men.

52. Taylor (1995) and Staggenborg (1995) have written about emotional expectations in feminist groups as a form of resistance in and of itself. These stories suggest exactly why this form of resis-

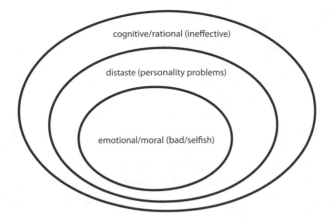

Figure 4.3 Relationship between social distance and evaluations of threatening action.

These stories suggest the dynamics by which well-intentioned people inadvertently reproduce the very inequality that they revile. By splitting their focus between local action and their distant relationships to global injustice or the divine, the Workers tended to miss the forest for the trees. In contrast, STOP's focus on growing their networks and political influence meant that STOP's leaders tended to miss the trees for the forest.[53] The differences between perspectives often persisted unnoticed, especially by those who occupied advantaged positions. When conflict halted the patterns that benefited the privileged in the groups, those with more power often felt betrayed because it appeared that those with less power had been "fake," meaning that the powerful actors assumed that their interactions with the less powerful actors were based in personal motivations, not motivations to avoid threats and losses. When such misunderstandings came to light, the emotional distress of the more powerful actors obscured *how* the conflicts that reproduced enduring inequality emerged. Instead, the more powerful actors tended to credit the conflict to the moral failings of those who were less powerful, by framing these conflicts as products of "personality problems."

tance would be appealing and important on an interaction level, even if it appears to be politically insignificant to those focused on inequality more easily recognized from a distance.

53. The fact that the Workers benefited from race privilege in interaction and STOP leaders benefited from gender privilege in interaction no doubt played a role in the dynamics to which they chose to pay attention. Undoubtedly, my own race and gender identities played a central part in what I saw and what felt important to me. For example, although there were moments at the Worker house when I felt that I deeply identified with guests or neighbors, there were plenty of moments that reminded me that the people who came for help rarely forgot the difference in power between helper and the helped.

Conclusion

The groups' expectations for interaction were based in their histories, so they rarely, if ever, fit the groups' immediate situations. For example, the Catholic Workers responded to numerous failed projects by developing aversions to righteous anger and planning. They learned to avoid focusing on the outcomes for particular neighbors or guests; instead, they focused either on the immediate environment or on their relationship to history or to the divine. STOP, on the other hand, had a history of internal conflicts; its leaders resisted any effort to focus the group's attention on internal processes. STOP's leaders responded to past threats by ignoring the internal running of the group and focusing on building their political influence.

Every failure the groups survived contributed to the increasingly elaborate set of shared expectations for how to avoid future failures. Subtle daily threats accumulated over time, creating increasingly complex labyrinths of expectations and prohibitions for emotion management within the groups. Strategies became denser, clumsier, and less rational as they became less responsive to the immediate context. As the groups lost flexibility, they lost both their agility for avoiding unanticipated conflicts and failures, and their ability to take advantage of unanticipated opportunities. Eventually the groups' strategies for avoiding threats became so elaborate that they went into energy debt anticipating and recovering from inevitable environmental disturbances. As energy dwindled, disruptions that once would have been brief repulsions or momentary dips became serious threats to continued involvement. Eventually the groups' increasingly elaborate strategies to avoid collapse *destabilized* the groups.

Observation over time provides a view of groups as cycling centers of action where patterns evolved from the continual reconciling of history and immediate context. These groups persisted by either forestalling collapse or developing tools to recover repeatedly from collapse. That is to say that the groups recovered by slowing to undermine the influence of past constraints, or speeding up the cycle of collapse and recovery so that a previously constraining force became irrelevant to involvement (cf. Allen and Star 1982; Simmel 1964, 66). The *scale of constraints* and the *direction* created by the history of the patterns of recoveries determined the *speed* and *trajectory* of the groups' involvement. If we were to understand the processes organizing these groups from inside the groups as they unfolded, the Catholic Worker house would feel like a roller coaster full of hair-raising drops, sharp turns, and disorienting spirals. STOP would feel like a merry-go-round for those at the center, and like standing in line for the roller coaster for the leaders—there was a sense of waiting for impending excitement.

A comparison of these two groups suggests that if we want to anticipate a particular type of action or the general persistence of such groups, we first need to understand the groups' local histories and how they generate evolving patterns that shift at different rates and rhythms. The symbolic content, the meaning of particular symbols, and relations between actors continually shift due to the open nature of these cycling processes. For example, focus of attention shifted depending on position in the cycle, changing what the groups saw, and, thus, the logic that shaped their action. There were different people, expectations, and resources in different parts of the cycles. Meanings were most consistent during periods of stability, but after collapse emerging meanings bumped against the restrictions of prior assumptions. Even highly resilient meanings gave way so that the groups' expectations for interaction eventually reflected their local histories far more directly than their movements' cultural histories.

Sociologists tend to look at how ideas are embedded in structural relations or how structural relations are embedded in ideas. By taking up an evolving cycle-of-organization perspective, we can think about when one of these relationships will be more constraining than the other and how and when this can switch.[54] Due to the continuously shifting meaning of symbols, it was impossible to anticipate the future meaning of any symbol, although identifying the rhythm and tempo of group involvement enabled those involved to anticipate, with some accuracy, when meanings would be more predictable or volatile and open to environmental influence.

Although the specific content of meaning changed over time, the style of approaching the work and meaning-making changed more slowly and provided a sense of consistency in interaction, even in chaotic environments where the meaning of a particular symbol is subject to potentially radical change at any moment. In general, we could predict that due to the groups' foci of attention, shifts in macro-political trends would have a more direct effect on STOP because the group was focused directly on the field of politics. Whereas, gaining or losing a member would likely have had a more substantial effect on the Catholic Workers because of their focus on their daily interactions with each other and their neighbors. That is not to say that changes in the interactional environment would not affect liberal reform outcome-focused groups, or that shifts in the political environment would not affect radical lifestyle-focused groups.

54. Harrington and Fine (2000) have similarly argued that localized theories of group action provide opportunities for understanding the processes that account for variation, conflict, and change.

However, these factors are not likely to be as significant because they have less direct influence on the foci of the groups and thus the patterns of interaction that constitute the groups' activity.

The stories across the previous chapters similarly present a picture of persistence in social movement groups that might be better thought of as resilience. In the ecological literature, a system is judged resilient when it is capable of maintaining at least some structures and functions despite disturbances (Carpenter and Cottingham 2002, 59); in other words, when involvement continues despite disturbances and produces at least a temporary pattern of oscillating limit cycles.[55]

This is very much the way these groups persist. These groups took risks that sometimes ended in great successes and other times ended in tremendous failures. Failures exacted both material and emotional tolls on the groups. If they survived, they did so by recovering emotionally, adjusting their evolving stories of who they were in order to account for such failures, and setting a new course for success. Recovery was always temporary and history shaped both periods of stability and the paths to recovery. Thus history tempered the groups. The tempering left them either more flexible if they sped up or more brittle if they slowed down.

A comparison of the long-term evolution of emotional dynamics in these groups reveals how the histories of such groups influence their focus, emotional expectations, understandings of themselves, and speed, which in turn generates the influences of future conditions on such groups. The unfolding cycles of involvement generate emotional rhythms over time. Faster emotional cycles support such groups' flexibility in the face of environmental changes. These more fluid groups maintain stability of meaning, particularly for those inside the group, but maintain little consistency in action. Slower emotional cycles increase such groups' capacity to resist the influence of environmental changes. These more rigid groups maintain the same pattern of action, although the meaning of this pattern may change for both those inside and outside the group.

---

55. Social movement scholars have long noted the importance of cycles for social movement activity. Noting the central concept of cycles in the social movement literature (Meyer 1993; Oliver and Myers 2003; Staggenborg 1995; Tarrow 1994), Jasper calls for further theorizing the multiple dynamics shaping cycles of social movements (1997, 39). He offers resources, strategies, culture, and biography, as well as other derivative macro-dimensions, as dimensions that need to be integrated into a theory of protest. All of these various dimensions that he identifies become integrated if we look at how they drive each other in patterned ways over time.

FIVE

Conclusion: Toward a Fluid Theory of Social Organization

Conditions both inside and outside of the groups were never static, but the process of change itself developed a regular pattern within these groups. Through referencing their histories in order to avoid future obstacles, the groups created cycles of involvement.[1] Movement through these cycles generated a rhythm of organization. Although it was impossible to predict how the relations and meanings within and between the groups and their environments would change, identifying the groups' foci of attention and their tempos of involvement enabled me to anticipate how and when relations and meanings were likely to change.

1. It may seem as though this relationship between speed of organization and distance of focus is almost tautological—high speeds keep the focus close, and a close focus speeds up organization. Although the relationship is self-reproducing during the stable periods of social organization, the two factors do not reproduce each other ad infinitum. After the collapse of patterns following crisis, where the group learns to look sets the speed of interaction. Once the groups stabilized, their speed of interaction constrained the distance of the groups' focuses. Thus, distance and speed do not constrain each other indefinitely; like the meaning of symbols, the relationship between speed and distance of focus will remain relatively stable until an unexpected event cannot be absorbed. Lefebvre describes this relationship between time and space. The temporal aspect is derived from the cyclical nature of the cosmos—seasons, waves, tides, et cetera—while the linear space orientation is developed in social practice (2004, 8). Both are measured against the other. In other words, people are subject to cyclical temporal events, but they learn how and where to look and move in space through their history of social interaction.

The analysis of the Catholic Worker house and STOP in the previous chapters illustrates the rhythmic quality of involvement and is suggestive of patterns of involvement in such groups, and in groups more generally. In this chapter, I begin by revisiting the patterns of organization within the Catholic Worker community and STOP.[2] I then argue that there is much that can be learned from viewing not only the Catholic Worker community and STOP but social actors more generally as the intermittent construction and decay of patterned action. From this perspective, actors are defined as centers of action with the capacity to exert force within some field of action.[3] I suggest this definition of entities not so much as a confident metaphysical assertion but as an epistemological strategy for conducting social scientific investigation.[4]

High Speed and Uneven Tempo at the Catholic Worker House

This Catholic Worker community was small; they helped those who happened to pass within their orbit with whatever resources they had at hand, and their material resources shifted radically from month to month and even day to day. Since the Workers could not always feed a family who asked for help, it was difficult for them to imagine a series of concrete actions that would result in the revolution they envisioned. In

---

2. In Apter's terms, STOP's leadership worked to maintain a telic state and the Catholic Worker community worked to maintain a paratelic state: "If in the telic mode, life seems to be like a game of chess, in which one has to think many moves ahead; in the paratelic mode, it is more like a game of roulette; planning is not likely to help, and pleasure (or displeasure) comes from the immediate effects of one's actions. Where the telic state is careful and constrained, the paratelic tends to be easygoing and casual. . . . In the telic state it is not just a question of looking forward towards a given goal, but of tending to see that goal as part of a route to a further goal, and that in turn as but a way station towards something more distant and perhaps more important again. . . . And this is another way of saying that everything one does is seen as having significance beyond itself, as partaking in a hierarchy of sub-goals and goals. In fact, the greater the *felt significance* that an action is experienced as having, the more the person will be pleased. In the paratelic state, however, life *is* seen as exactly like a game: what one is doing has no significance beyond itself and is done for its own sake. If the telic state is serious-minded, the paratelic state is light-hearted and fun-loving. . . . [The] activities of the paratelic state are turned inward on themselves, cut off from the rest of life and encapsulated in their own 'bubbles'" (italics in original; Apter [1989] 2007, 40–41).

3. See Abbott (2001b, 274).

4. By distinguishing between an ontological and an epistemological position, I am suggesting bracketing the question of what is actually and definitively happening—a question for metaphysical philosophers—and treating the position represented here as a starting point for empirical investigation. In other words, I am asking, "What can we know about the social world if we begin by assuming that social organization is a fluid process?" Omar Lizardo helped me develop clarity about this point over a number of long and interesting conversations about the relationship between social theory and empirical investigation.

response to uncertain conditions, the Catholic Workers accommodated fluctuations to sustain involvement. Rather than resisting failure, the Workers saw it coming, encouraged it for the intensity and momentum it offered, and rebuilt themselves in the ashes. They became experts at precipitating their own collapse and recovery. The practice may have appeared self-destructive to outsiders, but it provided a reliable method for preserving involvement in varying conditions.

The Workers' acute sensitivity to their unpredictable environment meant that a lot could happen within the group in a very short amount of time. A steady stream of unpredictable and demanding situations in uncertain conditions generated a shared focus that was close to the group in both time and space.

The Workers' tight and fast involvement effectively maintained the intense involvement of the same members; once a person got in, getting out was difficult. Involvement in the Worker house was like double-dutch jump rope: the scene moved quickly, and if potential participants could not pick up the rhythm, they could not get into the action. Once into the action, it became absorbing so that the world outside the group almost seemed to disappear.

The all-or-nothing nature of involvement meant that actors tended to lose involvement in other scenes, resulting in fewer and fewer points of reference outside the group with which to mark the passing of time, which generated a tight and rapid quality to involvement and a feeling of timelessness. I often lost track of time and stayed longer than I had planned. This happened in a more profound way for people at the heart of the community. For example, Linda initially planned to spend one year living in the house and ended up spending eight years in the community. Sometimes Joan and Linda reminded me of Rip Van Winkle; they seemed astonished by the number of years that had passed, as if time had somehow slipped away.

By keeping their focus close to the group and its boundaries, they continually pulled themselves into the center of action, which reinforced intense moral boundaries around the group. They felt joy when their boundaries expanded, betrayal when their sense of unity was threatened, awe when they felt unity with a larger history of sacrifice for righteousness or God, and grief when they felt the loss of unity. With all of this intensity, their greatest emotional risk was exhaustion. To ward off the ever-present danger of exhaustion, they dedicated much of their time and energy to identifying when they needed to pray, confess to each other, or tell energizing or funny stories in order to keep up their momentum. Their variable-dependent action—for example, praying when needed rather than at scheduled times—both supported and required a close focus on the group and its immediate surroundings. As a result, it was difficult for them to execute long-term plans in unpredictable circumstances.

All of the Workers liked to talk about abstract values and engage in immediate solidarity-generating activities, but none of them liked the mid-range-focused action, such as planning and preparing for holiday meals and neighborhood barbeques. Pulling off neighborhood barbeques or even small-scale public actions with Women's Ordination groups required huge and draining efforts. However, many of these mid-range activities, like producing the community newsletter, brought desperately needed money into the house.

These larger events also mollified the Workers' outside supporters. Those who donated money from afar often failed to see the moments the Workers identified as successes and had difficulty understanding the Workers' failures. For example, when the editor of a local Irish newspaper heard that guests of the Workers had been stealing from them, she stopped running free ads soliciting donations for the Worker house in the newspaper, saying that she could not, in good conscience, solicit money for them if they didn't have enough sense to protect what was given to them. Thus there was a tension between the Workers' emotional preferences and their material needs.

We can think of the Worker house as an ideal type of group involvement that is densely populated within a narrow range, and that pulls the focus and action into the center. Their focus on the group persisted over time, but the content of the group, both in terms of members and other material resources, could change quickly, as could the expectations about particular actors, roles, and responsibilities in the group. Between the fluctuating circumstances and the members' fluctuating contributions, there were few cognitive hooks for identifying whether a particular person was involved in a scene or not. They often become confused about who was where when, and their default assumption was that a particular person was involved in a situation when, actually, they were not.

Low Speed and Even Tempo at STOP

STOP began with a style that looked much like the Catholic Workers; they focused primarily on their own activities and maintaining their efforts. However, a history of internal conflicts discouraged an internal focus. At the same time the group enjoyed improving political conditions. This drew the leaders' attention farther from the group and enabled them to envision a clear course of action to reach their goals.[5] By shifting the focus away from the group, Todd transformed the group from an entity to a coalition and moved the action away from the physical space of STOP's offices. He diversified, knocked on more and different doors, and pursued multiple paths to ensure greater likelihood of surviving future instabilities.

In other words, Todd widened and slowed organization to avoid collapse. Todd and the other leaders' desire to extend their influence, both physically farther away and farther into the future, replaced their focus on maintaining feelings of unity and enthusiasm within the group. Most of the intense interactions took place at the margins of the group when members bridged the boundaries between STOP and other groups. We can think of STOP's involvement as pulling action away from the center. Members strained to move farther out against their network limits.

Despite the leadership's focus on the thrill of conquering new political territory, mundane tasks routinely required them to focus their attention on the internal management of STOP. Among other activities, they had to write grant proposals; solicit and keep track of donations; balance budgets; write and send out mass e-mails; produce a never-ending stream of flyers and posters advertising meetings and protests; solicit invitations to speak in classrooms, churches, and community groups; handle the logistics of planning and pulling off protests; and attend endless meetings with one another, the local chapter, and other activist groups.

STOP's leaders did not face routine anxiety about physical danger, fear that they would lose necessary material resources, or concerns that they were being used; rather, they feared that they did not matter in the larger political sphere or even matter to those they directly identified as their opponents. To ward off infighting and a sense of meaninglessness, the staff told stories about past successes and future glories, stories in which they were the mighty victors against the prosecutors and politicians who sought the death penalty and signed death warrants. These stories evoked righteous anger, which enabled them to smooth over internal conflict without releasing the internal tensions that frequently simmered just under the surface.

Growth created more pronounced divisions of labor within the group, which increased the differences in status between different positions

5. Mead (1934) notes that distant responses are at the basis for reflexive consciousness—the more distant the focus, the more reflexive involvement.

within the group. The leaders' efforts to coordinate activity across a growing group required ever-increasing amounts of mundane activity. The stars enjoyed most of the excitement while the support staff took care of most of the mundane details. Lower-status staff members had to manage internal conflict, tensions, and feelings of boredom. The exciting moments of risk grew fewer and the day-to-day responsibilities became a mundane drain.

Since participants occupied different positions, any disturbance tended to affect members differently,[6] which pushed their positions still farther apart. With little emotional glue holding actors together, internal conflicts sometimes led to the breaking off of involvement. As a result, the staff often smoothed over differences rather than risk confrontation. This was particularly true of issues that Todd believed to be powder-keg issues, like gender dynamics among the staff. Thus STOP stabilized as a *form*, but the involvement of particular participants became *less* stable. Eventually, Todd hired Edward to mitigate the tensions that led to high turnover rates among the lower-level staff, but Edward merely protected Todd by absorbing the tensions himself.

The larger STOP became in terms of space, material resources, and political networks, the more slowly time moved, especially for the lower-level people, like the volunteers and office managers. Compared to the Workers, involvement in STOP was like a single-twirl jump rope that was slowing down; the barriers to entering and exiting diminished over time. STOP organized its activities around regularly scheduled time-dependent action, which supported its growth by facilitating coordination between STOP and other groups and members' multiple involvements. But there were costs associated with keeping a regular schedule. Meetings could be boring if there were few new developments between scheduled meetings. At other times, the meetings were too infrequent to handle the workload. STOP's extensive and rigid structure also made it very difficult for the group to mobilize in response to specific events, such as a pending decision on the sentencing of a capital case.[7]

6. This is similar to a point Simmel made long ago: "The smaller the amount of essential compatibility between the elements of the group, the more probable is it that new agitations, new stimulations of consciousness, new occasions for resolves and for developments will force the contrasted elements still further apart" (1898, 831–32).

7. Time also mattered as a status distinction in STOP; to claim a history of involvement was to claim status within the group. Unlike the Catholic Workers, who had a difficult time remembering who was involved in any particular moment in the group, STOP had a very clear collective memory of who was involved in different stages of the group's development. The group had a sense of trajectory, so previous or continuous involvement was a claim of credit for current and future success.

Organization Emerges When the Pull toward Expansion
Meets Obstacles

If we compare the two groups from the most distant perspective, we can see them as examples of social organization. If we examine social organization over time, we see that social actors are moments of coherent action that emerge within a slower-moving field that offers some resistance. If we were to observe the emergence of organization from above, it would look like random growth that draws in involvement from previously ruptured patterns.[8] Growth of involvement continues until constrained by competing forces, external obstacles, or limitations of resources required for sustaining growth.[9] Other patterns that obstruct action, and that have a solid feel because they move more slowly and resist change, are the source of resistance.

The period between the initial frustration of action and the formation of firm patterns is relatively plastic, meaning many different potential paths are available. Once the growth of involvement hits its first significant obstacle and survives, it weeds out some paths to action and strengthens others. The effort to anticipate obstacles creates pockets of organization. Rather than imagining continually reproducing cycles, the process is better depicted as an evolving pattern of organization. History carries actors to an emerging moment, within particular physical parameters, with particular expectations, and with interactions with others who have expectations as well.

Organization acts as a filter and enables actors to have a sense of themselves in relationship to a field of action. In other words, obstacles spark control efforts,[10] which are the basis for the most fundamental reflexive awareness required for actors to proceed purposefully within their environment. Control is a sense of being mobilized over and against outside conditions, thus a sense of control is predicated on actors' internal sense of being an object vis-à-vis the objects in their environment.[11]

---

8. See Lewontin (2000, 38).

9. The importance of particular resources varies depending on the center of action; in some cases, growth is limited by the biological needs of bodies, the density of population, or the demands of other centers of involvement (Prigonine 1969). For example, involvement in social movements can be constrained by pulls toward involvement in school, work, or family. Cf. McAdam and Fernandez (1990), Ulanowicz (1997, 47, 108), and Zhao (1998).

10. White defines control as "both anticipation of and response to eruptions in environing processes" (1992, 5, 9).

11. A sense of a relationship between actors emerges from moments that generate the perception of bounded actors, in other words, a perception of distance between actors. Processes only appear as discrete entities from a distance; therefore, control requires a distant perspective. This sense of distance between stimulus and response is the basis of reflexive consciousness (Mead 1934).

When actors anticipate future environmental conditions, they manage environmental instability within themselves in order to create stability at their boundaries.[12] We can think of stability as increasing internal complexity that decouples the flow of social organization from its surrounding environment. In other words, by absorbing environmental flux, actors create temporary pockets of stability.

Stability Eventually Undermines Itself

Patterns collapse when they can no longer absorb the variation in their environment. Once a pattern ruptures, an actor can reemerge with updated strategies and increased organization, which may or may not maintain what would appear to be a stable pattern from a more distant point of observation. Or its constituent elements could become available for involvement in other patterns. As the previous chapters illustrate, two different conditions produce such ruptures: (1) extreme shifts in the surrounding environment, and (2) increasingly rigid internal responses. Understanding the conditions that induce extreme shifts in the surrounding environment is beyond the scope of this volume. However, the previous examples reveal a detailed picture of the process through which organization can become rigid enough to collapse.

As organization increases, the logic guiding the vast majority of interactions becomes progressively more local, and the time between change in the environment and response of the actor slows. Blocks to action, or failures, accumulate over time, damming up potential paths so that action is pulled toward the few remaining paths, which reduces the flexibility of the actor. This narrowing not only constrains ongoing action; it also keeps other actions out, which means that the established flow of action loses energy over time. Organization will increase until its structure becomes thick, granular, and eventually brittle.

The stories about the Catholic Worker community and STOP illustrate how actors search for logic, order, and predictability, but when they come closest to achieving these, they find them stifling and inadequate for expressing their full range of experiences. Organization feels increasingly constraining, and the chaos of disorganization becomes ever more

---

12. The claim here goes beyond observations of particular systems, such as neurons and brains, to suggest that apparent stability in any social system is only possible because of the temporary absorption of considerable variation within apparently stable patterns.

attractive.[13] Eventually, the actors' rigidity becomes the biggest threat to stability. Even minor contingencies move the threshold of collapse ever closer. Finally patterns will collapse and dissipate. Organization creates the very conditions that appear to frustrate it.

On the surface, the fact that organization undermines itself is a paradox, but closer examination reveals this goal of emergence can only be realized in such *unstable* and *uncertain* conditions. A desire for expansion is founded in change, a process that has no meaning in completely stable conditions.

The Relationship between Culture and Social Actors

As explained in chapter 2, the perspective here counters the assumption that actors are synonymous with biological individuals, although they can be biological individuals.[14] For example, when a school district proposes closing a school, a loose network of parents can become an organization with a clear sense of itself as a political actor. Similarly, schools across a state that previously had little sense of shared identity may become a coalition in response to state-level changes in education standards.

If actors are not limited to biological individuals, and the experience of what constitutes an actor can shift in response to environmental conditions, we cannot assume that the sense of indeterminacy and agency that is associated with actors is a product of anything essential and enduring (Emirbayer and Mische 1998). In other words, if actors do not arise in response to a constant internal essence, they must arise in response to external conditions. However, it is equally problematic to assume that actors merely reflect their immediate surroundings. Actors are not only characterized by a sense that they are independent and can exert some control over their environment; they are also characterized by the sense that they exist over a history and will continue to exist in the future.[15] The actors' sense of duration enables them to draw on previously

---

13. Douglas gives an elegant description of the creativity inherent in the impending collapse of a pattern and why actors may lean toward a collapse if they have felt acute awareness of the restrictions of prevailing patterns. "Granted that disorder spoils pattern, it also provides the material of pattern. Order implies restriction; from all possible materials, a limited selection has been made and from all possible relations a limited set has been used. So disorder by implication is unlimited, no pattern has been realized in it, but its patterning is indefinite. That is why, though we seek to create order, we do not simply condemn disorder. . . . [I]t has danger and power" (1966, 117).

14. See Mead for discussion of how types of social actors other than biological selves arise in the same way that selves associated with biological individuals arise (1934, 144).

15. See Bergson ([1912] 1999) and Abbott (2001b, 274).

established meanings to anticipate and negotiate changing conditions. This capacity becomes a buffer between the immediate unfolding environment and the actor. Thus, while actors are not grounded in an enduring essence, the role of their history in determining their action prevents them from being a mere reflection of the immediate environment.[16] Indeed, it is the capacity to reflect on their own history that gives actors the ability to understand themselves as independent actors who can exert some control over their environment.[17]

Continued independence from the immediate environment requires historical referencing and anticipation. Referencing a continuous line of history to anticipate future obstacles creates intentions and expectations,[18] which then lump perceptions, reactions, and actions into types. For example, in the Catholic Worker community, middle-class do-gooders either "get it" or do not. For Todd, in the STOP community, other activists are either "serious" or not. By limiting perceptions and the meanings actors make of them, intentions and expectations generate patterns of activity that can influence the surrounding environment and, in turn, can be influenced by the surrounding environment.[19] As organization increases, the actors become increasingly capable of influencing their environment by disrupting the flow of other action.

As actors reference their histories to anticipate future obstructions to their action, they become centers of symbolic accumulation and preservation. All the following are examples of centers of preservation: people, organizations, museums, libraries, legal systems, religious institutions, and governments. In the present Western context, individuals are particularly key sites of accumulation. That is to say that they are crucial for pulling history into unfolding contexts. Every time a doctor checks a medical chart, a gun shop employee checks police records, a judge sentences an individual to prison, or an individual goes through psychoanalysis or

16. As Fine suggests, local culture mediates between external constraints and the behavior in response to these constraints (1979, 737).

17. Mead refers to actors' understanding of themselves in relationship to a particular field as the generalized other (1934, 154). He argues that it is only the capacity to view one's self from the perspective of the generalized other that allows for the capacity to consciously reflect and act (156).

18. If we examine the relationship between actor and context over time, it is clear that they are mutually constitutive (Mead 1934, 309; Sewell 1992). However, if we pay attention to *how each is modified over time*, it is clear that not only do external obstacles organize an actor into being, but that obstacles continue to shape that being over time. Thus both in the emergence of the actor and in the development of the actor, external obstacles determine the conditions under which the actor will have the capacity to exert control over its environment. This is to say, although the actor and its environment exist in an open system of mutual influence, there is no chicken-and-egg problem. Obstacles are of primary importance in both the initiation of the mutually constitutive system, the modification of that system, and the ultimate collapse of that system (Bourdieu [1997] 2000, 130).

19. See Kelso (1995, 141).

situates explanations for behavior in themselves or other individuals, biological individuals are reinforced as the relevant lines along which symbolic meanings accumalate and action unfolds.[20]

Dynamics of Influence Across Actors

The cycles of action that are actors are embedded in other cycles of action and overlap with still others. Thus, stable patterns require interlocking activity between the processes internal to and external to the actor.[21] Stability, then, is based not only in the dynamics of the center of action, but also the dynamics of the neighboring, overlapping, embedded, and embedding centers of action that make up the boundaries of the actor (Abbott 2001, 261–79). Knowing the location and general dynamics of action is insufficient for anticipating relationships between actors and action; we must understand the rhythm and tempo of action. The stories in this volume about the Catholic Workers and STOP reveal the ways in which differences in tempo and rhythm can create various relationships between actors. Since social organization cycles, action is fundamentally intermittent. At some tempos, dynamics disappear; indeed, actors leverage this fact when they negotiate obstacles by speeding up or slowing down.[22]

Timing creates the boundaries among entities that share component processes and the same tempo; in such cases, actors move through the cycle of organization at a similar speed but at different times.[23] Under such conditions, action could happen in the same space but at different or rarely overlapping intervals. This is how the constituent processes that comprise a center of action can be taken up into multiple fields at the "same" time. For example, a baseball field is a constituent of a baseball league, but because baseball leagues coordinate their use of the ballpark, the baseball field can be drawn up into multiple leagues at once. Similarly, a human body is a constituent of a baseball fan, but the ways in which the different activities of a fan use the body as a space make it

20. This is not to say that because history could be organized in other ways that existing patterns are somehow not real. On the contrary, the centrality of the individual as a site for the organization of history has significant consequences for the interior of individuals and for the context within which they operate. For example, in the present context there are very real reasons to be concerned about individuals with violent histories gaining access to weapons.

21. See Simmel (1964, 15) and Lefebvre (2004, 17).

22 See relevant discussion on enduring patterns of inequality in chapter 4.

23. See Bergson ([1988] 2005, 209).

possible for a fan to watch every batter and also participate in the wave.[24] Social organization is generally far more complex than coordinating several baseball teams to use the same field or coordinating the watching of batters while doing the wave.

For example, *biological* individuals are only occasionally the focus of action for *social* persons and groups, yet biological individuals are vital constituent processes for both social persons and groups.[25] The fact that the biological individual is common to both types of action undoubtedly facilitates the translation of relevant information across the actors— social person to group and group to social person. However, the mere fact that they share the same biological individual does not eliminate the need for translation. For example, when I reflect back on group-based experiences, such as a weekly liturgy at the Catholic Worker house or a successful STOP demonstration, I am constructing a memory for myself as an ethnographer as though this ethnographer self experienced these moments directly. In actuality, my ethnographic self was peripheral to these experiences, so such a memory requires a translation between these different centers of action, a translation facilitated by the fact that my biological body played a role in the initial experiences and in my later analysis of these experiences.

Patterns at different speeds can coexist in balance, or they can develop competitive trajectories. Actors also can be partially oriented toward the same field but arranged at slightly different speeds or rhythms, in which case the actors are not in direct competition with one another; rather, they can be in competition to claim the nature of the field so that it suits their organizing dynamics. This sort of conflict would appear more ideological than direct competition for resources or influence. Cycles of organization that unfold at slightly different rhythms may intermittently overlap, and in doing so would create yet another type of opportunity for centers of action to shape and influence each other. The dynamics driving such moments of influence would make little sense according to standard narrative accounts of causal relationships.[26]

The relative speed at which a cycle of organization—that is, an actor—turns over marks the differences in scale between centers of action. Slower-moving processes generally constrain faster-moving processes

24. Chris Hausmann suggested these baseball examples to illustrate the more general point about timing in social organization.

25. Goffman suggests that individuals are a peg on which to hang biographical information (1959, 252–53), but the biological individual can be a peg to hang information for many other centers of action as well.

26. Spillman (2004) opens up more intellectual space for considering causal processes in broader terms than the well-worn debates between nomothetic and ideographic sociological approaches.

(Allen and Starr 1982), but even slower-moving processes will ultimately move through the cycle of stability, increasing rigidity, and collapse. The differences in scale may generally prevent faster-moving dynamics from influencing slower-moving dynamics, but faster-moving dynamics can influence slower-moving dynamics if they exploit the vulnerability inherent in rigid stability or collapse.[27] Even the most apparently stable pattern requires active dampening of environmental influence in order to endure.[28] As slower patterns head toward collapse, positive feedback looped within embedded faster processes could shift abruptly enough to disturb slower patterns.[29] That is to say, there are moments of vulnerability and opportunity across speeds of involvement that provide windows of opportunity when faster processes could influence slower processes.[30]

The Role of the Observer in the Perception of Stability

As long as the constraints and resources that generated a pattern of organization are relatively constant, the process will appear stable at its boundaries and beyond. In inconsistent contexts, a pattern would only appear to be constant when viewed from a distance. In other words, a particular center of action may look like chaos up close, a rhythmic pattern of organization from a greater distance, and a solid, even permanent, actor from an even greater distance. A moment of emergence for one pattern is the collapse of another. Depending on one's perspective, all destruction is creation and vice versa.[31] Thus stability is not only an internal characteristic of the actor; it is also a product of the distance of the observer from the observed.

Imagine moving toward the part of the cycle of involvement that looks like stable action, the period between the onset of organization

---

27. See Tarrow (1991, 4) and Erickson Nepstad (2004, 108).

28. This approach avoids the major weaknesses of the most infamous attempt to provide an integrative picture complexity in the history of sociology, Parsonian functionalism. Rather than understanding stability as a manifestation of natural equilibrium, this approach treats such moments of stability as fragile and temporary achievements that require work and energy to maintain.

29. Lefebvre similarly argues that "the discordance of rhythms brings previously eurhythmic organizations towards fatal disorder" (2004, 16).

30. For example, a rock of a certain mass dropped from a certain distance, from a certain place, in a certain pond will have varying consequences for the other side of the pond. If dropped on a calm day, the surface influence will be great; if dropped on a windy day, the disturbance will be absorbed. The potential for impact on the other side of the pond is not contained within the rock.

31. As Dewey notes, "In the process of living, attainment of a period of equilibrium is at the same time the initiation of a new relation to the environment, one that brings with it potency of new adjustments to be made through struggle. The time of consummation is also one of beginning anew" (1959, 16).

and collapse. Such a move would be much like moving closer to an eddy in a stream. Consider an eddy in a stream as an object.[32] Now consider the movement of the molecules of water around the eddy. It may be the case that the water molecules are pulled into involvement again and again, creating a history of involvement over many cycles. Or it may be the case that most of the water molecules move through involvement, so that there would be very little recognizable pattern. We would see only flow, emergence, from this perspective. We could look at the eddy over months or years and see it as a temporary structure in a larger pattern of disorder, and consider how the eddy emerges, stabilizes, and decays. We could also back up far enough to look at the stream as organization that has a flow, and the eddy as temporary disorganization of that flow. Apparent stability is nothing other than the process of emergence, stability, and decay appearing coherent from a particular distance.

Similarly, social organization is made up of multiple embedded relations that only have solid and natural-seeming boundaries when viewed from a distance. An apparently discrete center of organization from one perspective is the context for other centers from another perspective, and a constituent element of a cycle that creates other centers from yet another perspective.[33] Any observation is a slice out of time that could capture endless complexity through close observation or simple predictable relationships viewed from afar. There is no actual "thing" that we can see from a certain vantage point. The dynamics at a particular speed of observation may appear to share few points of overlapping involvement with distant entities, but that does not mean that they are not still entwined in relationships at yet another speed of organization. For example, the biological individuals appear distinct from one timescale, but if one is focused on the carbon cycle, they disappear as meaningful actors.[34] This is not to say that there are no "real" social dynamics some-

32. Andrew Abbott suggested the image of an eddy to me. This image offers a number of advantages over the image of a vortex, the analogy that I had been considering, namely, the importance of context for emerging and collapsing patterns.

33. Padgett and Ansell point to the multiple contradictory, but undoubtedly accurate, explanations for a single case, the actions of the Medici, and suggest that any particular explanation reflects the observer as much as the observed (1993, 1307–8).

34. We should not assume that patterns of organization that from some perspectives would appear to be larger are necessarily slower than patterns that appear to be smaller from the same perspective. For example, not only is it likely that the rhythm and emotional style of a whole group would be completely different from the rhythm and emotional style of subgroupings, but we should not assume that the speed of the group would be slower than the speed of the triad or dyad. In fact, it is the lack of perfect timing and coordination between overlapping and embedded cycles of organization that creates windows of opportunity when apparently smaller patterns can create huge changes in larger patterns. As Lefebvre notes, "The discordance of rhythms brings previously eurhythmic organizations towards fatal disorder" (2004, 16). "For there to be *change*, a social group,

where "out there," rather that we can only access the social world from the limits of our potential to perceive. No perspective is complete and no perspective is wrong.[35]

The constraints of human perception, at least for now, make it necessary for social scientists to bracket *most* complexity to see any patterns at all; we will undoubtedly solidify some aspect of organization that is fundamentally fluid from another perspective. Social scientists have to translate observed dynamics across social space, so their depictions of social organization are necessarily abstract and unrefined compared to direct experiences of the same social processes.[36] It would appear that in order to detect patterns, we need to envision a social world that is firmer and more solid than we can likely justify. These inevitably less-nuanced descriptions of social processes provide significantly different information about the observed dynamics from those generated by direct experience. The extent to which a social scientist's depiction of a dynamic resonates with those who are directly involved will vary with the researcher's distance from the scene. Depending on how closely, how long, and how often we observe, we will see some dynamics and not others. Any moment of change can feel like stability, and any moment of stability can feel like change, depending on our perspective. If any moment can be part of the collapse of one pattern, the beginning of another, or the maintenance of another,[37] where we look and for how long—that is, where and when we focus our attention—are crucial for what we see.

If we look closely, we see continually changing situations—total unpredictability and no persistence. At a distance, we see concrete and solid entities, a view that suggests that the question of persistence is irrelevant. If we take up a perspective that is somewhere in between and look at situations unfolding over time, we can begin to see organization as temporary patterns that emerge, stabilize, and collapse. Every point along this continuum of chaos to solidity overestimates the firmness of the

---

a class or a caste must intervene by imprinting a **rhythm** on an era, be it through force or in an insinuating manner. . . . Perspicacity, attention and above all an opening are required" (italics and bold in the original; 14–15).

35. That does not mean, however, that conclusions drawn from observations cannot be wrong.

36. This position shares some resemblance to Weber's use of ideal types as a basic method for investigating the social world. Indeed, this is the most basic assumption in sociology, one that I, among others, would argue is so basic that we have become blind to its implications for our own "findings." To use a well-charted sociological example, the notion of "the family" falls apart as soon as we focus on the complexity contained within this deceptively simple term, a point that has been the focus of many entertaining conversations with my colleague Juli Sobolewski.

37. Cf. Husserl ([1893–1907] 1991,78), Thelen and Smith (1994, 68), Kelso (1995), and Abbott (2001b, 243).

boundaries we envision in order to reduce complexity. This is to say that any perspective appears to reveal irreducible dynamics *and* predictable dynamics. The experience of fluidity or concreteness inheres in the perspective we take up relative to our focus of investigation, not in what we observe.[38] We can observe qualitatively different sorts of patterns when we draw boundaries in different ways. A situation that may be engaging and entraining for some may seem flat and boring for others, depending on where and when the actors focus their attention.

The farther an observer moves away from the action, the more they will perceive action according to a cognitive/rational logic and the less they will perceive according to an intuitive/emotional logic. Thus, from a distance, rational choice would appear to be the organizing motivation for behavior. For example, from a distance, an entity only appears during the phase in which the secondary motivation for organization and stability decouples action from the immediate context. This is the instant in which motivations for social organization come closest to those assumed by rational choice theories. However, rational choice assumptions could only predict behavior at a distance, and they would never be able to capture the dynamics that create this stability, nor the dynamics that lead to its collapse.

From a mid-range perspective, rational choice-motivated action is a periodic achievement that appears in rhythmic pulses. If we understand the dynamics driving the cycle observed, we can begin to anticipate the sorts of conditions that will generate pattern formation and destruction, which will indicate the conditions that likely will lead to periods of apparent rational or irrational action. Every perspective merely reveals what is available for perception from any particular location in space and time, meaning what is literally available to the actors' senses and what they will actively attend to based on their history of experience.[39] Thus, when we select a position from which to observe, we are ruling out the capacity to see certain aspects that are necessarily relevant to what is going on.

---

38. Ludwig, Walker, and Holling similarly argue that "the notion of resilience of a system depends upon our objectives, the time scale of interest, the character and magnitude of disturbances, and the underlying structure of the system, and the sort of control measures that are feasible" (2002, 23).

39. Thus our observations communicate information about our positions as observers as well as information about what we observed. As Lefebvre notes, "Our scale determines our place in the space-time of the universe: what we perceive of it and what serves as a point of departure for practice, and for theoretical knowledge" (2004, 82).

Assessing Outcomes

Understanding how distance affects perceptions of the observed undermines the taken-for-grantedness of the appropriate realm of outcomes. The social movements literature has tended to assess success in terms of political outcomes (Giugni, McAdam, and Tilly 1999; Polletta 2002), usually national politics, and tends explicitly to state or implicitly assume a rational motivation for action. Alternately, the burgeoning body of work on emotions in social movements (Jasper 1997; Goodwin, Jasper and Polletta 2001; Polletta 2002) focuses on expressive motivations and outcomes. The perspective presented here illustrates how that which counts as influence or success largely depends on the perspective of the observer. For example, the greater the distance between the observer and the processes being observed, the more rational motivations will be apparent. The lesser the distance between an observer and the processes being observed, the more emotional and cultural motivations will be apparent.

Distance also affects how we assess the persistence of a social movement group, a social movement, or a cycle of protest. That is to say that an observer will perceive a group as enduring when either a group's patterns of action changes slowly and gradually from the observer's perspective. The perception of endurance varies with the location of the observer. When a social movement runs up against unfavorable political conditions, such as the women's movement has, a field once consisting of multiple organizations and groups could split. Such a split could create a small number of increasingly rigid and slow-moving organizations; for example, NOW and countless small internally focused groups, such as informal feminist friendship networks. Those involved in either the longer organizations or friendship networks could miss the relevance, or even existence, of the other types of groups and bemoan not only the death of a particular group but the death of the movement.[40]

Conclusion

The process of organizing does not seek the patterns that develop from it directly. They are the product of problem solving in anticipation of future obstacles. Once a pocket of organization forms, it gains the capacity

---

40. See Taylor (1989).

to obstruct other action. By establishing a rhythm of organization that responds indirectly to context but has the capacity to directly affect a context, actors exert a force of their own. They do this by decoupling patterns they encounter, or by transforming forces through changing their direction or strength. In other words, when actors reference their histories in an attempt to control their environments, they pull their histories across unfolding scenes. In doing so, they cut grooves that run opposite to the otherwise constant flux of the environment.[41] These grooves temporarily smooth and stabilize some paths to action while disrupting others.

Taking up the perspective presented in this volume shifts the social scientist's focus from asking about the roles of symbols versus relations, or conflict versus stability,[42] to asking: When do social actors move from one basin of attraction to the other? Such a question highlights the role of rhythm in social organization and the importance of timing in shaping the influence of both ideologies and patterns of relations. The capacity to exert force is the product of multiple indirect forces, so action can only be understood over time. If we want to anticipate the actions or persistence of groups or other actors, we would first need to identify these rhythms and understand their local history of moving through their patterns.

This is neither a cultural constructivist nor a structural determinist approach; rather, this is a theory about how local expectations and values, as well as structural relations, are products of historical path-dependent involvement. History does more than constrain the material and cultural conditions of interaction; it also influences the rhythm of interactions and the capacity to absorb disturbances. From this perspective, history

41. This is merely a more general version of Abbott's point that individuals shape unfolding social organization precisely because they are important sites for encoding historical information (2005b, 4–5).

42. Thinking in terms of "structure" and "culture" draws social scientists' attention to static moments of social organization rather than change over time. When we focus on structure (the moments when constraints on various resources undermine or create new symbolic meanings) or culture (the moments when symbolic meanings organize expectations and actions), we can find limitless examples of how the other is subordinate. Thus when social scientists assume that either culture or structure is the primary force organizing social life, they are able to find more than enough evidence to support their claims (Bourdieu 1977; Eliasoph and Lichterman 2003). However, when we focus on how patterns of social organization change over time, we can see that culture and structure are two basins of attraction for social organization, and actors move between these basins over time. Obstacles block action and, in doing so, create the motivation for control in the actor. Similarly, we can see that conflict and functionalist perspectives are also two sides of the same coin (Sewell 1992). One focuses on how actors impinge on other actors to shape unfolding environments; the other focuses on how such blocked action creates actors and how such actors persist by managing future blocks. Action and obstacles are central to both stories, with the stories merely told from different vantage points.

cannot be measured in some standard time; it can only be measured in the amount of accumulated organization created by blocked paths to action.

As I said at the beginning of this chapter, my expectation is that the theoretical perspective presented here will be treated as an epistemological strategy rather than an ontological claim. Much like the Catholic Worker community's and STOP's evolving expectations, this theoretical perspective probably will not generate accurate predictions about the future, but it just may prove useful.

Methods Appendix

Working within the Limits of Observation

Any of the perspectives that an observer or researcher could possibly take up relative to the observed could provide rich empirical detail, but only at the cost of losing other information.[1] For example, the previous chapters illustrate how the greater the distance between the observer and the observed, the slower and more solid the observed dynamic will appear to the observer. Likewise, the closer an observer is to the observed, the more fluid the observed will appear.

Relationships between the observer and the observed inevitably change over time. Unanticipated environmental changes can move observers or the observed toward or away from each other, altering even the most apparently stable patterns in both the observer, the observed, and the observer's perception of the observed. Beyond the potential for random shifts in relationships, the stories and analyses in this volume illustrate how a researcher would likely end up shifting positions over the course of their fieldwork. This ethnographer's journey of intimacy within their sites is not so different from other newcomers. This trajectory of intimacy shapes both an observer's perceived distance from the observed and their sense of time; therefore, understanding that relationships change over time is crucial for interpreting field notes from varying points across fieldwork.

1. Polanyi argues that "our attention can hold only one focus at a time and that it would hence be self-contradictory to be both subsidiarily and focally aware of the same particulars at the same time" ([1958] 1962, 57).

In addition to the complexity of the relationship between the observer and the observed within any particular research project, one social scientist may not take up the same position as another in relation to the flow of the observed: Some observe from a distance; others are right in the mix. When researchers fail to account for how their position and trajectory influence their perception, they lose the capacity to understand how these differences can account for apparently fundamental incompatibilities between meticulous accounts of the same phenomenon.[2] Information gathered from a much closer or farther distance from a particular observer's perspective will reveal little that is immediately useful for that observer.[3] When observers from different perspectives find inconsistencies across their work, it is all too easy for researchers to dismiss "the other" perspective as "wrong" or even "wrongheaded."

There are numerous ways of handling all of this complexity and potential for miscommunication. The most obvious is to insist that researchers develop a reflexive understanding of their trajectory, speed, and distance in relation to the observed. By cultivating a reflexive awareness of both the limits of their perspectives as researchers and, more generally, the inescapable limits of any perspective they could take up, researchers will not have to be reminded that the pictures they present *cannot* be correct if they claim them to be total.[4] Although the academic world appears to re-

2. Kuhn (1996) and Mead (1932) both point out that knowledge becomes problematic for scientists when unexpected findings arise. However, the ethnographer, adhering to grounded methods of theoretical sampling, *chases* unexpected findings. As soon as a pattern is identified and a story about the logic of the pattern begins to emerge, we go back to the field in order to *prove ourselves wrong*. We work to prove ourselves wrong in an ongoing effort to ferret out the implicit assumptions that all people rely on when negotiating their daily lives. For example, social scientists' perceptions of stability and predictability of social organization is a product of the duration of their observation. Compared to the Catholic Worker community, STOP's day-to-day activities were far more predictable. If, however, we compare stability over years, STOP's goals and procedures changed radically compared to the Catholic Worker community's. There are many factors that render the ethnographer's perspective different from the subjects of study, but this continual testing and refining of theories is one of the most important.

3. It is important to note that we cannot replace "close" with "micro" and "distant" with "macro"; some forms of content analysis are examples of a distant perspective on what are traditionally viewed as micro-dynamics in sociology; whereas some historical accounts are close perspectives on what are traditionally viewed as macro-dynamics in sociology.

4. Polanyi argues that researchers must make a commitment to a perspective: "Like the tool, the sign or the symbol can be conceived as such only in the eyes of a person who *relies on them* to achieve or to signify something. *This reliance is a personal commitment which is involved in all acts of intelligence by which we integrate some things subsidiarily to the centre of our focal attention.* Every act of personal assimilation by which we make a thing form an extension of ourselves through our subsidiary awareness of it, is a commitment of ourselves; a manner of disposing ourselves" (italics in original; [1958] 1962, 61). He also argues that the view from any particular commitment is limited. "Subsidiary or instrumental knowledge, as I have defined it, is not known in itself but is known in terms of something focally known, to the quality of which it contributes; and to this extent it is unspecifiable. Analysis may bring subsidiary knowledge into focus and formulate it as a maxim or as a feature in a physiognomy, but specification is in general not exhaustive" (88).

ward strong claims that defend definitive positions, acknowledging limits can potentially allow researchers to *conceptually* integrate perspectives and enjoy a multidimensional view that is impossible from the point of a single human observer.

Researchers could turn an awareness of the limited view offered from every position into a conscious strategy for gaining analytic leverage. If researchers acknowledge the limits that constrain every point of observation, and allow room for the influence of these dynamics, they can develop suggestive theory about the relationships between dynamics revealed at different points of observation. I have attempted to do exactly that in this volume. For example, the stories convey the close experience within the groups, and the theory sections convey the detached experience of a distant comparison across the groups. By comparing my field notes from within each site over time, I was able to detect patterns that were not obvious to me while I was deeply involved in those scenes, because they cycled at timescales that I was not able to perceive directly. In providing views from closer and more distant perspectives and leaving the relationship between the two perspectives open for consideration, this volume offers an example of how to clarify the perceptual consequences of the relationship between the observer and the observed. It also provides one example of how social scientists can simultaneously contribute to about particular substantive questions while contributing to a more subtle understanding as to how distance and trajectory shape observations, analysis, and conclusions.

Investigating the Emotional Rhythm of Social Organization

This volume highlights the role of emotional rhythms and timing in the organization of the social world. In terms of the discussion above, the emotional rhythmic perspective is a close perspective. In order for researchers to get a feel for the rhythmic organization of a scene, they must do more than watch.[5] The quote below describes what it feels like to

---

5. Lefebvre (2004), like Mead (1934), points out that we need distance to perceive reflexively and analytically, but he argues that to understand a rhythm we must be grasped by it and give ourselves over to its duration (2004, 27). Field notes provide an ethnographer an opportunity to both step within duration and watch from a distance (personal communication, Chris Hausmann). Lefebvre says, "To grasp a rhythm, it is necessary to have been grasped by it; one must *let oneself go*, give oneself over, abandon oneself to its duration . . . In order to grasp this fleeting object, which is not exactly an *object*, it is therefore necessary to situate oneself simultaneously inside and outside" (italics in the original; Lefebvre 2004, 27).

be sensitive to not only the content of a scene, but also to the rhythmic organization of it:

The rhythm analyst calls on all his senses. . . . He thinks with his body, not in the abstract, but in lived temporality. . . . He must simultaneously catch a rhythm and perceive it within the whole, in the same way as non-analysts, people, *perceive* it. He must arrive at the **concrete** through experience. (Italics and bold in original; Lefebvre 2004, 21)

By definition, scholars work in the realm of analytical reflection. Scholars interested in investigating the emotional rhythms of social organization must give themselves over to the sensory experiences that reveal the visceral dynamics and the implicit assumptions that shape such rhythms. Only after experiencing multisensory information directly can a researcher report these experiences in the world of analytical reflection upon their return.[6]

To a large extent, this is what field researchers have always done. In order to successfully join a scene, a researcher has to learn to sustain the flow of interaction.[7] Eventually, researchers will experience their attentions being pulled into alignment with the rhythmic processes that constitute the scene.[8] However, even if ethnographers have always used all of their senses, academic conventions have not always encouraged ethnographers to fully capitalize on their rich sensory knowledge of their

6. Bergson suggests that our capacity to gain a living feel for a scene is entirely different from our capacity to name it as a solid thing: "Instinct is sympathy. If this sympathy could extend its object and also reflect upon itself, it would give us the key to vital operations—just as intelligence, developed and disciplined, guides us into matter. For—we cannot too often repeat it—intelligence and instinct are turned in opposite directions, the former toward inert matter, the latter toward life" ([1988] 2005, 194). The fundamental difference in the two types of knowledge suggests that the ethnographer's translation from one to the other is far from a simple or straightforward task.

7. See Goffman (1967, 9).

8. In Bourdieu's terms, we need to be able to stay until we begin to gain the practical knowledge necessary to negotiate the scene. He describes practical knowledge in this way: "Each agent has a practical, bodily knowledge of her present and potential position in the social space, a 'sense of one's place' as Goffman puts it, converted into a *sense of placement* which governs her experience of the place occupied, defined absolutely and above all relationally as a rank, and the way to behave in order to keep it ('pulling rank') and to keep within it ('knowing one's place,' etc.). The practical knowledge conferred by this sense of position takes the form of emotion (the unease of someone who is out of place, or the ease that comes from being in one's place), and it is expressed in behaviours such as avoidance or unconscious adjustments such as the correction of one's accent (in the presence of a person of higher rank) . . ." (italics in original; [1997] 2000, 184). Similarly, James argues that discourse is only the surface logic of social life. "Our impulsive belief is here always what sets up the original body of truth, and our articulately verbalized philosophy is but its showy translation into formulas. The unreasoned and immediate assurance is the deep thing in us, the reasoned argument is but a surface exhibition. Instinct leads, intelligence does but follow" ([1902] 2007, 77).

field sites in their scholarly work. Consciously nurturing multisensory knowledge would support the development of more complex under-standing of areas that social scientists have historically neglected, like the role of emotions, timing, sensory experiences, and the body in social organization.[9]

Embracing complexity means that rather than attempting to predict order, disorder, or the influence of any particular force, we understand the closest we can come to predictability is understanding how the mul-tiple forces that push and pull patterns toward order and disorder change over time. To understand from this perspective is to see how change and stability are inextricably linked. We could think of the potential for ac-tion as a vast turbulent soup of energy that cannot be contained. It can be trapped for a while, but social organization cannot truly hold it. Energy escapes in fits and starts, not slow, steady deflations. Some patterns have more pull, a wider basin of attraction, and a longer history, but that does not mean that we should mistake their stability for essence, entrainment for lack of resistance, or predictability for inevitability. General theories that are based on assumptions of stability will never provide us with useful specificity.[10] Rather, the awareness of the life cycle of organization

9. Social theorists have continually emphasized the importance of context, time, and feedback relationships for connecting processes at different levels of social systems, but even empirical work in the relational tradition has often failed to capture these dynamic connections. Clearly, action happens within a context, some of which can be thought of as relatively stable compared to the action. Yet conceptualizing context as a field or a network misses the fluid nature of even relatively slow-moving processes. Recent methods developed by network researchers take time into account, but as a series of events. This approach assumes one could identify a meaningful and consistent duration for any particular measurement (Walker et al. 2000, 332; Moody 2002; Moody, McFarland, and Bender-deMoll 2005), which seriously undermines the capacity for investigating the dynamics that influence most action. Attempting to account for time through a series of slices misses the most crucial questions for understanding processes of organization: What *are* the relevant interlocking temporal dynamics of organization and how do these dynamics change over time? If we were to take a slice out of time, an actor would be nothing more than a set of relationships between its constitu-ent elements that may or may not be representative of patterns that unfold over time. As Lefebvre points out, "Things matter little; the thing is only a metaphor, divulged by discourse, divulging rep-resentations that conceal the production of repetitive time and space" (2004, 7). If we look at actors over time, they are defined less by the elements that comprise them than by the action of organizing itself. By thinking of contexts as centers of action behaving as basins of attraction that push and pull other action into temporary patterns, we can think of boundaries as differences in speed, which allows for a more fluid and dynamic conceptualization on which to build relational theories.

10. We can see this same pattern in grand theorizing, or what might more precisely be called efforts to generate abstract widely applicable descriptions. By chasing coherent logics, we actually create contradictions (Douglas [1966] 2002, 200). Generating theory that explains why any general theoretical project may very likely be a waste of time could inspire an aspiring general theorist to call it a day, or at the very least have a good laugh at his or her own expense. Honesty and openness about these contradictions can protect us from the tendency to concretize and reify knowledge generated from farther and apparently more objective perspectives.

should help us to turn our attention toward the dynamics that generate perceptions that some things are solid, essential, or inevitable. Looking for the dynamic action that generates such firm perceptions will enable social theorists to better understand the conditions that make action that goes against the grain possible, less likely, or less visible.

Rather than the functionalists' visions of social organization as dominant patterns that reinforce each other and somehow find their way back to the prevailing equilibrium when disrupted, empirical work reveals patterns of organization as fragile and constantly in flux.[11] Instead of giving the impression of a monolithic integrated whole, we can see how very contingent and unstable the whole is. If one assumes dynamic and open organization, it is impossible to assume stability of size, boundaries, embeddedness, or relationships between actors—even the constitution of actors themselves.[12] The potential for sudden and drastic shifts in response to minor disturbances does not mean that we must give up entirely on the potential for anticipating future action. If we are to investigate complexity, we must be content with sketching rather than drafting; even sketching requires bracketing some complexity for the sake of explanation.

The general pattern of organization and the basic rhythmic quality to social organization implies self-similarity across timescales. However, this could only be true in the most basic sense. If social scientists are to understand how social organization emerges out of local dynamics over time, they must investigate social patterns in their own space and on their own timescale. Thus, the bulk of sociological work will always be in the empirical details, asking: When and where do we find the action that is relevant to our concerns? What are the relevant patterns of action? How have these patterns changed over their history? What does this history suggest about the likely influence of different types of environmental shifts? Once into a scene, a researcher can look for the moments when expectations for focusing attention shift and how changes in context both shift and are shifted by patterns of temporal expectations. They can ask: What are actors' expectations for control? What are the ranges of temporal focus? What are the sequences of temporal focus? And, finally, how do these ranges and patterns shift over time? They must also observe patterns long enough to see how fluctuations are folded into the larger

---

11. Frankl suggests that tension is preferable to equilibrium. "I consider it a dangerous misconception of mental hygiene to assume that what man needs in the first place is equilibrium or, as it is called in biology, 'homeostasis,' i.e., a tensionless state but rather the striving and struggling for a worthwhile goal, a freely chosen task" ([1946] 1984, 126).

12. As Abbott points out, "Previously constituted actors enter interaction, but have no ability to traverse it inviolable. They ford it with difficulty, and many disappear" (2001b, 266).

patterns, and hopefully how the patterns themselves are transformed. Only observation over time can reveal local histories of attractions and repulsions that shape cyclical embedded, overlapping, and interlocking patterns.[13]

Through observing patterns and processes that sustain involvement, we can anticipate how a particular shift in context would shape unfolding patterns, as well as how general variations in context would trigger shifts in these patterns. If one observes long enough, context will shift, and so will the pockets of stability within it. If we watch a pattern respond to a series of disturbances and the resulting narrowing paths for action, we should be able to gain a sense of the flexibility, energy, and types of events that might result in the collapse of a pattern. We also could anticipate the likelihood that the center of action would be reestablished after such a collapse.

Understanding complexity is therefore, at least to some extent, an issue of selecting one's focus of attention so as to avoid drowning in complexity or smoothing organization into deceptively simple relationships. If we chart this course between Scylla and Charybdis, we can see a general cycle of organization with turning points analogous to phase changes.[14] We can bracket enough complexity to discern patterns if we focus on what provides the environmental disturbances that push and pull other centers of action through their cycles of development. As illustrated in the previous chapters, this mid-range perspective highlights patterns of action that are composed of synchronized and competing attractions to, and repulsions from, involvement. Such patterns create other patterns' boundaries as they emerge, become forces in their environment as they stabilize, and free up elements for involvement in other patterns when they collapse.

Representing the Emotional Rhythm of Social Organization

Social scientists and readers who associate analysis with tables that allow them to see numerical relationships between independent and dependent

13. Following the basic assumptions of the argument I have presented, whether the perspective presented here is hopeful or distressing is likely a product of where one stands in relation to it. From my position, I believe there is much to be gained in remaining flexible and training oneself to flip perspectives, to practice changing positions of observation so that one sees the eddy as object, then process, and then object again. I also think there is tremendous potential in more distant standpoints that suggest sharper boundaries between actors and more stable patterns of organization. The predictability of organization that such distant perspectives suggest, however, will disappear as soon as an observer moves closer to the action.

14. See Abbott (2001b, 250).

variables may feel that stories about the carrying on of relations over time seem underanalyzed. However, I suggest that when a social scientist's goal is to convey emotional and embodied experiences, stories are a particularly effective form of analysis and representation. Bateson argues that "logic and quantity turn out to be inappropriate devices for describing organisms and their interactions and internal organization" (2002, 19). As a solution, he offers up stories as an alternative, pointing out that a story is a complex of connectedness, "which we call *relevance*" (emphasis in the original; 2002, 12). Stories proceed according to plots, imitations of actions and life that are connected series of events where events follow as consequences of earlier events (Aristotle 1996, 11). Park notes that social evolution proceeds according to a punctuated equilibrium; stories depict the complication of stability and the resolution of this complication (Aristotle 1996, 29). All this is to say that if literary tools have generally been outside the scope of social science, borrowing literary tools in order to draw on their strength for communicating worldviews, emotions, and personal experience will enable social science to explore hitherto underexplored aspects of social organization. As Mead argues, analysis—or what he refers to as "the attainment of knowledge"—occurs when we move from *collecting* data to *representing* our data in some sort of ordered whole (1932, 94). A story is most definitely one type of ordered whole.

To be clear, proposing the usefulness of literary tools is not a call for giving up on the potential for an objective understanding of social processes. On the contrary, I propose incorporating literary tools in order to open up new areas of human experience for social scientific investigation. I suggest these tools are not only useful for conveying particular scenes, but for building general theory. However, readers may need encouragement to understand how storytelling can be a form of analysis and communication of findings. Using stories to convey an evolutionary perspective is like an engineer's choice to use dynamic models to represent analysis of a particular system. Engineers not used to the technology that allows for depictions of dynamic processes may feel that such dynamic pictures are somehow unfinished. The end result is not the expected static representation of the data. Similarly, social scientists not used to analysis presented in story form may feel that such analysis is somehow unfinished. Where is the static vision of the world that we are used to? Where are the neat propositions that can be stated in a single sentence?

If the stories I tell were merely an account of my experience in the field, the above concerns would be valid. I could make a claim to journalism, but not social science. The stories I tell, however, represent only a small fraction of my time spent in the field. In order to convey particular patterns of social organization in each of the groups, I selected each event and sequence of events from a number of similar circumstances. Although the events that I depict could have been used as events in other stories with different points to make, their multivocality does not detract from the purpose of the storytelling, which, as Aristotle argued, is to convey the unity of a particular action (1996, 15) or, as social scientists would say, the unity of a particular social dynamic (Mead 1932, 34). If the social dynamic is emotional, stories offer the necessary tools for efficiently and effectively communicating social scientific insights.

References

Abbott, Andrew. 2001a. *Chaos of disciplines.* Chicago: University of Chicago Press.

———. 2001b. *Time matters: On theory and method.* Chicago: University of Chicago Press.

———. 2005a. Linked ecologies: States and universities as environments for professions. *Sociological Theory* 23:245–74.

———. 2005b. The historicality of individuals. *Social Science History* 29:1–13.

Allahyari, Rebecca Ann. 2000. *Visions of charity: Volunteer workers and moral community.* Los Angeles: University of California Press.

Allen, T. F. H., and Thomas B. Starr. 1982. *Hierarchy: Perspectives for ecological complexity.* Chicago: University of Chicago Press.

Anderson, Douglas R. 1995. Peirce's agape and the generality of concern. *International Journal for Philosophy of Religion* 37: 103–12.

Apter, Michael. [1989] 2007. *Reversal theory: The dynamics of motivation, emotion and personality.* Oxford: Oneworld Publications.

Aristotle [1925] 1990. *The Nicomachean Ethics.* Trans. David Ross. Rev. J. L. Ackrill and J. O. Urmson. Oxford: Oxford University Press.

Aron, Arthur, and Elaine Aron. 2000. Expansion motivation and including other in the self. In *The social psychology of personal relationships,* ed. W. Ickes and S. Duck, 105–28. New York: Wiley.

Arrow, Holly, Joseph E. McGrath, and Jennifer L. Berdahl. 2000. *Small groups as complex systems: Formation, coordination, development, and adaptation.* Thousand Oaks, CA: Sage.

Bales, Robert. 1955. Adaptive and integrative changes as sources of strain in social systems. In *Small groups: Studies in social interaction*, ed. A. Hare, E. Borgatta, and R. Bales, 127–31. New York: Alfred A Knopf.

Bandy, Joe, and Jackie Smith. 2005. Factors affecting conflict and cooperation in transnational movement networks. In *Coalitions across borders: Transnational protest and the neoliberal order*, ed. Joe Bandy and Jackie Smith, 231–53. New York: Rowman & Littlefield.

Bartky, Sandra. 1990. *Femininity and domination: Studies in the phenomenology of oppression*. New York: Routledge.

Bateson, Gregory. 1972. *Steps to an ecology of mind: Collected essays in anthropology, psychiatry, evolution, and epistemology*. Chicago: University of Chicago Press.

———. [1979] 2002. *Mind and nature: A necessary unity*. Cresskill: Hampton Press.

Becker, Penny Edgell. 1998. Making inclusive communities: Congregations and the 'problem' of race. *Social Problems* 45(4):451–72.

Bender, Courtney. 2007. Touching the transcendent: Rethinking religious experience in the sociological study of religion. In *Everyday religion: Observing modern religious lives*, ed. N. T. Ammerman, 201–18. Oxford: Oxford University Press.

Berger, Peter, and Thomas Luckmann. 1967. *The social construction of reality: A treatise in the sociology of knowledge*. New York: Anchor.

Bergson, Henri. [1988] 2005. *Matter and memory*. New York: Zone Books.

Bergson, Henri. [1912] 1999. *An Introduction to metaphysics*. Trans. T. E. Hulme. Indianapolis: Hackett.

Bordo, Susan. 1995. *Unbearable weight: Feminism, Western culture, and the body*. Berkeley: University of California Press.

Borer, Tristan Anne. 1996. Church leadership, state repression, and the "spiral of involvement" in the South African anti-apartheid movement, 1983–1990. In *Disruptive religion*, ed. Christian Smith, 125–43. New York: Routledge.

Bourdieu, Pierre. 1977. *Outline of a theory of practice*. Cambridge: Cambridge University Press.

———. 1984. *Distinction: A social critique of the judgment of taste*. Trans. Richard Nice. Cambridge, MA: Harvard University Press.

———. [1997] 2000. *Pascalian meditations*. Trans. Richard Nice. Stanford, CA: Stanford University Press.

Carpenter, Steven R., and Kathy L. Cottingham. 2002. Resilience and the restoration of lakes. In *Resilience and the behavior of large-scale systems*, ed. L. H. Gunderson and L. Pritchard Jr., 51–66. Washington, DC: Island Press.

Clark, Andy. 1997. *Being there: Putting brain, body, and world together again*. Cambridge, MA: MIT Press.

Clark, Candace. 1997. *Misery and company: Sympathy in everyday life*. Chicago: University of Chicago Press.

Clemens, Elisabeth, 1997. *The People's Lobby: Organizational Innovation and the Rise of Interest Group Politics in the United States, 1890–1925*. Chicago: University of Chicago Press.

Collins, Randall. 1988. The micro contribution to macro sociology. *Sociological Theory* 6:118–30.

———. 1990. Emotional energy as the common denominator of rational action. *Rationality and Society* 5:203–30.

———. 1998. *The sociology of philosophies: A global theory of intellectual change.* Cambridge, MA: Belknap Press of Harvard University Press.

———. 2004. *Interaction ritual chains.* Princeton, NJ: Princeton University Press.

———. 2008. *Violence: A micro-sociological theory.* Princeton, NJ: Princeton University Press.

Damasio, Antonio R. 1994. *Descartes' error: Emotion, reason, and the human brain.* New York: Putnam.

Day, Dorothy. 1939. *House of hospitality.* New York: Sheed & Ward.

Desjarlais, Robert R. 2003. *Sensory biographies: Lives and deaths among Nepal's Yomo Buddists.* Berkeley: University of California Press.

Dewey, John. 1910. *How we think.* Boston: D.C. Heath.

———. 1934. *Art as experience.* New York: Minton, Balch.

———. 1939. The individual in the new society. In *Intelligence in the modern world: John Dewey's philosophy*, ed. Joseph Ratner. New York: Modern Library.

———. 1959. *Dewey on education: Selections, with an introduction and notes.* Ed. Martin S. Dworkin. New York: Bureau of Publications, Teachers College, Columbia University.

Dilthey, Wilhelm. 1996. *Selected works volume V: Poetry and experience.* Princeton, NJ: Princeton University Press.

DiMaggio, P., and W. Powell. 1983. The iron cage revisited: Institutional isomorphism and collective rationality in organizational fields. *American Sociological Review* 48:147–60.

Douglas, Mary. [1966] 2002. *Purity and danger: An analysis of concepts of pollution and taboo.* London: Routledge.

Durkheim, Emile. [1912] 1995. *The elementary forms of religious life.* Trans. Karen E. Fields. New York: Free Press.

———. [1933] 1997. *The Division of Labor in Society.* New York: Free Press.

Ekman, Paul. 1992. *Telling lies: Clues to deceit in the marketplace, politics, and marriage.* New York: Norton.

Eliasoph, Nina. 1998. *Avoiding politics: How Americans produce apathy in everyday life.* Cambridge cultural social studies. Cambridge: Cambridge University Press.

———. 2005. Theorizing from the neck down: Why social research must understand bodies acting in real space and time (and why it's so hard to spell out what we learn from this). *Qualitative Sociology* 28(2):159–69.

Eliasoph, Nina, and Paul Lichterman. 2003. Culture in interaction. *American Journal of Sociology* 108:735–94.

Emirbayer, Mustafa, and Ann Mische. 1998. What is agency? *American Journal of Sociology* 103(4):962–1023.

Erickson Nepstad, Sharon. 1996. Popular religion, protest, and revolt: The emergence of political insurgency in the Nicaraguan and Salvadoran churches of the 1960s–80s. In *Disruptive religion*, ed. Christian Smith, 105–24. New York: Routledge.

———. 2004. Persistent resistance: Commitment and community in the Plowshares movement. *Social Problems* 51(1).

Escot, C., S. Artero, C. Gandubert, J. P. Boulenger, and K. Ritchie. 2001. Stress levels in nursing staff working in oncology. *Stress and Health* 17:273–79.

Farrell, Michael P. 2001. *Collaborative circles: Friendship dynamics and creative work*. Chicago: University of Chicago Press.

Fine, Gary Alan. 1979. Small groups and culture creation: The ideoculture of Little League baseball teams. *American Sociological Review* 44:733–45.

———. 1987. *With the boys: Little League baseball and preadolescent culture*. Chicago: University of Chicago Press.

———. 1990. Organizational time: Temporal demands and the experience of work in restaurant kitchens. *Social Forces* 69:95–114.

Fine, Gary Alan, and Corey Fields. 2008. The anthill and the veldt: Culture under the microscope. *American Academy of Social and Political Science* 619: 130–48.

Fine, Gary Alan, and Brooke Harrington. 2004. Tiny publics: Small groups and civil society. *Sociological Theory* 22:341–56.

Fine, Gary Alan, and Sherryl Kleinman 1979. Rethinking subculture—interactionist analysis. *American Journal of Sociology* 85:1–20.

Fine, Gary Alan, and Kent Sandstrom. 1993. Ideology in action: A pragmatic approach to a contested concept. *Sociological Theory* 11:21–38.

Fine, Gary Alan, and Randy Stoeker. 1993. "Can the circle be unbroken? Small groups and social movements." In *Social psychology of groups: A reader*, ed. Edward J. Lawler and Barry Markovsky, 225–52. Greenwich: JAI Press.

Flaherty, Michael. 2003. Time work: Customizing temporal experience. *Social Psychology Quarterly* 66:17–33.

Flam, Helena, and Debra King, eds. 2005. *Emotions and social movements*. London: Routledge.

Frank, Robert H. 1990. A theory of moral sentiments. In *Beyond self-interest*, ed. J. J. Mansbridge, 71–96. Chicago: University of Chicago Press.

Frankl, Viktor E. [1946] 1984. *Man's search for meaning: Revised and updated*. New York: Washington Square Press.

Freud, Sigmund. [1920] 1990. *Beyond the pleasure principle*. Trans. Peter Gay. New York: Norton.

———. [1923] 1960. *The Ego and the Id*. New York: Norton.

Gamson, William A. 1992. The social psychology of collective action. In *Frontiers in social movement theory*, ed. Aldon Morris and Carol Mueller, 53–76. New Haven, CT: Yale University Press.

Garfinkel, Harold. 1967. *Studies in ethnomethodology*. Englewood Cliffs, NJ: Prentice-Hall.

Gibson, James. J. 1966. *The senses considered as perceptual systems.* Boston: Houghton Mifflin.

Giugni, Marco, Doug McAdam, and Charles Tilly, eds. 1999. *How social movements matter.* Minneapolis: University of Minnesota Press.

Glaeser, Andreas. 2005. An ontology for the ethnographic analysis of social process: Extending the extended-case method. *Social Analysis* 49(3):16–45.

Goffman, Erving. 1959. *The presentation of self in everyday life.* Chicago: Anchor.

———. 1963. *Behavior in public places: Notes on the social organization of gatherings.* Glencoe, IL: Free Press.

———. 1967. *Interaction ritual: Essays on face-to-face behavior.* 1st ed. Garden City, NY: Anchor Books.

———. 1974. *Frame analysis: An essay on the organization of experience.* Boston: Northeastern University Press.

———. 1986. *Stigma: Notes on the management of spoiled identity.* New York: Touchstone.

Golding, William. 1954. *Lord of the flies, a novel.* London: Faber and Faber.

Goodwin, Jeffrey, and James M. Jasper. 2006. Emotions and social movements. In *Handbook of the sociology of emotions*, ed. Jan E. Stets and Jonathan H. Turner, 611–35. New York: Springer.

Goodwin, Jeff, James Jasper, and Francesca Polletta, eds. 2001. *Passionate politics: Emotions in social movements.* Chicago: University of Chicago Press.

Gopnik, Alison, and Andrew N. Meltzoff. 1997. *Words, thoughts, and theories (Learning, development, and conceptual change).* Cambridge, MA: MIT Press.

Haidt, Jonathan. 2006. *The happiness hypothesis: Finding modern truth in ancient wisdom.* New York: Basic Books.

Hallett, Tim. 2003. Symbolic power and organizational culture. *Sociological Theory* 21:128–49.

Hare, A. Paul, Edgar Borgatta, and Robert Bales. 1955. *Small groups: Studies in social interaction.* New York: Knopf.

Harrington, Brooke, and Gary Alan Fine. 2000. Opening the "black box": Small groups and twenty-first-century sociology. *Social Psychology Quarterly* 63(4):312–23.

———. 2006. Where the action is: Small groups and recent developments in sociological theory. *Small Group Research* 37:4–19.

Hatfield, Elaine, John T. Cacioppo, and Richard L. Rapson. 1994. *Emotional contagion.* Cambridge: Cambridge University Press.

Hayes, Diana L. 1998. "Introduction: We've come this far by faith." In *Taking down our harps: Black Catholics in the United States*, ed. D. Hayes and C. Davis. New York: Maryknoll.

Hervieu-Léger, Danièle. 2000. *Religion as a chain of memory.* Trans. Simon Lee. New Brunswick, NJ: Rutgers University Press.

Heuven, Ellen, Arnold B. Bakker, Wilmar B. Schaufeli, and Noortje Huisman. 2006. The role of self-efficacy in performing emotion work. *Journal of Vocational Behavior* 69(2):222–35.

Hochschild, Arlie Russell. 1979. Emotion work, feeling rules, and social structure. *American Journal of Sociology* 85(3):551–75.

———. 1983. *The managed heart: Commercialization of human feelings*. Berkeley: University of California Press.

Howard, Jenna. 2006. Expecting and accepting: The temporal ambiguity of recovery identities. *Social Psychology Quarterly* 69:307–24.

Husserl, Edmund. [1893–1907] 1991. *On the phenomenology of the consciousness of internal time (1893–1917)*. Trans. John Barnett Brough. Boston: Kluwer Academic Publishers.

James, William. 1890. *The principles of psychology*. New York: H. Holt.

———. [1902] 2007. *Varieties of religious experience: A study in human nature*. Charleston, SC: BiblioBazaar.

Jasper, James M. 1997. *The art of moral protest: Culture, biography, and creativity in social movements*. Chicago: University of Chicago Press.

Jawahar, I. M., Thomas Stone, and Jennifer Kisamore. 2007. Role conflict and burnout: The direct and moderating effects of political skill and perceived organizational support on burnout dimensions. *International Journal of Stress Management* 14(2):142–59.

Joas, Hans. 2000. *The genesis of values*. Chicago: University of Chicago Press.

Kanter, Rosabeth Moss. 1972. *Commitment and community: Communes and utopias in sociological perspective*. Cambridge, MA: Harvard University Press.

Kelso, J. A. Scott. 1995. *Dynamic patterns: The self-organization of brain and behavior*. Cambridge, MA: MIT Press.

Kelso, J. A. Scott, and David A. Engstrøm. *The complementary nature*. Cambridge. MA: MIT Press.

Kemper, Theodore D. 1990. *Research agendas in the sociology of emotions*. Albany: State University of New York Press.

Koffka, Kurt. 1922. Perception: An introduction to the *gestalt-theorie*. *Psychological Bulletin* 19:531–85.

Kuhn, Thomas S. 1996. *The structure of scientific revolutions*. Chicago: University of Chicago Press.

Lamont, Michele, and Virag Molnar. 2002. The study of boundaries in the social sciences. *Annual Review of Sociology* 28:167–95.

Lawler, Edward. J. 2002. Micro social orders. *Social Psychology Quarterly* 65:4–17.

Lefebvre, Henri. 2004. *Rhythmanalysis—space, time and everyday Life*. London: Continuum.

Lewontin, Richard C. 2000. *The triple helix: Gene, organism, and environment*. Cambridge, MA: Harvard University Press.

Lichterman, Paul. 1995. Piecing together multicultural community: Cultural differences in community-building among grass-roots environmentalists. *Social Problems* 42(4):513–34.

———. 1996. *The search for political community: American activists reinventing commitment*. Cambridge: Cambridge University Press.

Lizardo, Omar. 2004. The cognitive origins of Bourdieu's habitus. *Journal for the Theory of Social Behaviour* 34:375–401.

Ludwig, Donald, Brian Walker, and C. S. Holling. 2002. Sustainability, stability, and resilience. In *Resilience and the behavior of large-scale systems*, ed. L. H. Gunderson and L. Pritchard Jr., 21–47. Washington, DC: Island Press.

McAdam, Doug. 1988. *Freedom summer.* New York: Oxford University Press.

McAdam, Doug, and Roberto M. Fernandez. 1990. Microstructural bases of recruitment to social movements. *Research in Social Movements, Conflicts and Change* 12:1–33.

McAdam, Doug, Sidney Tarrow, and Charles Tilly. 2001. *Dynamics of contention.* Cambridge: Cambridge University Press.

McCarthy, John D., and Mayer N. Zald. 1977. Resource mobilization and social movements: A partial theory. *American Journal of Sociology* 82:1212–41.

McFarland, Daniel A. 2004. Resistance as a social drama: A study of change-oriented encounters. *American Journal of Sociology* 109(6):1249–1318.

McFarland, Daniel A., and Heili Pals. 2005. Motives and contexts of identity change: A case for network effects. *Social Psychology Quarterly* 68(4):289–315.

McGuire, Meredith. 2007. Embodied practices: Negotiation and resistance. In *Everyday religion: Observing modern religious lives*, ed. N. T. Ammerman, 187–200. Oxford: Oxford University Press.

McRoberts, Omar M. 2004. Beyond mysterium tremendum: Thoughts toward an aesthetic study of religious experience. *Annals of the American Academy of Political and Social Science* 595:190–203.

Mead, George Herbert. 1932. *The philosophy of the present.* Ed. Arthur E. Murphy. Chicago: University of Chicago Press.

———. 1934. *Mind, self and society from the standpoint of a social behaviorist.* Ed. Charles W. Morris. Chicago: University of Chicago Press.

Merleau-Ponty, Maurice. 1962. *Phenomenology of perception: An introduction.* Ed. Colin Smith. London: Routledge.

Meyer, David. 1993. Protest cycles and political process: American peace movements in the nuclear age. *Political Research Quarterly* 46(3):451–79.

Moody, James. 2002. The importance of relationship timing for diffusion. *Social Forces* 81:25–56.

Moody, James, Daniel A. McFarland, and Skye Bender-deMoll. 2005. Dynamic network visualization. *American Journal of Sociology* 110:1206–41.

Nakamura, Jeanne, and Mihaly Csikszentmihalyi. [2002] 2006. The construction of meaning through vital engagement. In *Flourishing: Positive psychology and the life well-lived*, ed. Corey L. M. Keyes and Jonathan Haidt, 83–104. Washington, DC: American Psychological Association.

Nash, June. 1996. Religious rituals of resistance and class consciousness in Bolivian tin-mining communities. In *Disruptive religion*, ed. Christian Smith, 87–104. New York: Routledge.

Nippert-Eng. 1995. *Home and work.* Chicago: University of Chicago Press.

Oliver, Pam, and Hank Johnston. 2000. What a good idea! Frames and ideologies in social movement research. *Mobilization* 5:37–54.

Oliver, Pamela E., and Daniel J. Myers. 2003. Networks, diffusion, and cycles of collective action. In *Social movements and networks: Relational approaches to collective action*, ed. Mario Diani and Doug McAdam, 173–203. Oxford: Oxford University Press.

Osa, Maryjane. 1996. Pastoral mobilization and contention: The religious foundations of the Solidarity Movement in Poland. In *Disruptive religion*, ed. Christian Smith, 67–86. New York: Routledge.

Padgett, John F., and Christopher K. Ansell. 1993. Robust action and the rise of the Medici, 1400–1434. *American Journal of Sociology* 98(6):1259–1319.

Pape, Helmut. 1997. The logical structure of idealism: C. S. Peirce's search for a logic of mental processes. In *The rule of reason: The philosophy of Charles Sanders Peirce*, ed. J. Brunning and P. Forster, 153–84. Toronto: Toronto University Press.

Park, Robert E. 1936a. Human ecology. *American Journal of Sociology* 42(1):1–15.

———. 1936b. Succession, an ecological concept. *American Sociological Review* 1(2):171–79.

Plutchik, Robert. 1980. *Emotion: A psychoevolutionary synthesis*. New York: Harper and Row.

Polanyi, Michael. [1958] 1962. *Personal knowledge: Towards a post-critical philosophy*. Chicago: University of Chicago Press.

Polletta, Francesca. 2002. *Freedom is an endless meeting*. Chicago: University of Chicago Press.

———. 2006. *It was like a fever: Storytelling in protest and politics*. Chicago: University of Chicago Press.

Prejean, Sr. Helen. 1994. *Dead man walking: An eyewitness account of the death penalty in the United States*. New York: Vintage Books.

Prigogine, Ilya. 1969. Structure, dissipation and life. In *Theoretical physics and biology*, ed. M. Marois, 23–52. Amsterdam: North-Holland.

Rappaport, Roy A. 1999. *Ritual and religion in the making of humanity*. Cambridge: Cambridge University Press.

Rawls, Anne. 2004. *Epistemology and practice: Durkheim's "The Elementary Forms of the Religious Life."* Cambridge: Cambridge University Press.

Riesebrodt, Martin. 1993. *Pious passion: The emergence of modern fundamentalism in the United States and Iran*. Trans. Don Reneau. Los Angeles: University of California Press.

Robinson, Dawn, and Lynn Smith-Lovin. 1992. Selective interaction as a strategy for identity maintenance: An affect control model. *Social Psychology Quarterly* 55(1):12–28.

Scheff, Thomas J. 1990. *Microsociology: Discourse, emotion, and social structure*. Chicago: University of Chicago Press.

———. 1992. Rationality and emotion: An homage to Norbert Elias. In *Rational choice theory: Advocacy and critique*, ed. by James Coleman and Thomas Fararo, 101–19. Newbury Park, CA: Sage.

Schutz, Alfred. 1962. *Collected papers I: The problem of social reality.* Ed. M. A. Natanson and H. L. van Breda. The Hague: Martinus Nijhoff.

———. 1967. *The phenomenology of the social world.* Trans. George Walsh and Fredrick Lehnert. Evanston, IL: Northwestern University Press.

Sewell, William F. 1992. A theory of structure: Duality, agency, and transformation. *American Journal of Sociology* 98(1):1–29.

Sikkink, David, and Mark Regnerus. 1996. For God and the fatherland: Protestant symbolic worlds and the rise of German National Socialism. In *Disruptive religion,* ed. Christian Smith, 147–66. New York: Routledge.

Simmel, Georg. 1898. The persistence of social groups. *American Journal of Sociology* 4:662–98, 829–36.

———. 1964. *Conflict and the web of group affiliations.* New York: Free Press.

Smith, Christian. 1991. *The emergence of liberation theology: Radical religion and social movement theory.* Chicago: University of Chicago Press.

———. 2007. Why Christianity works: An emotions-focused phenomenological account. *Sociology of Religion* 68(2):165–78.

Snow, David A., and Robert D. Benford. 1988. Ideology, frame resonance, and participant mobilization. *International Social Movement Research* 1:197–217.

Snow, David. A., Steven K. Worden, E. Burke Rochford, and Robert. D. Benford. 1986. Frame alignment processes, micromobilization, and movement participation. *American Sociological Review* 51:464–81.

Spillman, Lyn. 2004. Causal reasoning: Historical logic and sociological explanation. In *Self, social structure, and beliefs: Explorations in the sociological thought of Neil J. Smelser,* ed. Jeff Alexander, Gary Marx, and Christine Williams, 216–34. Berkeley: University of California Press.

Staab, Janice M. 1999. Questions concerning Peirce's agapic continuity. *Transactions of the Charles S. Peirce Society* 35(1):157–76.

Staggenborg, Suzanne. 1995. Can feminist organizations be effective? In *Feminist organizations: Harvest of the new women's movement,* ed. Myra Marx Ferree and Patricia Yancey Martin, 339–55. Philadelphia: Temple University Press.

Stets, Jan E., and Jonathan H. Turner, eds. 2006. *Handbook of the sociology of emotions.* New York: Springer.

Stoller, Paul. 1997. *Sensuous scholarship.* Philadelphia: University of Pennsylvania Press.

Stolte, John F., Gary Alan Fine, and Karen S. Cook. 2001. Sociological miniaturism: Seeing the big through the small in social psychology. *Annual Review of Sociology* 27:387–413.

Summers-Effler, Erika. 2002. The micro potential for social change: Emotion, consciousness, and social movement formation. *Sociological Theory* 20: 41–60.

———. 2004. Defensive strategies: the formation and social implications of patterned self-destructive behavior. In *Theory and research on human emotions: Advances in group processes,* vol. 21, ed. Jonathan H. Turner, 309–25. Boston: Elsevier.

————. 2006. Ritual theory. In *Handbook of the sociology of emotions*, 1st ed., ed. Jan E. Stets and Jonathan H. Turner, 135–53. New York: Springer.

Tarrow, Sidney. 1991. Collective action and political opportunity in waves of mobilization: Some theoretical perspectives. *Kolner Zeitschrift fur Socologie und Sozialpsychologie* 43(4):647–78.

————. 1994. *Power in movement: Collective action, social movements, and politics*. Cambridge: Cambridge University Press.

Taylor, Verta. 1989. Social movement continuity: The women's movement in abeyance. *American Sociological Review* 54:761–75.

————. 1995. Watching for vibes: Bringing emotions into the study of feminist organizations. In *Feminist organizations: Harvest of the new women's movement*, ed. Myra Marx Ferree and Patricia Yancey Martin, 223–33. Philadelphia: Temple University Press.

Taylor, Verta, and Leila J. Rupp. 2002. Loving internationalism: The emotion culture of transnational women's organizations, 1888–1945. *Mobilization* 7:125–44.

Thelen, Esther, and Linda G. Smith. 1996. *A dynamic systems approach to the development of cognition and action*. Cambridge: MIT Press.

Tilly, Charles. 2001. Do unto others. In *Political altruism? The solidarity movement in international perspective*, ed. Marco Giugni and Florence Passy, 31–50. Lanham, MD: Rowman & Littlefield.

Turner, Jonathan H. 2000. *On the origins of human emotions: A sociological inquiry into the evolution of human affect*. Stanford, CA: Stanford University Press.

————. 2002. *Face to face: Toward a sociological theory of interpersonal behavior*. Stanford, CA: Stanford University Press.

————. 2007. *Human emotions: A sociological theory*. New York: Routledge.

Turner, Jonathan H., and Jan E. Stets. 2005. *The sociology of emotions*. Cambridge: Cambridge University Press.

Turner, Victor. 1969. *The ritual process*. Ithaca, NY: Cornell University Press.

Ulanowicz, Robert E. 1997. *Ecology, the ascendent perspective: Complexity in ecological systems series*. New York: Columbia University Press.

Van Gennep, Arnold. 1960. *The rites of passage*. Chicago: University of Chicago Press.

Wacquant, Loic. 2004. *Body and soul: Notebooks of an apprentice boxer*. Cambridge: Cambridge University Press.

Walker, Henry A., Shane R. Thye, Brent Simpson, Michael J. Lovaglia, David Willer, and Barry Markovosky. 2000. Network exchange theory: Recent developments and new directions. *Social Psychology Quarterly* 63:324–37.

Weber, Max. [1914] 1978. *Economy and society: An outline of interpretive sociology*. New York: Bedminster Press.

Wertheimer, Max. [1945] 1982. *Productive thinking*. Chicago: University of Chicago Press.

White, Harrison C. 1992. *Identity and control: A structural theory of social action*. Princeton, NJ: Princeton University Press.

Whitehead, Alfred N. 1971. *Process and reality*. New York: Free Press.

Wiley, Norbert. 1994. *The semiotic self*. Chicago: University of Chicago Press.

Williams, Rhys H., and Jeffrey Blackburn. 1996. Many are called but few obey: Ideological commitment and activism in Operation Rescue. In *Disruptive religion*, ed. Christian Smith, 167–86. New York: Routledge.

Wuthnow, Robert. 1991. *Acts of compassion: Caring for others and helping ourselves*. Princeton, NJ: Princeton University Press.

Wuthnow, Robert, and Marsha Witten. 1988. New directions in the study of culture. *Annual Review of Sociology* 14:49–67.

Yamane, David. 2000. Narrative and religious experience. *Sociology of Religion* 61:171–89.

Zerubavel, Eviatar. 1981. *Hidden rhythms: Schedules and calendars in social life*. Chicago: University of Chicago Press.

Zhao, Dingxin. 1998. Ecologies of social movements: Student mobilization during the 1989 prodemocracy movement in Beijing. *American Journal of Sociology* 103(6):1493–1529.

Index

Abbott, Andrew, 172n41, 184n3, 197n37, 209n14; on competition in urban development, 114n25; on constitution of actors and interaction, 208n12; on duration, experience of, 167; on eddy image, as context for emerging and collapsing patterns, 196n32; on failure, 109n10; on group dynamics, xn3; on individuals shaping social organization, 200n41; on past and present, 164n14, 191n15, 200n41; on speed and framing, 173; on stability and action, 193; on timing, xvii

absorption, 67, 107–8, 110, 165, 190n12

accidents, 172n40

action: and behavior, 167n24; and conscious awareness, 119n50; context for, 207n9; and control efforts, 122n61; coordinated vs. separate, 5n9; defined, 113n22; and failure, future, 109n10; and failure, generally, 15–17, 18–19, 68, 69–70, 90–102; 127; and failure, theory, 106–27; field of, 112; by groups, 107n3, 181n54; influence on, 21; new, 172n39; observation of, 114n26; and obstacles, 65n33, 107n3, 108, 118n40, 200n42; paths of, 112; and processes, 181n54; and recovery, 106–27; and risk, 61n16; source of, 112;

and stability, 193; strategies for, 122n61; telic vs. paratelic, xvn10, 114n22, 184n2; and transformation, 64n28; types of, 166n22. *See also* political action; social actors

actors. *See* social actors

agape: and boundaries opened, 79; defined, 64n29; and failure, 111–12; and gratification, 64n29; and grief/joy, 63n23, 116; moments of, 37–40, 63n23, 67

Allahyari, Rebecca Ann, 27n2, 28n3, 107n2

Allen, T. F. H., xvii, 169n32, 180, 194–95

altruism, and expansion, 65n33

altruistic social movement groups, generally, ix, ixn1, xiv–xv, xvii, 1–6, 14–17, 16n15. *See also* Catholic Worker community; small groups; social movement groups; STOP

Amnesty International, 49

Anderson, Douglas R., 64n29

anger, 135–36; and boundaries, 78–79, 111; righteous, 18, 19, 66, 78, 96, 111, 114, 117–18, 117n38, 138, 160, 169n30, 180, 187; shared, 106

Ansell, Christopher K., 196n33

apathy, 116n34

Apter, Michael: on behavior as means vs. ends, 61n17; on telic vs. paratelic action, xvn10, 114n22, 184n2

INDEX

Gestalt psychology, x, 122n59, 128n1
Gibson, James J., 60n10, 61n14, 62n19,
    116n31, 120n49, 121n56, 122n58,
    124n64; on proprioception, 176n46; on
    senses trained through experience, 176
Giugni, Marco, 199
Glaeser, Andreas, 16n15
Goffman, Erving, 119n44, 206n7; on ac-
    tion, 114n22; on biological individuals,
    194n25; on coordination and timing,
    172n40; on framing, 112n18, 173; on
    group dynamics, xn3; on interaction,
    xvii, 172n39; on interaction, traffic laws
    analogy, 5n9, 172; on involvement, 173;
    on personal identity, 162; on practical
    knowledge, 206n8; on risk, 61n16, 167;
    on social space, 206n8
Goodwin, Jeffrey, 5n10, 19, 127n71, 199
Gopnik, Alison, 119n45, 120n52
gratification, and agape, 64n29
grief, 60n12, 143, and agape, 111, 116; and
    awe, 18, 116; boundaries, destroyed,
    111; as forbidden emotion, 116; and
    helplessness, 66; and horror, 19; and
    joy, 62, 63n23, 111; and laughter, 18,
    142; and loss of unity, 185; and shame,
    110; and suffering, 60; and tragedy, 117
group action. See action
group dynamics: and culture, 121n57; and
    individuals precipitating out, xn3; ob-
    serving, ixn1; unfolding over time, xn3.
    See also dynamics
group evolution, 2n1, 16n15, 17n16,
    161–66, 182
group structure and style, 2n2, 17, 159n5,
    162n10
Guevara, Che, 131

Haidt, Jonathan, 63n24, 64n29, 116n32–33,
    181n54
Hallett, Tim, 126n69
Hare, A. Paul, ixn1
harmony, 62n21, 109n13
Harrington, Brooke: on civil rights move-
    ment, 162n12; on conceptual and
    complexity of groups, 16n14; on group
    action, 181n54; on groups and political
    life, 4n7; on interaction, 16n14; on
    small groups, ixn1, 16n14; on social
    organization, ixn1
Hatfield, Elaine, 119n50

Hausmann, Chris, 194n24, 2055
Hayes, Diana L., 178n50
helplessness, 25–42
heroes and heroism, 59, 65n31, 66–67, 111,
    125, 178. See also saints and saintliness
Hervieu-Léger, Danièle, 18n18
Heuven, Ellen, 62n21
Hierarchy (Allen and Starr), xvii
Hochschild, Arlie Russell, 59n8, 60n13
Holling, C. S., 172n38, 198n38
homeostasis, 208n11
honor, and stability, 160–61n9
Howard, Jenna, 108n6
Human Emotions (Turner), xvii
humility, 39, 87n1, 137; and disappoint-
    ment, 87; vs. failure, 69; and grief, 117;
    and joy, 66; and laughter, 143; and
    moral superiority, 79; mystical, 87
Husserl, Edmund, 108n7, 109n11, 112n21,
    162n11, 168, 168n27, 176n47, 197n37
hysteresis, 176

identity: collective, 64n27; personal, 15n12,
    64n27, 162; shared, 191; social and
    bodily, 64n27; of sympathizers, xivn10
Identity and Control (White), xvii
ideological commitment, 3–4, 5n10, 6, 117,
    119n43, 121, 127, 163, 171; emotional
    logic embodied, 119–22
ideology: and day-to-day practice, 119n43;
    formal and operative, 118n41; and
    goals, 115n30, 120, 171n36; of groups,
    110n14; and ritual, 115n30; and
    solidarity, 85, 106; and time, 200; and
    transformation, 173
individualism, and expansion, 65n33
inequality: and abolition, 90; enduring
    patterns of, 193n22; and expectations/
    persistence, 177–79, 178n53; and inter-
    action, 178n52; racial, gender, ethnic,
    class distinctions, 126, 177, 178n50;
    structural, 126, 177n49. See also equality
influence: on action, 21; and social actors,
    193–95; on social movement groups,
    20–21
initiative, 63, 63n26
instinct, 206n6
integration, 166n23, 177n49
intellectual commitment, xiiin8
intelligence: emotional, 116n32; and
    instinct, 206n6

MORALITY AND SOCIETY SERIES

Edited by Alan Wolfe

Cultural Dilemmas of Progressive Politics: Styles of Engagement among Grassroots Activists
Stephen Hart

For the Sake of the Children: The Social Organization of Responsibility in the Hospital and the Home
Carol A. Heimer and Lisa R. Staffen

Money, Morals, and Manners: The Culture of the French and the American Upper-Middle Class
Michèle Lamont

Streets of Glory: Church and Community in a Black Urban Neighborhood
Omar Maurice McRoberts

The Making of Pro-Life Activists: How Social Movement Mobilization Works
Ziad Munson

God and Government in the Ghetto: The Politics of Church-State Collaboration in Black America
Michael Leo Owens

The Catholic Social Imagination: Activism and the Just Society in Mexico and the United States
Joseph M. Palacios

Citizen Speak: The Democratic Imagination in American Life
Andrew J. Perrin

Speaking of Abortion: Television and Authority in the Lives of Women
Andrea L. Press and Elizabeth R. Cole

The Ironies of Affirmative Action: Politics, Culture, and Justice in America
John David Skrentny

Public and Private in Thought and Practice: Perspectives on a Grand Dichotomy
Edited by Jeff Weintraub and Krishan Kumar

Soft Patriarchs, New Men: How Christianity Shapes Fathers and Husbands
W. Bradford Wilcox

Faith in Action: Religion, Race, and Democratic Organizing in America
Richard L. Wood